DOING TIME LIKE A SPY

HOW THE CIA TAUGHT ME TO
SURVIVE AND THRIVE IN PRISON

A VIREO BOOK | RARE BIRD BOOKS
LOS ANGELES, CALIF.

DOING TIME LIKE A SPY

HOW THE CIA TAUGHT ME TO SURVIVE AND THRIVE IN PRISON

JOHN KIRIAKOU

This is a Genuine Vireo Book

A Vireo Book | Rare Bird Books
453 South Spring Street, Suite 302
Los Angeles, CA 90013
rarebirdbooks.com

Set in Minion Pro
Printed in the United States

PAPERBACK ISBN: 9781947856325

Whistleblower John Kiriakou is number six in a series of ten works of art that John
Dingler calls "Prosecuted Whistleblowers." Not all of them were prosecuted and not all
were whistleblowers, however, their contributions toward whistleblowing are significant
enough to be included in the group: Philip Agee, Daniel Ellsberg, Julian Assange,
Jeremy Hammond, Thomas Drake, John Kiriakou, Jeffrey Sterling, Aaron Swartz,
Chelsea Manning, Edward Snowden.

johndinglerart.com

(Philip Agee served as a role model for other whistleblowers;
Jeremy Hammond and Aaron Swartz were facilitators.)

10 9 8 7 6 5 4 3 2

Publisher's Cataloging-in-Publication data
Names: Kiriakou, John, author.
Title: Doing time like a spy : how the CIA taught me how to survive and thrive in prison
/ John Kiriakou.
Description: A Genuine Vireo Book | New York, NY; Los Angeles,
CA: Rare Bird Books, 2017.
Identifiers: ISBN 9781945572418
Subjects: LCSH Kiriakou, John. | United States. Central Intelligence Agency—Officials
and employees—Biography. | Spies—United States—Biography. | Whistle blowing—
United States. | Prisons—United States. | Prisoners—United States—Biography. |
BISAC BIOGRAPHY & AUTOBIOGRAPHY / Personal Memoirs |
BIOGRAPHY & AUTOBIOGRAPHY / Law Enforcement |
BIOGRAPHY & AUTOBIOGRAPHY / Political.
Classification: LCC HV9468 .K57 2017 | DDC 365/.6/0924—dc23

For my brother and sister, Emanuel Kiriakou and Tina Moulis,
and for my father-in-law, Dr. Michael Armentrout.
Thanks for everything.

Every current and former CIA officer must submit his book manuscript to the CIA's notorious and politicized Publications Review Board (PRB) for clearance to ensure that the book does not contain classified information. Well, every current and former CIA officer is *supposed* to submit the manuscript. Many don't. The ones who are famous or who are friends with the president get away with it. The little guy who doesn't ends up getting crushed in a court of law. I submitted my manuscript. And despite the fact that the federal courts have mandated that the CIA has thirty days to review it, my book took more than eight months. Still, I played by the rules, even if the CIA didn't.

In the end, the CIA necessitated the following disclaimer:

This does not constitute an official release of CIA information. All statements of fact, opinion, or analysis expressed are those of the author and do not reflect the official positions or views of the Central Intelligence Agency (CIA) or any other US Government agency. Nothing in the contents should be construed as asserting or implying US Government authentication of information or CIA endorsement of the author's views. This material has been reviewed solely for classification.

Introduction

I LIKE TO THINK that I'm a pretty nice guy. In fact, people tell me all the time that I'm friendly and easy to get along with. I consider myself a good father, a good husband, a hard worker, and a patriot.

But in prison I had a reputation for being an asshole. I was comfortable in prison plotting against people, cutting off those who crossed me, and trying, constantly, to stay one step ahead of the Corrections Officers (COs) and the prison administration.

I am an experienced, highly trained former CIA operations officer. It was my job to recruit spies to steal secrets and to run counterterrorist operations to break up and foil terrorist plots. I'm very proud of my CIA career. I spent nearly fifteen years there, and I played a role in the country's response to the September 11, 2001, attacks. I spent the first eight years of my CIA career working in analysis and specializing on Iraq. My final seven years were spent on the ground in counterterrorism. I resigned from the CIA in 2004.

Despite my career, which included a later stint as the senior investigator for the Senate Foreign Relations Committee, and nearly a half-century of being a law-abiding citizen, I eventually found myself as the target of a federal investigation. At the end of the ordeal I was sentenced to thirty months in prison.

I was determined to get through my prison experience unscathed, and I thought the best way to do that would be to rely on what the CIA had taught me over the years. After all, prison couldn't possibly be tougher than Afghanistan, Pakistan, Iraq, Yemen, or any of the other dumps in which I'd served over the years. I resolved to make the best of a bad situation, to stay safe, and to make sure that I remained at the top of the social heap.

When I came to prison, I didn't know what to expect. Nobody among my friends had ever been to prison, and I had nothing to go on other than what I had seen on TV. What I did not expect, however, was that the training and experience that I had amassed in my CIA career would prepare me to survive and thrive in prison. As you will see, I wasn't the typical federal prisoner.

A CIA psychiatrist once told me that the Agency looks to hire people who exhibit "sociopathic tendencies." CIA recruiters are not interested in sociopaths, who have no consciences or empathy, and who can easily pass a polygraph exam. Sociopaths are too hard to control. Instead, they are interested in people who are comfortable working in ethical, moral, and legal grey areas. I had no problem bending some rules if it was in the interest of national security.

Some researchers have gone further in their analysis of the typical CIA officer than the CIA psychiatrist who told me about "sociopathic tendencies." New Mexico State University professor Peter Jonason published a paper entitled "Who is James Bond?" which found that successful intelligence officers have a "specific triumvirate of personality traits—the stratospheric self-esteem of narcissism; the fearlessness, ruthlessness, impulsivity, and thrill-seeking of psychopathy; and the deceitfulness and exploitativeness of Machiavellianism." That's a little harsh. An actual psychopath or sociopath, according to Dutton, "seeks reward at any cost, flouting consequence and elbowing risk aside." That's not at all what a CIA officer does. He tries to get the job done while not making waves or attracting undue attention. That's exactly what I did in prison.

The CIA recruited me in graduate school in the late 1980s for a reason. I was, and remain, very patriotic, and I was very interested in public service. I also had a bachelor's degree in Middle Eastern Studies and a master's degree in legislative affairs, as well as a facility for foreign languages. A retired CIA officer teaching at my alma mater, George Washington University, spotted me, made a few introductions, and, after a battery of tests and a comprehensive background investigation, I found myself at CIA headquarters in Langley, Virginia.

I'm glad I joined the CIA. The CIA taught me great survival skills. I'm not just talking about how to break into houses, how to surreptitiously gather information, or even how to use weapons in dangerous situations. I'm talking about how to survive—and even thrive—when surrounded by idiots, dangerous criminals, crooked cops, corrupt administrators, sexual perverts, and the scum of society.

You see, this is prison.

How Could This Happen?

I BEGAN WORKING AT the CIA in January 1990. After a week of orientation, I was assigned to an office in the Directorate of Intelligence (DI)—the Agency's analytic arm—that focused on doing long-term psychological profiles of foreign leaders. My assignment was to cover Iraq and Kuwait, which I was told were "training accounts." As a senior analyst explained to me, "Nothing ever happens in Iraq or Kuwait. They've had the same leaderships since the nineteen sixties. The same cabinets are still in place. Learn your analytic tradecraft and you can move onto something interesting, like Romania." That was eight months before Iraq invaded Kuwait and started the Gulf War.

The Gulf War made me a star in the DI. I became one of the Agency's "go to" analysts on Iraq. I was Saddam Hussein's biographer for the Intelligence Community, and I was called on to brief presidents, cabinet secretaries, members of Congress, and foreign leaders. I traveled to more than sixty countries and wrote analyses that helped to form the basis for US policy in the Middle East.

But I got bored. By 1997 it was clear that Saddam Hussein wasn't going anywhere. I wanted to go back overseas, where I had served in the early 1990s. I spoke both Greek and Arabic, which was unique in the Agency, and I decided that I wanted to switch to counterterrorism operations.

A move from analysis to operations was highly unusual at the time. There was normally a Chinese wall between the CIA's two most important functions. But the Counterterrorism Center thought that I showed promise and that my language skills were unique, and they allowed me to make the switch.

I didn't have to do interim one-month assignments around headquarters, what people call CIA 101, because my colleagues and I in the Special Operations Training Course (SOTC) were all mid-career officers. Instead, I dove right into operations, first at a secret facility in northern Virginia, and then in the CIA's famous training facility known as "the Farm."

SOTC was a deep, involved, and difficult course. It was also the most fun I've ever had. Besides learning the fundamentals of operational writing, clandestine meetings, disguises, and other espionage basics, there were other components. These included "Crash and Bang," a course on how to avoid kidnappings and car-borne terrorist attacks; weapons training with a variety of handguns, long guns, and even some heavy weaponry; surveillance, countersurveillance, and surveillance detection; and parachute jump school.

But it was the other courses that I really took to. The most interesting and professionally important one was how to spot, assess, develop, and recruit spies. Unless you plan to make your career as an ass-kicker in places like Afghanistan, Iraq, or Pakistan, recruitment skills would be the most valuable for a career in CIA operations. These skills proved to be the most valuable to me in prison.

Operational meetings could be held anywhere—in a restaurant, in a hotel, in a car, literally anywhere. I've even done operational meetings in a men's restroom and behind a garbage dumpster. The idea at first is to spot a target and to assess his access to protected information. Once you find the right person, you cultivate and develop a friendship so that, over time, the target becomes more and more comfortable speaking openly with you. The final phase in the relationship is recruitment. Here you establish a formal relationship between the CIA and the target. There are lots of reasons people would consent to being recruited. These are called vulnerabilities. Maybe the target needs money—he can't afford his lifestyle, he can't afford to send his kids to college, or he has large medical bills. Revenge is a good motivator. Maybe the target has been passed over for promotion or has a beef against his bosses. Another motivator may be patriotism. The target loves the US and wants to help. Whatever the motivation, though, every recruitment comes down to the relationship.

In this kind of clandestine relationship, trust and a personal "connection" are paramount. After all, the goal is to convince someone to commit espionage—treason, even—for you. Why? Because he likes you, he believes he can work with you, and he gets something that he needs out of the relationship—money, revenge, even just a shoulder to cry on. This is the very foundation of CIA operational work.

I had no idea at the time, of course, but it was these skills that would allow me to protect myself and my interests in prison. I learned in my CIA training that almost everybody has a vulnerability. Almost everybody and every situation can be manipulated. I honed these skills in the Middle East and Europe virtually as soon as I finished training.

I had to live by my wits while serving overseas. There were two assassination attempts made against me abroad—one in Greece, where a terrorist group called Revolutionary Organization 17 November set out to kill me, but murdered my neighbor, the British Defence Attaché, instead. The second was in a Middle Eastern country where I was handling a double agent. The enemy country he was working for ordered him to kill me in our final meeting. We were tipped off, we grabbed and disarmed him, and we cracked his organization.

Then the September 11 attacks occurred. Like everybody else at CIA headquarters, I volunteered to go to Afghanistan and fight. That wasn't really my thing—I have no military experience—but patriotism dictated that I do my part. I volunteered repeatedly, and finally, after making enough of a pest of myself, I was sent to Pakistan to run counterterrorist operations. I spent most of 2002 there.

The highlight of my time in Pakistan was the late-March 2002 capture of Abu Zubaydah and dozens of al-Qaeda fighters at a string of safehouses in Faisalabad. This was a major catch. Our government thought at the time that Abu Zubaydah was the third-ranking official in al-Qaeda. But that turned out to be untrue. While Abu Zubaydah had certainly done a lot of logistical work for al-Qaeda, and he created and ran the group's training camps in southern Afghanistan, he had never actually joined al-Qaeda. He had never pledged loyalty to Osama bin Laden, and he knew less about al-Qaeda's leadership than we thought he did.

I didn't have any idea at the time how important Abu Zubaydah would be to my life over the next decade. Frankly, I wish I had never been in Pakistan that night. You can keep the medals and awards. In the end, as you'll see, it wasn't worth it to me.

When I got back to CIA headquarters in the summer of 2002, a senior officer in the Agency's Counterterrorism Center asked me if I wanted to be certified in the use of what he called "Enhanced Interrogation Techniques." I didn't know what that meant, so I asked. He told me, "We're going to start getting rough with these guys," and he explained the various torture techniques that had recently been approved by President George W. Bush. I told this officer that "this sounds like torture to me," and I said that I had a visceral opposition to it. Count me out.

But just to make sure I was thinking correctly, I went to a very senior CIA officer and asked for his guidance. He said, "First, let's call it what it is. It's torture. Second, somebody is going to go too far and they're going to kill a prisoner. Third, there's going to be a Congressional investigation and somebody's going to go to prison. Do you want to go to prison?" I said no and I went back to the Counterterrorism Center and said in no uncertain terms that I didn't want to be involved. In the end, I was the only person with any connection to the CIA's torture program that went to prison, not because I tortured anybody, but because I blew the whistle on the CIA's torture program. I aired the Agency's dirty laundry in public.

On August 1, 2002, CIA interrogators began torturing Abu Zubaydah. At first he was slapped, punched, kicked, stripped naked, and humiliated. Later he was chained to an I-bolt in the ceiling and kept awake for weeks at a time, while ice water was thrown on him.

Abu Zubaydah exhibited an irrational fear of insects, so he was put in a dog cage with cockroaches to see how crazy he could become. Most famously, or infamously, he was waterboarded eighty-three times. The Senate Select Committee on Intelligence said in its torture report in 2014 that none of these techniques resulted in Abu Zubaydah ever giving the CIA any actionable intelligence that disrupted terrorist attacks or saved a single American life.

While all of this was going on, CIA officers speaking out of school were telling me and others that Abu Zubaydah had been waterboarded once, that he had cracked, and that he had provided actionable intelligence that foiled terrorist plots and saved lives. This was a lie. But it was what was being circulated around CIA headquarters. It was a lie that helped to perpetuate the torture program.

I resigned from the CIA in 2004. I was divorced and I had remarried—this time to a CIA officer—and I wanted to be able to spend quality time with my two sons from my first marriage. I was tired of going overseas, and my boys were young at the time, eleven and eight. They needed me in their lives and I needed them. So I left the CIA and went into the private sector.

Things were going gangbusters for me until December 2007. At the beginning of that month I received a call from Brian Ross, the senior investigative reporter for ABC News. Ross said that he had a source who had told him that I had tortured Abu Zubaydah. "Absolutely untrue," I said. "I was the only person who was kind to Abu Zubaydah." Indeed, after we had captured him, I sat at Abu Zubaydah's side for fifty-six consecutive hours. We talked about religion, poetry, our families, even the September 11 attacks. At one point, in tears, he asked me to smother him with his pillow.

I told Ross that his source was dead wrong. "Well, you're welcome to come on the show and defend yourself," he answered. I had no idea that this was an old reporter's trick. I should have hung up on him. Instead, I went to my boss, and my boss's boss, and asked what to do. "Go on the show, but don't mention the firm or any of the firm's clients" was the answer. So I went on the show.

I had honestly stopped following news about al-Qaeda after I left the CIA. I was burned out and I was excited to start a new life. I was vaguely aware that the non-governmental organization Human Rights Watch had issued a report saying that Abu Zubaydah had been tortured and that Amnesty International had issued a report saying the same thing. So in my mind, the news was out there. Everybody knew we were torturing prisoners, right? Wrong. Brian Ross asked me directly during the course of the interview whether the CIA had tortured Abu Zubaydah. Yes, I said. Was he waterboarded? Yes. Were others? Yes. I told the whole story.

Ross went on to ask me for my own feelings about waterboarding. I said that I thought it was torture and that as Americans we shouldn't be in the business of torture. I made three major revelations during that interview. I said the CIA was torturing its prisoners, that torture was official US Government policy, and that the policy had been approved personally by the president. By saying that, I became the first CIA officer, past or present, to confirm the torture of prisoners. The CIA was enraged.

The next morning, the CIA filed a "crimes report" against me with the FBI, saying that my revelations were illegal, and asking the FBI to begin a criminal investigation. I read about this filing in the newspapers, and I hired an attorney.

The FBI took a full year to investigate me. In the end, they elected not to charge me with a crime, finding that I had not revealed any classified information. The case against me was officially closed. But the CIA was livid. Four weeks after the case was closed, Barack Obama, the self-professed "most transparent president in history," was inaugurated. The CIA asked him secretly to reopen the case against me. He did, and the secret investigation proceeded for another four years. I didn't know it at the time, of course, but the FBI was all over me—carrying out surveillance against me, collecting my telephone metadata, even intercepting and reading my emails. Again, I didn't know it at the time, so I just continued on with my life.

Despite having my bosses' permission to go on ABC in 2007, I was asked to resign from the private company I was working for. I hired another attorney and, after the provision of a generous severance package, I offered my resignation. Still, the timing could not have been worse. I left my job just as the worst recession since the Great Depression hit the country. I was out of work for all of 2008, other than a little consulting work here and there, until finally in February 2009 I got an offer.

A friend with ties to then–Senator John Kerry offered me a job as the senior investigator on the Senate Foreign Relations Committee staff. It was a senior position on the most prestigious committee on Capitol Hill and I was thrilled at the prospect. I just had to get through an interview with Kerry, who had just been elevated to the Committee's chairmanship.

I met with Kerry in his office in February 2009. I was immediately struck by his friendliness and informality. Kerry gets a bum rap for his reputation as a stiff patrician politician. I liked him. He was very intelligent, accomplished, and a bona fide war hero. I was struck by a couple of things during that meeting. First, he had his medals—a Silver Star and three Bronze Stars—in a shadow box on a credenza. (The press had reported in great detail in the 1970s that Kerry had thrown his medals over the White House fence to protest the Vietnam War. That was a publicity stunt. He threw copies over the fence and kept the originals.) He also had pictures of himself with John Lennon, Mary Travers of Peter, Paul, & Mary, and a wide variety of 1960s- and 1970s-era celebrities. It was a fun office.

Kerry and I had a great conversation about the Middle East and South Asia. He asked my opinion on the Iraq War, on the occupation of Afghanistan, and on strategies for getting out of both of those countries. The interview went exceedingly well. At the end, I got up and shook his hand, and I thanked him for not asking me about waterboarding. "I hate being 'the waterboarding guy,'" I told him. Kerry smiled and said, "Nobody in this country has taken it on the chin from the press like I have. I know the truth of your story. I'm happy to have you onboard." I started working two weeks later.

I was blessed with great leadership for the first year of my stint at the Senate Foreign Relations Committee. We tackled some important issues, and I took very seriously our oversight responsibilities. I thought that hard work and tough investigations were what was expected of me. I was wrong, wrong, wrong, and all I did was stir up a hornet's nest of troubles.

I didn't realize it at the time, but even before I joined the Senate Foreign Relations Committee staff I was ruffling feathers at Langley. First, before I joined the SFRC, I had written an op-ed for the *Los Angeles Times* saying that the next president, whether it was Barack Obama or John McCain, should work to improve US relations with South America because Iran already was doing that. I sent it to the CIA's Publications Review Board (PRB) for clearance before submitting it to the *Times,* and it was cleared quickly. My sources for the piece were two reports from United Press International's Spanish-language service and the Foreign Ministry website of one of the countries I mentioned in the piece.

A couple of days after the op-ed ran, my wife was called into the CIA's Office of Security as part of an "inquiry." The officer, who videotaped the interview, said, "I noticed that your husband had an op-ed run in the *LA Times* over the weekend." My wife responded that I had had the op-ed cleared. "Well," the officer continued, "that op-ed contained highly classified information." My wife answered calmly that I did not have access to classified information. "But you do," the officer retorted.

My wife and I had a hard-and-fast rule at home. We never talked about Iran. Ever.

The officer told her that we could dispense with the entire episode if she would fax him my sources. I emailed them to her immediately and told her to pass the CIA a message from me: First, apparently nobody at the CIA spoke Spanish. Second, they appeared to have a source who was selling them press and calling it intelligence. She forwarded the source material to the officer, and she never heard anything about it again. In retrospect, I should not have just put this incident behind me. I should have assumed that the Agency was paying intensely close attention to me, even through my wife. But I didn't. And I continued to poke that hornet's nest.

Soon after I started working on the Committee, I got a call from a human rights activist who said he had some explosive information to give me. We met later that day in a small classroom at Johns Hopkins University's School of Advanced International Studies on Massachusetts Avenue in Washington.

The activist asked if I had ever heard of the Dasht-i-Leili massacre. I had. On November 30 and December 1, 2001, the US-backed Northern Alliance captured two thousand Taliban soldiers near Dasht-i-Leili outside Mazar-i-Sharif in northern Afghanistan. It just so happened that December 1 was the same day that John Walker Lindh, the "American Taliban," was captured nearby during an uprising at the Qalat e-Jhangvi fort. CIA officer Johnny Michael Spann was killed in the uprising.

US forces were preoccupied with what was happening at Qalat e-Jhangvi. Northern Alliance leaders, meanwhile, did not know what to do with the two thousand Taliban prisoners, all of whom had given up peacefully. The Northern Alliance leader, General Abdul Rashid Dostum, a man who had repeatedly switched sides in Afghanistan over the years and who had an absolutely dismal human rights record, ordered that the prisoners be loaded into shipping containers and trucked out into the desert until somebody could figure out what to do with them. The trucks drove eight hours into the desert. When they finally stopped, and the drivers opened their containers, "the bodies fell out like sardines from a can," according to one of the only sixteen survivors. Nearly everybody was dead.

Whether on purpose or by accident, no air holes were made in the containers. There was no food or water, either. General Dostum hated the Taliban. Had he suffocated these soldiers on purpose? I wanted to find out. And my human rights activist source was offering me an eyewitness. The eyewitness was twelve years old at the time of the "box-up," and had hidden behind a rock when the prisoners were loaded into the containers. He had seen the entire thing happen, and he said that there were two other people there—two "white men," wearing blue jeans and black shirts, and speaking English. CIA? I wanted to know.

I began by calling a contact who had been a senior State Department official during the George W. Bush administration and asking if he knew anything about the allegation that the CIA may have known about the Dasht-i-Leili box-up. He referred me to a retired ambassador who would have known something if the box-up had occurred the way the witness said it had. I interviewed him at his law firm in Washington. He said that he had heard the allegations, but had never seen any proof. He referred me to a retired assistant secretary of state, who was happy to speak on the record. He recalled the massacre and said that he had "assumed Agency folks were in the area," but there was no smoking gun.

The assistant secretary, in turn, referred me to one of former secretary of state Colin Powell's closest advisors. The advisor sat with me in the Foreign Relations Committee's conference room and told me a story about US acquiescence in the massacre that infuriated me. He suggested that I call Secretary Powell personally, which I did the next day. I never got through to Powell, but his secretary called me back a day later to say that "Secretary Powell stands behind whatever (the senior advisor) said."

That was good enough for me. I decided to begin a formal investigation into what was probably indirect US involvement in the Dasht-i-Leili massacre. But before I could even make my first appointment one of Senator Kerry's top aides called with a message: "kill this investigation right now." There would be no explanation. To me it was obvious that word had gotten back to the CIA. I was looking into things that shouldn't be looked into. The investigation was over.

A year passed. I received a call from a national security journalist who said a source had told him that the CIA was placing officers associated with the torture program undercover with a certain government entity in order to shield their identities from journalists. If true, this would have been a violation of the cover agreement that the CIA had with this entity.

I sent a letter to the CIA, under Senator Kerry's signature, asking for clarification. About six weeks passed without any response. Finally, one of my colleagues walked into my office and said nonchalantly, "The Agency sent a response to your letter." I told him that I hadn't seen any response, and that I had just checked my mail an hour earlier. He told me that the response had been marked "Top Secret." At the time, I had only a "Secret" security clearance. I asked what the letter said. "It said 'Go fuck yourself,'" my colleague responded. *Well*, I thought. *I guess I'm not the most popular guy at CIA headquarters.*

One of the nice things about a job like the one I had on the Foreign Relations Committee is that you get to meet diplomats from all over the world. And one of the perks is that you get to have lunch with these interesting people, within the confines, of course, of the Senate Ethics Committee rules. One day I got a call from a Japanese diplomat inviting me to lunch at a nearby restaurant on Capitol Hill. We got together and talked about the Middle East, Turkish elections, and Afghanistan. I remember it being a very nice lunch. Just before we finished, the diplomat asked what I thought I would be working on in the coming months. I told him that I thought I might resign from the Committee. "I promised Senator Kerry that I'd give him two years. It's been two-and-a-half. I'm ready to move on." "No!" he responded excitedly. Then in a whisper, he said, "I can give you money if you give me information."

I was stunned at this bold operational approach. This is what we intelligence officers call a "cold pitch." It is when an intelligence officer just goes up to a target without even trying to develop him, and says, essentially, "I'm an intelligence officer and I want you to work for me." I responded to the pitch, "Shame on you. Do you have any idea how many times I've made that pitch?" I thanked him for lunch, got up, and walked out.

I went directly to the office of the senate security officer, a secure facility underneath the new Capitol Visitors Center, on the east lawn of the Capitol building. I told him that a foreign intelligence officer had just pitched me and that I wanted to report it. The senate security officer listened to my story, and then asked me to write it as a memo to the FBI on a standalone computer in his office. I did that, and he said he would get back to me in the next couple of days.

The security officer called me two days later and said that two FBI agents were coming to talk to me. Could I come to his office in an hour? So an hour later, I walked to the Senate Security Office and met two young FBI agents. They asked me to repeat what had happened with the Japanese. When I finished the story, one of them said, "Here's what I want you to do. Call him back and invite him to lunch. Tell him that you're thinking about his offer. Then try to get him to tell you exactly what information he wants and how much money he's willing to pay you for it." He went on to say that the FBI would put two agents at a nearby table so they could listen to the conversation.

I called the diplomat, who readily agreed to get together. But on the morning of the lunch, one of the FBI agents called me to say that something had come up and the FBI would be unable to send two agents to the restaurant. I should just do the lunch without them, and then write them another memo. I did that. And they asked me to do it a third time, and a fourth, and a fifth. Finally, after lunch at an out-of-the-way Georgetown café, the Japanese diplomat said that he was being transferred to Cairo. He went on and on about what a great move this was for his career and how much he was looking forward to it. I congratulated him, shook his hand, and left. I never saw him again.

It wasn't until a year later, four months after my arrest, that I learned from a friend in the FBI that there never was any Japanese diplomat. He was an FBI agent, and the whole "pitch" was a setup. The FBI was trying to trap me into committing espionage—real espionage. But I kept foiling their efforts by repeatedly reporting the contact, not only to the senate security officer but also right back to the FBI. So they abandoned the operation.

In the meantime, I was confronted with the most obvious red flag. I received an email from a reporter for a conservative national newspaper. I had heard bad things about this reporter and I simply deleted his email. But he was persistent, and he emailed me three times. I finally went to my boss, who was a Pulitzer Prize–winning journalist earlier in his career. "I'll authorize the contact," he said. "Have lunch with him and see what he wants."

I got together with the reporter at a small, nearly empty restaurant just off Capitol Hill. Even though the place was practically deserted, he spoke in a whisper. "I have a source in the FBI," he said. "You're under surveillance." My heart began to race. "Why?" He continued in a whisper. "The FBI thinks you're the source for the John Adams Project." I leaned in toward him. "What's the John Adams Project?"

The reporter just sat there looking at me. "That's not really the response I expected."

"I'm serious," I said. "I don't know what you're talking about, and I don't know what the John Adams Project is." He explained that the John Adams Project was an effort by the American Civil Liberties Union (ACLU) and the National Association of Criminal Defense Lawyers (NACDL) to support the attorneys representing Guantánamo defendants. I told the reporter that his source was wrong. I had never had any contact with anybody from the John Adams Project or anybody having anything to do with Guantanamo defense attorneys. I thanked him for lunch and went back to the office.

I found my boss in his office and I told him what had happened. He was puzzled by the approach and repeated what I had heard about the reporter's reputation. He put me at ease by saying that if I had been under FBI investigation, Senator Kerry would have heard about it. And if Senator Kerry had been told, then he, too, would have been told. Still, I conducted a sophisticated surveillance detection route home that evening, even utilizing the extensive network of tunnels under the Capitol building. I saw nothing.

On January 16, 2012, I got a call at home from the FBI. "Remember that [Japanese diplomat] case you helped us out with last year? Well, we need your help again." Remember, I didn't know yet that the Japanese diplomat was a fake. So the first thing that came to mind was that the FBI needed my help to expose his replacement. It was my patriotic duty to help them. I agreed immediately to meet with them at the FBI's Washington Field Office on January 19. It wasn't until we were an hour and twenty minutes into the interview that I realized that the investigation was of *me*. One FBI agent finally looked me in the eye and said, "You should know that we are executing a search warrant on your house as we speak." I responded with, "I want to see my attorney."

That was the only thing that kept me from being arrested that day. I went directly from the FBI's office to my attorney's office. On Monday, January 23, I turned myself in to the FBI. I was arrested, booked, photographed, and taken to the federal courthouse in Alexandria, Virginia, for processing. I was charged with five felonies, including three counts of espionage, one count of making a false statement, and one count of violating the Intelligence Identities Protection Act.

I had the best attorneys in Washington; "legal titans," *The Washington Post* called them. They recognized the charges for what they were—political. The CIA never forgave me for saying that it was torturing prisoners. The espionage charges, especially, were ridiculous on their face. Attorney General Eric Holder said in a press conference announcing my arrest that I had exposed "Top Secret information that has been declassified solely for the purpose of Mr. Kiriakou's prosecution." What was that "Top Secret" information? It was that the CIA had a program after the September 11 attacks to kill or capture members of al-Qaeda. Seriously.

The other two espionage charges were equally ridiculous. A reporter from *The New York Times* and another from ABC News had asked me how to get in touch with a former CIA colleague of mine. This colleague had resigned and had taken a job with the two psychologists who had created the CIA's torture program. He had given me his business card several years earlier, and I gave the reporters the contact information from the business card. This colleague had never been undercover. The business card was unclassified. But the Justice Department made me defend myself against two espionage charges for that business card.

All three of the espionage charges were eventually dropped, as was the false statements charge. I was never actually clear about what the false statement was that I had supposedly made. It had something to do with my first book. But it was eventually dropped, too.

My problem was with the Intelligence Identities Protection Act. In the summer of 2008 I received an email from Matthew Cole, a freelance reporter who was writing a book, he claimed, about the CIA's rendition, detention, and interrogation program. He sent me a list of names and asked if I could introduce him to anybody on the list who might agree to an interview. I didn't know anybody. He followed up with a second list, and then a third. I wrote back that he obviously knew this issue much better than I did. I didn't know a single name on any of the lists.

Finally, Cole wrote, "What about the guy you wrote about in your first book?" There was a passage in my first book, *The Reluctant Spy*, in which I said that I had run into an old boss of mine on the tarmac of an airport in Pakistan. He was there to take Abu Zubaydah to a secret prison for interrogation and, it turned out, torture. Cole said, "Wasn't his name [John]?"

"Oh, you mean, [John Doe]," I said. I don't know what happened to him. He's probably retired and living in Virginia somewhere. That conversation was a felony. I should never have provided John Doe's last name to Cole. It was a mistake that I'll regret for the rest of my life.

To compound my problems, although I didn't know it at the time, Cole was the source for the John Adams Project. Cole wasn't writing a book about the CIA. He was collecting as much information as possible about the CIA's rendition, detention, and interrogation program, especially names, and passing that information secretly to a John Adams Project investigator. Cole, in turn, had had another CIA source, a disgruntled former employee who gave him the names and photos of ten more undercover CIA officers. My attorneys and I knew this because our investigator was able to procure personal notes on these officers written by one of Abu Zubaydah's attorneys after a conversation with Cole. Why hadn't this other CIA officer been arrested and charged with espionage and with violating the Intelligence Identities Protection Act? Because he hadn't blown the whistle on torture.

In my case, Cole passed Doe's name to the John Adams Project investigator, who passed it to the Guantanamo defense attorneys. The attorneys filed a classified motion with the court asking to interview Doe. When the judge received the motion, he called the FBI. How the FBI tied the name back to me is still something of a mystery. The conventional wisdom is that the FBI got into the Guantanamo defense attorneys' emails and traced the name to the investigator. They then either got into the investigator's emails or the investigator cooperated, and they traced the name to Cole. The FBI then either went into Cole's emails or Cole cooperated with the FBI to incriminate me. So either the FBI spied on a journalist or Cole turned rat. He's never spoken about it publicly.

I wanted to go to trial. In fact, that's exactly what I prepared to do until October 2012. But it came down to an economic decision. I had given my attorneys everything I had, and I still owed them $880,000. A trial would have added another $2–$3 million. I would never have that kind of money. I could never pay the bill. In the meantime, the government was offering me a sentence of thirty months in prison. If I had gone to trial and had been convicted, I would have received a likely sentence of twelve to eighteen years. That would have been generous. I was actually facing forty-five years. It would have been a death sentence.

I concluded that this could be a blip in my life or the defining event of my life. I elected to take the blip. I would likely do about two years. With the help of friends and family, my wife and five children could make it two years without me. I had to cut my losses.

So on October 22, 2012, I took a plea to one count of violating the Intelligence Identities Protection Act. I was formally sentenced in January 2013 and arrived at the Federal Correctional Institution at Loretto, Pennsylvania to begin my sentence on February 28.

A few nights before my departure, the peace group Code Pink held a going away party for me on the roof of Washington's storied Hay-Adams Hotel. Nearly two hundred people attended, and they even serenaded me with a personalized version of Peter, Paul, & Mary's 1960s-era hit "Have You Been to Jail for Justice?" I told the crowd that I didn't fear prison. I was tougher than the CIA thought I was. I would not be broken. I would not be institutionalized. Here's what I said:

Good evening and thank you for coming.

Last month I was sentenced to thirty months in a federal correctional institution for violating the Intelligence Identities Protection Act. The prosecutors—and the judge—insisted that my case was about leaking. It was not. I was targeted for prosecution for protesting torture before opposition to torture was kosher. The government's purpose in prosecuting me was to frighten critics into silence.

As every American knows, leaking classified information by marquee executive branch officials is as routine as the rising and setting of the sun. If my case was about leaking, we would have seen simultaneous prosecutions of people like former CIA director David Petraeus[1], who provided classified information to his girlfriend; like Defense Department Undersecretary Michael Vickers, who federal

---

1   Petraeus eventually took a plea to a misdemeanor charge of unauthorized removal and retention of classified information. He was sentenced to eighteen months of unsupervised release and a fine of $100,000. He did not lose his security clearance, and the day after his sentencing he traveled to Iraq on a consultation contract for the White House.

investigators say leaked classified information to the producers of the film Zero Dark Thirty; like the Navy Seals who divulged classified information for profit to the makers of a video game; and like Seal Team Six member Matt Bissonnette, who profited by publishing his classified account of the Osama bin Laden killing without clearance. But none of them uttered a single word critical of the government.

My attorneys also found documentary evidence that another former CIA officer provided the names of some ten covert officers to journalist Matthew Cole, and classified information on counterterrorist operations. But the FBI declined to investigate, and the Justice Department declined to prosecute him. Why? Because he didn't blow the whistle on torture.

A year ago, the Justice Department, at the insistence of the CIA's leadership, charged me with three counts of espionage, in addition to other felonies, despite admitting privately that I had not committed espionage. I became the sixth person charged by President Obama under the Espionage Act, double the number of prosecutions made under all previous presidents combined. So far, every espionage case that has found its way into a courtroom has either been dismissed or has crumbled, but the targets have still been destroyed in their careers and lives by the ordeal and the staggering expense of investigation and accusation.

Former Attorney General and Supreme Court Justice Robert Jackson warned of cases like mine more than seven decades ago when he said, "With the law books filled with a great assortment of crimes, a prosecutor stands a fair chance of finding at least a technical violation of some act on the part of almost anyone. In such a case, it is not a question of discovering the commission of a crime and then looking for the man who has committed it, it is a question of picking the man and then searching the law books, or putting investigators to work, to pin some offense on him. It is in this realm—in which the prosecutor picks some person whom he dislikes or desires to embarrass, or selects some group of unpopular persons and then looks for an offense—that the greatest danger of abuse of prosecuting power lies."

Let me be clear: I am a patriotic American. I love our great country. I love the CIA. I always will. I believe that the CIA is largely made up of dedicated men and women who want nothing more than to protect the country. But a true patriot, as Thomas Paine wrote, saves his country from his government.

Certainly Congress has neglected its oversight duties. Where are the voices of outrage when the new CIA director designee maintains a "kill list" with American citizens on it? Where is the outrage when those citizens are denied their Fifth Amendment rights to due process and instead are vaporized by drones without even a formal accusation of a crime? Didn't even the Nuremburg defendants receive a trial, and Adolph Eichmann in Jerusalem?

At the CIA, we are taught that everything is a shade of grey, that nothing is black or white. But this is wrong. Torture is black and white, and we as Americans should not be involved in it. Torture is a crime, both in the US and according to international law. There is no excuse for it. Its use is never appropriate for civilized peoples.

But today, I will be the only person to go to prison for any crime related to torture. The torturers are free. The men who conceived of the torture are free. Those who implemented the torture policy are free. And those attorneys who justified the torture with warped legal opinions are free.

I took a plea to violating the Intelligence Identities Protection Act for five reasons: their ages are nineteen, sixteen, eight, six, and one. My wife and children are proud of me, and that is what matters.

My whistleblowing also accomplished something very important. Despite the fact that I was prosecuted, my protest against torture is now the law of the land. I'm glad that I had a role in that.

I would like to thank my wife and family, my attorneys, my advisors Jesselyn Radack and Bruce Fein, and the dozens of former and current CIA officers, FBI agents, and assistant US attorneys who both publicly and privately encouraged me to stand up and fight. Thank you for your emails, calls, cards, and donations to my defense fund.

My journey has just begun. Thirty months is not a long time. When my sentence passes, I will continue to speak out against torture and in support of the civil rights and civil liberties that we as Americans have fought and died for at Valley Forge, Cemetery Ridge, Omaha Beach, and elsewhere.

As President Obama so eloquently said earlier this week, "We, the people, still believe that our obligations as Americans are not just to ourselves, but to posterity."

Thank you.

My wife Heather was and is my strongest supporter and a never-ending source of level-headed wisdom for me. On the day of my arrest, she said, "You have to embrace this. You are not a criminal. You're a whistleblower. They are doing this to you because you're a champion of human rights. You embarrassed them. You have to fight back." She said later, when I was thinking about doing something to myself that I'm too ashamed to even discuss here, she said, "You're strong. You're tough. You can fight them. They have consistently underestimated your toughness. You can get through this and we'll be stronger for it on the other side."

It was because of Heather's support and steadfastness that I decided to fight. And I would do other things, too. Heather and my friend and attorney Jesselyn Radack said that I should work hard while in prison to remain "relevant" to the national debate on torture. They said that I had a unique, experienced, and respected voice on the issue, despite the fact that the government had worked so hard and had spent millions of dollars of the taxpayers' money to silence it. I should write, they said.

I already had success writing for the *Los Angeles Times* and *The Huffington Post*. I should keep that up, they said, and I decided to continue writing for major publications, even if I had to do it by hand. One night, in the week before I went to prison, I was at an informal dinner at the home of firedoglake.com publisher Jane Hamsher. Jesselyn, NSA whistleblower Tom Drake, journalist Kevin Gosztola, and godfather of all whistleblowers Daniel Ellsberg also were there and all urged me also to write about my prison experience. After all, they said, Americans really don't have any idea what prison life is like, other than what they see on television, and that is so skewed toward violence that it's not a comprehensive or truly honest picture.

I agreed and decided to write an open letter to my supporters that Jane would publish on her website. I would do that as soon as I felt comfortable enough to sit down and collect my thoughts. I figured it would take only a few minutes and it would give me something to do to pass the time. A few months later, I was left speechless by the response.

But in the near term, I had one final goal. I made one last-ditch attempt to avoid prison about a week before I was due to turn myself in. I wrote Senator Kerry a long, heartfelt email and sent it to his personal email account. I asked if he would speak to the president for me and ask him to commute my sentence. The conviction would still be on my record, but I could stay home with my family and work to support them. I received his terse reply a few days later: "Do not ever attempt to contact me again."

Day 1:
"This Has to be Some Kind of Mistake"

ON THE MORNING OF February 28, 2013, Jesselyn Radack, Tom Drake, Jim Spione, my cousin Mark Kiriakou, and his son-in-law Matt McCarthy drove me to prison in Loretto, Pennsylvania, to drop me off. When we pulled into the parking lot and I saw the big blue water tank, the double fences with concertina wire, and the roving guard vehicles, I said, "Holy shit! This is a *real* prison!" I was thankful that I was assigned to the minimum-security work camp on the other side of the parking lot.

I walked through the front door and announced to the first guard I saw that I was John Kiriakou and I was there to turn myself in. I got to the prison at 10:30 a.m. Because the judge and prosecutors both recommended that I serve my time in the minimum-security Federal Work Camp at Loretto, that's where I went when we pulled into the parking lot. A CO there told me that all self-surrendering inmates had to go across the street to the Federal Correctional Institution (FCI) low-security prison to check in first. I went there, said I was there to self-surrender, and said goodbye to my family and friends. A CO then had me go through a metal detector. So far so good. I had brought nothing but the clothes on my back and a driver's license.

The CO asked if I was ready. "I am," I said, although I wasn't quite sure what he meant. We walked out of the main entrance, turned right, and began walking around the building to the back of the prison, away from the camp. "Wait a minute," I said. "I think there's been a mistake. I'm supposed to be in the camp."

"Not according to *my* paperwork," he said. "Welcome to prison."

I told myself to stay calm. *You can call the attorneys on Monday and get this worked out*, I thought. In the outbuilding at the back of the prison I went through a more rigorous body check and a more sensitive metal detector. From there, the CO escorted me to Receiving & Discharge (R&D) inside the main prison building. I was strip-searched again, given a cursory medical exam, my fourth DNA swab, and a set of khaki XXXXL pants and shirt (which for the next three days I had to use one hand to hold up—"sorry, but that's the only size we have"), a pair of blue canvas slippers, a pair of underwear, a pair of socks, and a roll of toilet paper. The CO took a mug shot photo for my ID, and put me in a holding cell for forty-five minutes. My new first name was "inmate." I was also now known as prisoner number 79637-083.

A second CO finally arrived and took me to my housing unit, Central 1, trying to be helpful along the way by saying things like "You only have thirty months? That's good. A lot of guys die here because their sentences are so long." He offered one word of advice: "If anybody comes into your room without being invited, that's an act of aggression." *Great*, I thought. *I've been here for forty-five minutes and I'm going to get my ass kicked.* He pointed out the hall I needed to take to get to the cafeteria and said that I would probably have an easy time of things.

We arrived in an overcrowded cubicle with three bunk beds. He pointed at a top bunk, said "home sweet home," and walked away. I didn't really know what to do at that point, so I climbed up into the bed and fell asleep. The truth was that I was in shock. I figured I would get my bearings when I woke up. I would introduce myself to my cellmates, generally keep my mouth shut, and figure out the lay of the land.

Two hours later I awoke and introduced myself to my cellmates: three Mexican drug smugglers, one of whom was a major prison gang leader, a black drug dealer from Virginia, and a Chinese drug dealer who, despite having been in American prisons since 1988, could barely speak a word of English besides "muthafucka."

Soon after awakening, I was sitting in a chair next to my bunk when two neo-Nazis walked in. The first one, a tall, pale skinhead, had a swastika tattoo that took up his entire neck. The other was small and fat, with a swastika and "WHITE POWER" tattooed on his arms, along with a small skull on his left cheek.

I jumped out of the chair and put up my dukes. "What do you want?" I shouted.

"Take it easy," the big guy said. "Are you the new guy?"

I kept my fists up. "Yeah. So?" The big guy leaned in.

"Are you a fag?"

"No," I responded.

"Are you a rat?"

"No. I didn't have anybody else in my case."

"Are you a chomo?" I had never heard the term before.

"I don't know what that means," I told him.

"Cho-mo," he said slowly, like I was stupid. "Child molester."

"Of course I'm not a child molester," I said, outraged.

"OK," he continued. "You can sit with us at the Aryan table in the cafeteria." *Great*, I thought. *I guess now I'm with the Aryans.*

Some time later I was sitting in the chair again when two hugely-built African-Americans wearing skullcaps walked into the room. I recognized them immediately as members of the Nation of Islam. The first one was holding a newspaper. Again I jumped up. Again I heard, "Take it easy. Are you the dude from the CIA?"

"I am," I said warily.

He handed me the newspaper. "Reverend Farrakhan says you're a hero of the Muslim people. We want you to know you won't have any problems with us." I thanked them and they went on their way. We never spoke to each other again.

(About a year later, after I had struck up a friendship with a senior captain from one of New York's five organized crime families, the captain stopped me in the hall. "Let me ask you a question. Why in the world do you sit with those Nazi retards in the cafeteria?" I shrugged. "I don't know. On my first day they said I should sit with them." He looked at me like I was the one with a mental handicap. He put his finger in the air dramatically. "From today...you're with the Italians!" And from that day I sat with the Italians. I attended every Italian party and dinner, we exercised together in the yard, and we became good friends.)

I had missed lunch and the laundry work hours that first day, so I didn't eat and I had to wait until Monday for real clothes. I sat in my cell for two hours before Robert Vernon, an Australian arsonist, approached me. He's the Australian I mentioned earlier. I'll get into more detail about Robert in coming chapters. Suffice it to say that Robert makes a very good first impression. He's warm, friendly, outgoing, and helpful. He mentioned that I would have to meet Dave Phillips, with whom Robert said I had "a lot in common," Frank Russo, and Art Rachel. He would introduce me to them. He also said I needed to find a job immediately, or I'd be placed in the kitchen, the worst job in the prison. I was very grateful for Robert's help in those first few days. For all his faults I would soon learn about, he helped me a lot.

As I said, I "self-surrendered" to prison. That is, I literally drove up to the prison, walked in the front door, and said, "Hi. I'm John Kiriakou. I'm here to turn myself in." Being brought into the actual prison confused me because the prosecutors in my case, my attorneys, and the judge all agreed that I would go to a minimum-security federal work camp. Camps have no fences, no barbed wire, and some prisoners even work in town at the local university.

As it turns out, judges can only make *recommendations* as to prison assignments. The Bureau of Prisons, in its infinite wisdom, decided that I should do my sentence in a real prison. No club fed for me. This was going to be hard time. I finally got telephone privileges five days after I arrived. My first call was to my attorney to tell him that the Justice Department had put me in the actual prison, not the minimum-security work camp. "Oh, my," he said. "Well, we can file a motion asking the judge to move you. But it'll be two years before we even get a hearing, and you'll be home by then. I'm sorry. You're just going to have to tough it out."

I understood immediately that I would have to "adapt to my current environment," as the CIA had taught me. I took the first days and weeks to get the lay of the land.

No two prisoners' experiences are the same. Certainly, prisons vary from location to location within the same security level. For example, Loretto has a reputation as being a haven for pedophiles. They walk freely around the yard, hang out in the TV rooms without being bothered, and generally carry on as if they own the place. In other low-security prisons, pedophiles are frequently banned from the TV room and have to stand in the hallway to watch TV, they're subject to an occasional "thumping" in the yard, or they're banned from the yard altogether. Many are not even allowed by their roommates in their own rooms except to sleep and during count times. There are no pedophiles in medium-security prisons or in penitentiaries because it's too dangerous for them, unless, of course, they killed the children they molested, in which case they spend their sentences in a medium-security prison's solitary confinement unit.

Low-security prisons have double fences topped with concertina wire, motion detectors, and roving patrols. But there are no guard towers in lows, and none of the COs are armed. There is very little violence other than the occasional fisticuffs over what show to watch on TV. Sexual violence is even more rare. I was surprised to learn that there is "situational homosexuality," which is consensual (and still illegal), but that, too, is unusual.

I never served in a medium or a pen. Violence is a way of life in those institutions; serious, injury-inducing fights are routine occurrences, and prisoner movements are tightly controlled. The day before I arrived at Loretto, a CO was murdered at the nearby US Penitentiary Canaan. The rumor was that he had mocked an inmate and took a shank to the heart. I lost count of the number of times fellow prisoners who had worked their way down from a higher-security prison told me, following a tiff with a CO, "If this were a medium or a pen, I would have cut his head off." That kind of violence simply doesn't happen in a low.

With that said, prisoner movement in lows is also pretty tightly controlled. Prisoners can only go from Point A to Point B during "ten-minute moves." Once the ten minutes have passed, you're locked down wherever you happen to be. If you want to go somewhere else, you have to wait fifty minutes.

The daily schedule is set in stone. Breakfast is at 6:00 a.m. and "work call," where everybody heads out to do their "jobs," is at 7:30 a.m. "Recall," where everybody must return to their respective housing units, is at 10:20 a.m. Lunch is at 11:00 am, and then afternoon work call is at 12:20 p.m. Afternoon recall is at 3:00 p.m. Dinner is at 5:00 p.m. Evening work call is at 6:00 p.m., and final recall is at 9:00 p.m. That's also when all prisoners are locked down for the night. "Lights out" is at 11:00 p.m. The only change on weekends and holidays is that breakfast is at 7:00 a.m. and there's no work call.

Interspersed throughout the day (and night) are "counts." "Standing counts," where all prisoners must stand silently next to their bunks and be counted to ensure that nobody has escaped, are at 4:15 p.m. and 9:30 p.m. There is also a standing count at 10:00 a.m on weekends and holidays. Non-standing counts are at midnight, 3:00 a.m., and 5:00 a.m. Since most everybody is asleep at these times, COs go from bed to bed shining a ridiculously bright flashlight in your face, again to make sure that you haven't escaped. I never really understood that, as we'd been locked in since 9:00 p.m., and it's impossible to get through concrete, steel bars, and bulletproof glass, over two twelve-foot fences topped with concertina wire, past the night-vision security cameras and motion detectors, and into the night. But that's just the way it is. I had a lot to learn in those first days. There is no "orientation." You just have to pick things up on your own. It's all part of a broader "prison culture," where nobody is expected to help anybody else. I had to remind myself to keep quiet, watch my back, and try to elicit the information I needed.

There are no "cells" in the common sense of the word in low-security prisons. Instead, there are different housing setups depending on the unit in which one lives. Loretto was originally built as a Catholic monastery, and the original housing unit, North Unit, was made up of individual rooms with a closet and a small sink. When Loretto became a prison, the walls dividing each pair of rooms were knocked out, so one-man rooms became two-man rooms. Unfortunately, because of overcrowding, those two-man rooms now hold six men in bunk beds.

South Unit had smaller rooms, meant for two men, which when I was there held four or six. Larger rooms, which used to hold card or game tables or pool tables, became housing rooms and now hold fourteen to twenty-eight men each.

Central Unit, where I lived, was built to look like a prison housing unit. It was a large, no-nonsense unit divided into sixteen-by-twenty-nine-foot cubicles, each of which was separated by six-foot-high concrete block walls. Each cube was designed to hold four men, but held six. The two former game rooms held twenty men. In total, Central 1 had 198 men, 12 showers, 10 sinks, and 5 toilets. It was crowded and very loud. (Central 2, which was up one floor, had about fifty more men than Central 1.) Central 1 was also the only unit without any windows, so I never knew if it was night or day, raining, snowing, cloudy, or sunny, and there was no circulation of fresh air.

Roommates are another issue entirely. There's actually a lot of work involved with finding the right roommates. When I first arrived, I was just plopped into the first available bed. But once you've been in prison six months, you can ask to move to a different cubicle.

There's a great sense of working against the clock when a bed comes open, or is about to come open, in your cube. The goal is to find the best possible roommate and to invite him to move into the cube before the "counselor," a prison officer with jurisdiction over bed assignments, puts a lunatic, a child molester, or a filthy pig in the bed. Pedophiles certainly are not optimal roommates, unless they're clean, quiet, and never, ever have visitors. (Cell rules for most pedophiles are that they can never have visitors, nor may they ever talk about their crimes.) Once a prisoner is chosen for a room, the other potential roommates interview him and vote (except pedophiles, who are cut out of the entire process.) If he is acceptable, one of the roommates and the prospect go to the counselor together and fill out the paperwork for the move. You have a new roommate the next day.

Jobs are another major issue. There are lots of nonsense jobs all around the prison. "Stand-by orderlies," who are technically on call in case of a janitorial emergency of some sort, make $0.60 a month. They literally do nothing. The worst possible jobs are in food service, although prisoners who work in the kitchen get larger portions and can steal whatever they want. Landscaping and snow removal are also terrible jobs. The work call, when it's snowing, is 4:00 a.m. No thanks.

Every prisoner, within one week of arrival, must find a job. The truth is that there are four times as many prisoners as there are jobs, so most of the jobs are make-work or no work. After a brief moment of idealism, when I volunteered to be a GED tutor and was immediately slapped down by my "counselor," who shouted, "If I want you to teach a fucking class, I'll ask you to teach a fucking class!," I decided to do as little work as humanly possible. I also made a commitment to myself: I would not help these crooked cops run their prison. I would not be a clerk. I would be an orderly, and I would otherwise do what I could for other prisoners by helping them with legal work.

My first job was in the library, one of the very, very few air-conditioned rooms in the entire prison. I reported to work at 7:30 a.m. "work call" and then I sat there like a bump on a log until 10:30 a.m., when all the other prisoners moved to their housing units to wait for "lunch call." From 10:30 a.m. to 10:40 a.m., I had to wipe down the library's tables and chairs, and then return to my unit. My salary was $16.00 a month.

I hated the job from the second I got there. It really wasn't the job itself that was bad; it was the office. The library is part of the "Education Department," which, in reality, educates no one. The

CO staff was made up of a collection of lazy slobs, malcontents, and bullies. What I hated most were their attitudes. Who did these maroons think they were? They get to tell me that I'm a piece of shit because I'm a prisoner? I quit after six weeks. When they asked me why, I told them the truth. They told me to never come back. No problem there.

I transferred to the chapel, where the atmosphere was much more welcoming (although it, too, was filled with pedophiles). My job was to dust, vacuum, and get books from the chapel library for any prisoner who wanted one. I got a lot of personal work done during my hours at the chapel. Otherwise, I spent a good deal of my time helping prisoners write letters to judges, attorneys, or groups that work to defend prisoners' rights. I helped illiterate prisoners write letters or emails home. And I even designed one prisoner's website. My pay there was only $1.08 a month, but it was worth it.

Besides education and the chapel, a prisoner can also work in recreation, medical, laundry, plumbing, facilities, woodshop, the psychology library, manufacturing (UNICOR), the barbershop, or the kitchen. In and of itself, the kitchen was by far the worst job in the prison. The morning shift began at 4:00 a.m., conditions were harsh, and the COs in charge were a collection of the biggest douchebags in the entire prison.

With that said, an enterprising prisoner could make a good living in the kitchen, not from the salary, but by stealing. There were two ways to do it. Most kitchen workers just stole whatever was available that day (donuts, bagels, scones, cookies) then went from unit to unit selling them two for a bag of mackerel ("mack"). The butchers and cooks had a better scam going. They would take "orders" for a certain amount of meat per month, whether it was chicken, beef, or pork, and steal that amount for their customers. Then each month, the recipient's family would transfer $100 or $150 into the butcher's or cook's commissary account. It was good for them, but for the rest of us it was chicken potpie with no chicken, hot dogs instead of roast beef, and sloppy joes instead of pork loin.

Some guys are very entrepreneurial. One prisoner made a handsome living selling used shoes on which he took a commission. Some prisoners had "convenience stores" in their lockers. They sold sodas, candy, and chips with a standard 30 percent markup. There were a dozen bookies in the prison (a good friend of mine being the most successful), some of whom made thousands of dollars a month that they sent home as a nest egg for their releases. Some guys repaired radios, some did unofficial, unlicensed chiropractic work, and some sold underwear, socks, and T-shirts stolen from the laundry.

Others were even more enterprising. One person provided "tantric" massages, complete with an index finger slathered in Vaseline, behind the rec building for a book of stamps. Another prisoner, for a book of stamps, would let you watch as he shoved a Dial roll-on deodorant up his ass. Yet another sold his "turnkey" business and list of a dozen clients for sixty-five books of stamps. His service offerings were a hand job for one book of stamps, a blowjob for two books, or you could pound him in the ass for five books. Ah, capitalism! I was happy to take my $1.08 a month and to otherwise rely on the generosity of family and friends.

Factions are another important issue that every new prisoner has to come to grips with immediately. Whether you like it or not, whether you consider yourself culturally progressive or not, you are confronted by every racial stereotype society has to offer while you're in prison. I'm not saying this to be glib. There is very little mixing of the races in prison, other than during sporting events. Whites eat with whites, blacks eat with blacks, and Hispanics eat with Hispanics, for example. You can, of course, have friends of different races, but you won't eat together. And you won't watch TV together. The TV room is also segregated.

Everybody is divided into factions, and each faction has its own "shot-caller." The shot-caller is the person you go to to mediate any dispute you may have with another prisoner, whether of your own race or another. That way, problems are worked out before they lead to violence. It almost always works. Indeed, the only violence I saw in prison was a result of three separate disagreements over what to watch on TV, and once because one white guy called another white guy a "rat."

The factions are what you might expect them to be. They include Aryans/hillbillies, blacks, Hispanics, Muslims, Italians, and rats/child molesters. Each faction has its own shot-caller, except the Italians, and its own table or tables in the cafeteria.

Most whites in prison call themselves Aryans. They're not. They're generally toothless, stupid, redneck hillbillies who have spent most of their lives in prison, almost always for manufacturing meth or dealing in huge quantities of marijuana. Their tattoos are prolific: lots of swastikas, German SS insignias, and meaningless clichés like "Death b4 Dishonor," "Bloodline of Champions," "Last of a Dying Breed," and other nonsense. If you want to talk to them about something other than making meth, NASCAR, weightlifting, or get-rich-quick schemes, you're out of luck. The white shot-callers tend to be big, patient guys who speak a little Spanish.

The blacks tend to have three shot-callers: an overall boss, a representative of the Bloods gang, and a representative of the Crips gang. The Bloods and Crips generally stay away from each other (remember, this was a low-security prison, and most prisoners didn't want to risk going back to a medium or a penitentiary), and if a dispute pops up, the head shot-caller will mediate. With that said, most of the violence was black/black or black/Hispanic. Like I said, the issue was always what to watch on TV.

The Hispanics were complicated. Every Hispanic prisoner *must* belong to the prison gang "Pisces." If they don't join, they get a good beating before checking themselves into protective custody and getting shipped to another prison, where the experience would likely repeat itself. All Pisces members MUST work out every day, including calisthenics, weightlifting, and cardio. When the weather is good there's soccer and baseball. Every day. This is so that in case of a race riot, the Hispanics would be able to hold their own.

But the Hispanics were not monolithic. Hispanic prisoners also identified by country of origin and by street gang. For example, Dominicans tended to associate only with other Dominicans, Mexicans with Mexicans, and Puerto Ricans with Puerto Ricans. Puerto Ricans and Mexicans generally looked down on each other ("Dirty Mexican!" "Dirty Puerto Rican!") Everybody looked down on the Dominicans. The Costa Ricans, Venezuelans, and Colombians thought they were better than everybody else, nobody respected Salvadorians or Hondurans, etc. Each ethnicity thus had its own shot-caller, and there was a shot-caller council of all Latino ethnicities to mediate disputes among them.

On top of that, there was a myriad of gangs: MS-13, Norteños, Burachos, Mexican Mafia, Zetas, you name it. There were gangs from all over Latin America. On the street they're deadly rivals, but in the prison, their gang identities were subjugated to Pisces. There could be no in-fighting. If there was, it would have led to chaos. I have to admit to a grudging respect for how this system worked. And it did work. It was very labor intensive, with strong personalities, ethnicities, and gang affiliations at play. But violence was rare. I made it a point to befriend several of the shot-callers. It went a long way toward building mutual respect.

The Muslims were also a diverse group. There were several Arab, Kurdish, Indian, Afghan, and Pakistani prisoners at Loretto who were adherents to mainstream Sunni and Shia Islam. Believe it or not, they were a small minority among prison Muslims. Most prison Muslims are African-American converts to the Nation of Islam (NOI), a group that the Grand Mufti of Saudi Arabia, the seniormost religious figure in Sunni Islam, has branded a cult.

As I mentioned earlier, I had more respect and closer ongoing contact with the Italians than with any other group in prison. I found them to be honest, honorable, and generous. Sometimes I felt like I was in a movie: dinner at 8:00 p.m. It was frequently pasta with three cheeses, shredded chicken, fresh tomatoes, mushrooms, and basil, lots of garlic, a delicate white wine sauce, and maybe even some sweet and hot Italian sausage. I never asked how they got it into the prison. I didn't want to know. What I do know is that my friend Mark Lanzilotti made fine dining, restaurant-quality Italian food with a garbage bucket full of water and a live electrical wire. It was amazing.

Most of New York's five families were represented in Loretto: Gambino, Bonnano, Luchese, Colombo, and Genovese. There was a sizable contingent from Philadelphia (Bruno/Scarfo), northern New Jersey (Decavalcante), Boston, and upstate New York. A half dozen were "made men." The rest were not. The Italians didn't need a shot-caller because the made guys worked together, ate together, and socialized together. The Italians commanded far more respect than their small population otherwise would have warranted. Because they were direct and honest in their dealings with others, they commanded respect and admiration. They were by far my favorite people with whom to hang out. I'll get into more detail about the Italians later.

As crazy as it might sound, the pedophiles also had something of a "shot-caller," not that any other shot-caller would sit down with him. They wouldn't. But the "chomo shot-caller," as he was known, gave pedophiles a feeling of representation, kind of like belonging to a weak labor union in a strong industry. The chomo shot-caller could do nothing to prevent a pedophile from having ice water poured on him while he was sleeping, from being thrown out of the TV room, or from being bullied in his cell. But he was there every other Friday to meet the bus from other prisons and to provide each newly-arrived child molester with soap, shampoo, toothpaste, a toothbrush, and shower shoes. He was more like a welcome wagon than anything else.

The rats and snitches had nobody to look out for them. Except for the cops, of course.

As you might imagine, many prisoners were in constant search of a vice. Tobacco is technically banned in federal facilities. I say "technically" because it's freely available, albeit at a price. A major part of the problem is that seemingly every CO chews tobacco. Many of them walk the compound with small plastic or Styrofoam cups, or with empty plastic soda bottles, spitting tobacco-laden saliva into them as a disgusting reminder that they can have tobacco and prisoners cannot—federal regulations be damned! Even the captain's wife, who worked in the mail room, chewed tobacco like a truck driver.

That's not bad enough, however. When they are finished chewing, the COs normally just spit their wad of used tobacco on the ground, if outside, or into a trash basket, if inside. Enterprising prisoners retrieve the chewed tobacco, dry it out, wrap it in toilet paper, and sell the "spitterette" for ten dollars' worth of commissary goods. Matches are easily smuggled in by visitors or crooked COs, or prisoners use batteries and live wires as makeshift lighters.

Even more dangerous, smokeless tobacco contains very tiny particles of fiberglass, meant to gently cut the inside of the lip, thus allowing the user to more easily take in nicotine. When a prisoner smokes this tobacco-fiberglass concoction, he draws the fiberglass into his lungs, making himself more susceptible to lung cancer, mesothelioma, and any number of potentially fatal lung diseases. All that for only ten bucks. Or, the prisoner can just pay a crooked CO to bring in chew or a pack of cigarettes, each of which cost one hundred dollars. (Your family just sends the crooked CO a money order.)

Illegal drugs are an even bigger problem. Every once in a while, somebody on the outside will throw a package containing drugs, and sometimes a cell phone, over the fence into the prison yard where a prisoner can retrieve it. This happened a couple of times while I was at Loretto. More unusually—it only happened once while I was there—somebody on the outside was stupid enough to actually mail drugs to a prisoner. The prisoner was then called down to the mail room, where he was arrested on new charges before being taken to solitary to await arraignment and transport to a higher-security facility. The idiot on the outside also got a charge.

Once, while being routinely strip-searched after a visit, I asked a chatty CO if he had ever caught anybody smuggling anything back into the prison. He said no, but added, "but that's how the drugs get in here." I laughed and said, "Wait a minute. Are you telling me that in the visiting room, in full view of three COs and six security cameras, a woman will take a bag of drugs out of her vagina, and give them to a prisoner, who will then insert them into his rectum, get through the strip search, and sell the drugs in the prison?" "Yep," he said. "Or," I continued, "does a crooked CO just bring them in?" He didn't respond.

Heroin was the drug of choice at Loretto. The overwhelming number of prisoners who were at Loretto on drug charges were in for cocaine (the Hispanics), crack (the blacks), or meth (the whites.) Most weren't there on heroin-related charges. But of the prisoners who tested positive during their random drug tests, it was heroin that did them in. That's not necessarily to say that there were any consequences. One prisoner in my unit tested positive for heroin on a number of occasions. But because he was a valuable rat for the COs, he was simply told to stop doing it. Eventually, he was transferred to a minimum-security camp, where he tested positive again. Because his use as a rat had run its course, he was sent to solitary for a while, then shipped out to another low-security facility. (Interestingly, this prisoner once complained to me that his parents never sent him any money because they thought he would use it to buy drugs. "Can you imagine that?" he asked incredulously. "Where would I find drugs in prison?")

One of the first prison slang terms that I learned at Loretto was "chomo." Short for "child molester," it's a catch-all for anybody with even a hint of child sex in his case. Chomos were divided into "clickers" and "touchers." Clickers were caught looking at child pornography. Touchers, well, you get the idea. Fully 25 percent of the prisoners in Loretto were pedophiles, according to BOP figures. This is typical of a low-security facility. There are almost no pedophiles in medium-security prisons or in penitentiaries, where it was too dangerous for them, so no matter how horrific their crimes or how long their sentences, almost all pedophiles go only to lows. (They are not eligible to serve their sentences in minimum-security camps.)

With the proliferation of child pornography on the Internet, it is much easier to catch pedophiles in the act of committing their crimes than it has ever been. Most of the pedophiles in the prison system are white. I'll let the sociologists and psychologists figure that one out. They range in age from eighteen to the middle eighties. Most of them profess to be very religious. Indeed, chapel services are normally packed to the rafters with pedophiles. Almost all of them shout about their innocence, the injustice of their incarcerations, and their own victimization. Other prisoners would just as soon kill them.

I decided to go to church on my first Sunday in prison. I'm not Catholic, but my wife is, so I went to the Catholic service with a very religious "made man" from the Genovese crime family who had invited me. We sat in the back. I had no idea that the two of us were practically the only non-pedophiles in the place until it was time for the "sign of peace," where you shake hands with those around you. One man put out his hand, only for my Italian friend to say, "Touch me and I'll break your neck, you fucking pervert." My friend then put his hand out for me to shake. "Peace be upon you, John."

"And peace be upon you, Steve."

I came into contact with many pedophiles. The first was on my first day in the library. The lead orderly there, William, asked me if I had just arrived and if I had ever been in prison before. I said I had gotten in a week earlier and that this was my first—and last—stint. I told him that I had thirty months, and he exhaled, saying, "I wish." I asked him what kind of sentence he had, to which he responded, "Twenty-four years, unfortunately." I was surprised at the length of the sentence. I didn't know anybody could have such a long stretch and be allowed to serve in a low. I asked him what he had done. He responded matter-of-factly, "I got caught looking at crime scene photos."

"What's that supposed to mean?" I asked.

"Well," he said. "Having sex with children is a crime. I got caught looking at the photos. But what really did me in was that subfolder."

"OK," I said. "I'll bite. What was in the subfolder?"

Excitedly, he said, "I like to masturbate to pictures of dead children. I have a friend who works at a morgue…"

I interrupted him. "Don't ever try to speak to me again. Never. Understand?" He never spoke to me again.

I knew in my gut when I first arrived that my biggest challenge would be the COs. I'm going to make some generalities about COs. The problem with generalities is that they don't apply to everyone. They're generalities, though, because they apply to most. There were certainly some COs I respected. One Recreation Department CO was a genuinely good guy—cheerful, friendly, and respectful. My regular afternoon unit CO for most of my sentence was also a good guy. He had twenty-three years of experience and he was respected by everybody because he showed respect. The COs who usually manned the visitors room were alright, too. They didn't take their jobs overly seriously, they engaged in small talk, and they responded to "hello," which was very unusual in prison.

The sad truth, however, is that most COs are assholes. They're power-mad bullies, passive-aggressive instigators, and just all-around dicks. I believe this is for several reasons. First, let's look at who becomes a CO. Dr. Peter Moskos, a professor of criminal justice at New York's John Jay College, author of the book *In Defense of Flogging*, and a former Baltimore policeman, says that the Bureau of Prisons is really little more than an employment agency for unemployed, uneducated, rural whites. He is 100 percent correct. Most prisons are in the boondocks, heavily white, rural areas where there is no industry and no opportunity for work. The BOP is thus a multi-generational savior. Sign up, go through a short training program, hang around for ten, twenty, twenty-five, or thirty years, and get a nice pension. Because of the mistaken belief that COs are somehow "law enforcement," the job attracts former military grunts and rejects from the local police academy. And the qualifications to be a CO are basic, at best: you must be an American citizen, at least eighteen years old, with no felony convictions, and you must be at least *working* on a GED. The cream of the crop this is not.

Daily prison life often came down to "us" versus "them." That is, it was the prisoners versus the COs. Relations between the two were proper at best and openly hostile at worst.

I was consistently awed by how many COs were barely literate. Mail call was often a nightmare with different variations on people's names every time a letter was handed out. Jose became "Joezee," Socrates was "Sow-crates," and so on. My last name had a hundred pronunciations.

My own personal policy was to mind my own business and to have no contact with COs unless I had to. But that didn't stop one CO from whispering "scum" every time I walked past him in the cafeteria. Another looked at me and said "traitor" as I passed him in the yard. Class acts, both. And remember, if this had been a medium or a pen, they might have ended up with knives coming out of their throats.

Several COs could also join the ranks of the inmates in the not-too-distant future. Just after I arrived at Loretto, one female case manager was escorted to her car in tears and fired after being caught *in flagrante delicto* with a prisoner. Her humiliated CO husband, who was an investigator in the Special Investigative Service (SIS) and was supposed to have a foolproof network of informants to keep him updated on goings-on around the prison, had to take time off, lest he have to face the ridicule of the prisoners.

This is not to say that all COs are bad people. They aren't. One senior CO discreetly pulled me aside once and said he had followed my case, he thought I had been wronged, and he thought I had done a service to the country. Another CO said that he had "great respect" for what I had done, and that he would always treat me with respect. He did. One CO once discretely pulled me aside and asked how he could go about applying for a job at the CIA. I told him that there was nothing sexy about it. He just had to go to the CIA website and click "Apply." After pondering the idea, he said that he was just dreaming. His mother, father, and grandfather had all been COs, and his wife would never agree to move out of Loretto, population 1,200.

This is not an unusual situation. A large minority of COs have parents, brothers, sisters, sons, daughters, and cousins who were or are COs. The insular environment that is every rural prison makes for a very incestuous culture. And that often leads to a lot of trouble.

I personally saw several of these sexual situations, unique to prison, but unheard of elsewhere in government (except maybe at the CIA, where the culture encourages Agency romances because both parties have security clearances). At Loretto, though, there's something grosser and more primal about those relationships, something I never saw anywhere else in government.

Two COs, married to each other when I first arrived, went through something I consider to be rather typical. The wife had a reputation as being "friendly" with prisoners. Too friendly, actually. One of my closest friends in the prison told me that she would come into his room, order everybody out except one prisoner, manually pleasure that prisoner under the sheets, then go about her rounds. She was finally caught months later, after the prisoner had been transferred to another prison, when their love letters were intercepted. The CO was fired and escorted out of the building. Needless to say, she and her husband soon divorced. Several months later, the husband and a colleague were escorting me to a local hospital for an x-ray. I overheard the husband tell the other CO, "If you can introduce me to somebody who might be interested in a recently-divorced guy with a four-inch dick, I'd really appreciate it."

I've mentioned that I left my job in the library for one in the chapel only six weeks after I arrived in prison. The library is run by the Education Department, and I had a real problem with the CO's attitudes there. We never exchanged a word; the vibe was unspoken. But when I was leaving on my last day, I overheard one of the COs say about me, "I could never stand that fucking guy." The feeling was mutual.

Oddly, the three COs in Education looked alike. One was tall and thin with a shiny bald head. We called him "Dr. Evil." One was short and thin with a shiny bald head. We called him "Mini Me." And the third was tall and fat with a shiny bald head. We called him "Fat Slob." These three COs were "teachers," although they didn't actually teach anybody. They technically led the GED program (even though prisoners, as tutors, taught the classes.) Besides, with a GED passage rate of 17 percent, calling oneself a "teacher" was a real stretch.

A few days after I arrived at Loretto, I was sitting in the library during my shift, when a Pennsylvania state trooper walked in and asked to see Dr. Evil. They whispered to each other for a minute, then walked out of the library, it turned out, to go to the lieutenant's office. Another fifteen minutes passed, and several of us stood stunned as we watched Dr. Evil being led away handcuffs. His crime? He had allegedly beaten his wife to a pulp. But the next day, there he was at work, albeit in a terrible mood. Remember, to be a CO, you can't have been *convicted* of a *felony*. He wasn't. His wife later dropped the charges.

Mini Me was still reliving his glory days as a grunt in the military. Every Monday he would brag about how many cases of beer he had consumed over the weekend and about how far he had jogged. He ran every race that Pittsburgh, two hours to the west, had to offer, and he would crow about the marathons he had run with nothing more than a stomach full of brew. He was finally humbled when he was arrested at 6:00 a.m. one Sunday, drunk, and jogging butt naked a few miles from the prison. This had no effect on his job.

When I first arrived, several of my cellmates warned me to stay away from a CO assigned to the cafeteria. They told me he was a "pervert" and that he preyed on prisoners. When I asked around, I learned that this CO had something of an "agreement" with several kitchen workers. If he could perform oral sex on them, they could steal whatever they wanted from the kitchen and sell it on the compound. At some point, though, the deal fell apart, and somebody told on him. A week or so later he was escorted out of the prison, and we never saw him again.

I had nothing but contempt for COs as a group. In my personal experience, the vast majority are stupid, lazy bullies, in some cases sadistic, and in nearly all, untrustworthy. Do you remember being in seventh grade? There was always a kid who was bullied and teased by others. But he wasn't smart enough, aggressive enough, or skillful enough to make something out of himself as an adult. Well, that kid grew up to be a CO. He's no smarter than he was in seventh grade, but he's just as pissed off now as he was then. And although he can't exact revenge on the bullies who beat him up in seventh grade, he can take it out on prisoners who have absolutely no recourse and no way to protect themselves.

More experienced officers and prisoners who have worked their way down from a penitentiary told me that disrespectful COs obviously started in low-security prisons. If they had treated prisoners in the pens the way they treat them in the lows, they wouldn't have lived to see the end of the shift.

One administrator told me that when he was working in a pen there was a Hispanic prisoner with the first name "Undi." One day Undi was walking past a CO when the CO shouted, "Hey you! Come here!" Undi walked over to the CO to see what he wanted. The CO said, "What's your fucking name? Undi? Like underwear? Who gave you that fucking name? Your mommy?" Without saying a word, Undi pulled out a shank and plunged it into the CO's neck. Repeatedly. He bled to death on the spot.

The same administrator told me that he had a CO friend at the pen that caught an inmate cooking with a stinger. A stinger is a piece of metal, like the faceplate from a wall plug, that is then attached to two live wires. The faceplate is placed in a bucket of water, and the wires are put directly into a wall outlet. The electricity causes the water to boil, then food is placed into a plastic bag, which is then placed in the boiling water. Pasta can go directly into the water without the plastic bag. It's an incredibly dangerous way to cook.

This happens every single day, and ninety-nine out of one hundred times COs will just ignore it. This CO, for some reason, decided to make a scene. He berated the prisoner for cooking, shouting, "Are you fucking stupid? How many fucking times do

I have to tell you? No fucking cooking!" The prisoner pulled the stinger out of the water by the wire, still attached to the wall socket, and tossed it to the CO. The CO, without thinking, caught it and was electrocuted. He died in a hospital three days later. Both COs and prisoners in pens learn to respect one another. The COs don't want to die, and prisoners don't have anything to lose. Most of them are doing between twenty years and life anyway. So there's an uneasy truce. Not in a low, though.

I was so taken aback by the filthy language the COs used with prisoners, including me when I first arrived, that I went to the law library to look up the regulations on abusive language. The reg is crystal clear: "In their official capacities, employees may not use profane, obscene, or abusive language when communicating with inmates, fellow employees, or others. Employees shall conduct themselves in a manner that will not be demeaning to inmates, fellow employees, or others." The penalties for verbal abuse are "official reprimand" for a first offense, fourteen-day suspension for a second offense, and removal from the job for a third offense.

I saw prisoners verbally abused almost every day of my incarceration. I was luckier than most other prisoners, though. A few months after I arrived, I began writing my "Letters from Loretto." I wrote about daily life, challenges, and what I saw as inefficiencies, hypocrisies, and illegalities within the Bureau of Prisons (BOP). Much to my surprise, the blog took off, and the first two postings garnered more than a million hits each. Several were picked up by the mainstream media, and were reported on CNN, Fox, MSNBC, ABC News, BBC, and elsewhere. I planted a message with a friendly CO, one I knew he would repeat: mess with me and see it on CNN in the morning. Most COs stayed out of my way. Some, the semiliterate bullies, tried to bait me. I gave as well as I took, but I was always careful not to cross the line, and the COs always knew when to back down. I could say things that landed other prisoners in the SHU—the Special Housing Unit, also known as solitary confinement—but I was careful not to go too far.

Most of the COs have nicknames, and most of those, while descriptive, are not very nice. At Loretto we had Sarge, Big Dummy, Blue, Honey Boo Boo, Big Bottom, Horseface, and her daughter, Spawn of Horseface, among others. COs who showed prisoners respect in turn were shown respect and were referred to by their actual names. It was the COs who insisted on being bullies, know-it-alls, and tough guys who were shown the disrespect of a nickname.

There were a couple of other things that surprised me when I went to prison. These were things I had generally never given a thought to. Some were funny. Others were just puzzling. I got a chuckle, for example, out of many of the tattoos I saw in prison. I was pretty much the only person in the entire prison without tattoos. As for the handful of tattoos I saw that were actually well done—that is, were good art—they were exclusive to young guys who had gone to real tattoo artists. Most inmates had horrible, poorly-done prison tats. Picture lots of swastikas, spider webs, barbed wire, random tribal symbols, and tributes to "Paula," "Donna," "LaShawnda," and lots of homies who had been killed on the streets.

Even the gay guys had tats, which wasn't the case among my gay friends and relatives at home. One gay guy in my housing unit was covered with very high-quality and colorful tats that he had obviously gotten on the outside. As soon as he arrived I noticed a tattoo of a bright red cherry on the back of his neck, just under the hairline. One hot day during the summer, he took off his shirt while walking the track, revealing a lemon under the cherry, a grape under the lemon, and a gold bar under the grape. Odd. Below that were two cherries, followed by two lemons, two grapes, and two bars.

You really aren't supposed to stare at seminude guys in prison. You can catch a good beating if you look at the wrong guy. But I found the pattern fascinating. And it continued—three cherries, three lemons, three grapes, disappearing under his shorts. It wasn't until a unit-wide strip search months later that I saw the rest of the tattoo: three bars, the word "JACKPOT!" and an arrow pointing to his ass crack.

I thought this was weird, but not as weird as others I saw. One of my favorites took up one guy's entire back. It was Lady Justice in her flowing gown, lying on her side after being knocked to the ground, her blindfold askew, with her scales of justice on the ground next to her, her other arm up in the air as if to protect herself. Above her stood the owner of the tattoo with a .45 caliber handgun pointed at her. Above him was a text bubble with the words "Take that, bitch!" Classic.

A friend of mine had an elaborate tattoo done, which also took up his entire, ample back. The tattoo was of the federal courthouse in Boston, his hometown. Jesus Christ had burst through the roof of the building, holding an infant, but with the head of the tattoo's owner. One of the baby's arms was pointed skyward, where God himself was reaching down from a cloud to touch the baby's finger, a la God and Adam at the Sistine Chapel. Underneath were the words "Fuck the Justice Department!"

One prisoner, in what seemed to be a moment of religious discovery, got an elaborate tattoo of Christ carrying the cross. Above that tattoo were the words "Only God can judge…" Below it were the words "…so who the fuck do you think YOU is?"

Amid all the Nazi emblems, the literally thousands of devils, skulls, and nude women, there were some tattoos that were fun—and funny—just for their stupidity. One idiot had the crest of the Saudi royal family across his back. He thought it was cool looking. Another moron had "Fuck" on one eyelid and "You!" on the other, so he could send you a message every time he blinked.

One of my favorites was also in my housing unit. The owner was an idiot who had spent years in the Navy before becoming a really bad drug dealer; bad in that he kept getting caught. He also told everybody that he was a porn star. In reality, he just set up a webcam in his apartment and charged people fifty dollars a month to watch him masturbate and walk around naked. Anyway, he decided to get a new tattoo running down the length of his left arm. It was supposed to say, "If it doesn't make dollars, it doesn't make cents." Get it? He thought it was clever. He hired the unit tattoo guy to do the tattoo in one long sitting, and he ended up with "If it does'nt make dollars, it does'nt make sense." On top of misspelling "doesn't"—twice—the tattooist completely missed the pun. He ended up with a nasty black eye, and he gave him a refund. The new owner of the tattoo ended up looking even more stupid than when he set out to get some ink.

It's not hard to get a tattoo in prison, although it's illegal, painful, and carries serious health risks. (Rates of HIV and Hepatitis C are many, many times higher in prison than they are among the general public.) All you need is a Bic pen (thirty cents in the commissary) and an unfolded paper clip. You draw an outline of the tattoo on the skin, using lots of ink, then use the paper clip as a needle, forcing the ink under the skin. There's a lot of blood and pain, and most tattoos look like a child's drawing. You can get colored tattoos on the rare occasions when somebody can steal a red pen or a green, orange, or yellow highlighter. You also have to pay the tattoo artist between $20 and $150 worth of commissary.

If tattoos aren't your thing, you can also get a kind of body piercing. (Before I came to prison, I had never heard of this form of self-mutilation. Not only is it real, but it is also particularly popular among Hispanic inmates.)

They're called "cock rocks." Inmates take a domino out of a domino set and break it into pieces. (Dominoes are usually made out of wood or hard plastic.) The small pieces are filed down into shapes—circles, diamonds, whatever you want. Then you and the piercer go into the shower together, where he slits your penis with a razor blade taken from a shaving razor. He inserts the domino piece into your penis, then closes the cut either with a bandage or with stolen Krazy Glue. I'm told that this is done to "satisfy my woman when I get out." Apparently, it feels like the rib of a ribbed condom. But how the body doesn't just reject it over a period of time is a mystery to me. Honestly, I doubted at first that any of this was true until two guys in my cube, Luis and Julio, proudly whipped out their cocks and showed everybody in the room.

When I first arrived at Loretto, I thought that perhaps I should use my time constructively. There must be classes offered in things like plumbing, electrical work, or small engine repair, right? At least, that's what it said on the Internet. Instead, I was in for a surprise when I realized right off the bat that the "Education Department" was used for little more than teaching and running scams. Because the Education Department doesn't actually educate anybody, the prison relies on prisoners to teach classes of common interest. These Adult Continuing Education (ACE) classes were available to everyone and were supposed to be taught by experts in their fields. There were classes like Construction Management, taught by the guy who designed and poured the concrete steps at Dallas Cowboys Stadium; Creative Writing, taught by a prisoner who had never published anything in his life; History of Western Film, which was actually about Westerns and was taught by an old man who liked to watch them; Crochet; Gardening; Spanish; Typing; and others.

The most egregiously inappropriate classes were taught by scammers, who taught their scams, the mistakes they made, and how they could get away with it if they tried again. There were investment classes run by prisoners doing twenty years for running Ponzi schemes, classes on currency trading run by a former trader doing twenty years for not actually trading currencies but instead using client money to finance his lavish lifestyle, and a real estate class run by a guy doing ten years for selling shares in a condo development in New Hampshire that didn't actually exist.

My "favorite" ACE class was taught by a prisoner in my unit. A tax attorney and Baptist minister, he was also one of the most blatant and obvious con men I encountered at Loretto. His ACE class was on property development, and it was like reading a transcript of his case. This was the scam: the prisoner said he had a ninety-nine-year lease on a golf course in Coffee Bay, South Africa, on three miles of pristine, untouched Indian Ocean frontage. The course was eighteen holes, but was in need of TLC. He had hired a renowned golf course architect who had designed some of the best golf courses in America to fly to South Africa to conduct a feasibility study, site visit, CAD design, and cost study, along with an engineer, a golf pro, and a golf course builder. They concluded that the entire cost of renovation would be $2.2 million without a clubhouse and $3.5 million with a clubhouse.

The prisoner engaged Sotheby's International Realty in London to market and sell shares in the golf course and to sell twelve chalets that would be built along the beach. There would be a main lodge, restaurant, bar, and staff quarters. He also envisioned a two-star hotel on the edge of the property for backpackers—an "a la carte" option separate from golf. He asked potential investors for $500,000 each (or $10,000 a month) and showed a business plan estimating $2.2 million in revenue the first year against $1.2–1.6 million in costs. The business plan also allowed for future construction of a luxury eight-chalet camp with two private lodges set aside for investors, a small main lodge, outdoor and indoor dining, and a riverfront game viewing deck with no fences to separate it from the Kruger National Park.

The only problems a person could encounter, the prisoner said, were permits and financing. He told his students to hire the most experienced attorney they could find to deal with government regulations. He also explained that it's much, much easier to find individual investors than it is to go to a bank or investment company. In his case, he sought investors from his church in Virginia and quickly raised the first $2.2 million.

Soon after that, the plan expanded to include a third lodge, this one for big game hunters interested in bagging an elephant, lions, tigers, leopards, or water buffalo. When one of the students suggested that this was poaching and was illegal in South Africa, the prisoner responded, "Well, that's something you can work out with the South African government." The students were becoming skeptical.

The prisoner continued, though. "Once you have the money, you start developing. Once you develop, you sell shares. And once you sell shares, you open for business." The problem was that, while there was indeed a beaten-up old golf course on South Africa's Indian Ocean coast, the prisoner didn't have a lease on it, ninety-nine-year or otherwise. He flew the architect, engineer, and others to see the property as a ruse. He used the $2.2 million to buy a new house (for cash), a Mercedes Benz, and to put his daughter in private school. He was sentenced to twelve years and was ordered to pay back the $2.2 million. He was also disbarred. He is now studying for a minister's certificate from a mail-order Christian school.

The most egregiously inappropriate class that the Education Department had the unmitigated gall to sponsor was one called Reentry Benefits for Convicted Felons. It should have been called How to Scam Free Money from the Government. The informational handout stated things clearly in the first paragraph: "Supplemental Security Income (SSI) can best be described as a form of welfare that is paid through the Social Security office. There is no need to qualify. You automatically qualify because you are unemployed and are considered to be disabled. Be sure that you understand the situation concerning your disability. The government has declared that you are disabled because you have an emotional problem. If you had not had this emotional problem, you would have been able to conform to the rules of society, thus preventing the commission of your offense. Regardless of whether or not you feel, or accept the fact, that you are an offender, you do in fact have a disability. According to both federal and state policies, your mental and emotional problems constitute a hundred percent disability. You cease to be disabled when you become a productive member of society. You will qualify for $310 a month. But by law, you have only thirty hours after you're released to get to a Social Security office to put your application in.

"If you contact the Social Security Administration ninety days before your release date, and your application was processed, you will have a check waiting for you in the amount of $930 for three months' worth of benefits the afternoon after you report to the halfway house. This is black-and-white law under RCW 74.29.105 [sic]. Also, tell the Social Security counselor that you would like to apply for SSI Emergency Supplement benefits of $1,500 and show them your papers to prove you just got out of prison. You should have a check within seventy-two hours.

"The Small Business Administration (SBA) will loan you $24,000 to start any business you like. They will also give you $4,000 to get a car.

"Also, be sure to call the Food Stamp office's hotline and get $80 worth of food stamps. You can also apply for an F811 Food Stamp Grant that will get you another $160.

"Contact the federal Department of Vocational Rehabilitation [author's note: no such entity exists] and tell them you want to sign up for their assistance, thus you will be eligible for all kinds of free services, including schools, clothing, small business loans, financial aid for transportation, etc. You are a 'depressed minority' and the Department of Vocational Rehabilitation will give you $1,900 for a car or truck, $300 for work clothes, $400 for casual clothes, and $400 for new tools. Understand, again, that these are GRANTS and DO NOT have to be paid back at any time. These grants are available to you because you are a 'disadvantaged minority' because you just got out of prison. For more information, contact Mrs. H_____ in the Education Department."

I caught more grief complaining about this class than any other. The entire concept was a lie, and it did a disservice to every person who took it. In the end, I just kept my mouth shut.

Sometimes the scams were sophisticated, with some prisoners preying on the weakness and hopelessness of others. Pat Summer lived in my housing unit. He was a quiet, friendly guy, a devout Catholic with nine children. Pat was uncomfortable with bawdy talk and would literally walk away from a conversation if someone was swearing. Pat's problem was that he was a simpleton. At fifty-five years old, you'd think that he wouldn't have let his father-in-law talk him into burning down the family business for the insurance money. But that's what happened, and he got a very light three-year sentence for it. Pat was one of those guys who always seemed to be in a good mood and who trusted everybody. That was another of his problems.

One day Pat ran up to me and breathlessly announced, "Rocket's going home!" Rocket was a notorious child molester from Washington, DC. He had a long sentence and was most certainly not going home. That's what I told Pat. But Pat was insistent. "He renounced his American citizenship and he's moving to the Dominican Republic!" I laughed out loud. I had been a commissioned State Department consular officer, I said, and lesson number one was that an American citizen could renounce his citizenship only in a US consulate or embassy overseas—not from a prison cell in the US. Pat looked at me as though he pitied my ignorance. Then he described the most interesting scam I had ever heard. Here's how it worked.

"A guy in Central Two Unit who knows these things" was offering a service. For $25,000 he could get any prisoner Russian citizenship. He claimed to have contacts in the Russian Foreign Ministry who could process the paperwork and make anybody who applied a Russian citizen in one year. "This guy really has the inside track," Pat explained.

Once you got your Russian citizenship, you could apply for residency in the Dominican Republic, the Bahamas, Costa Rica, Aruba, or St. Kitts and Nevis. The Russian consulate would act as your power of attorney, and for another $10,000 they'd arrange your residency visa in any of those countries. The only other thing you had to do was to put $300,000 in a bank in the country you chose to go to and leave it there for five years. If you didn't touch it for the entire five years, you could have citizenship of that country, too. Even better, the Bureau of Prisons would pay for your airfare to the country you chose! "This is all in Article three of the Asylum Act," Pat insisted. (Note: there is no such thing as Article three of the Asylum Act. Besides, the US asylum law is for people who want to come *to* the United States, not run from it.)

Another great thing about this amazing opportunity, Pat insisted, was that once you got a Russian passport, your prison sentence, fine, and restitution were all canceled. Since you were no longer an American citizen, the US government had no right to hold you or fine you. The only downside was that you probably couldn't return to the US.

I listened to all this, dumbfounded that anybody in his right mind would believe any of it. I tried reasoning with Pat, first by telling him that you can't renounce your citizenship from the US. "Maybe the rules changed since you left government," was his reply. I told him that the BOP is holding thousands of foreign nationals who can only go back to their country after they've served their prison sentences. "But they came here illegally and they weren't originally Americans," Pat replied, as if that made any sense. "Pat," I said, "it's insane to believe that the Russian government has a program to sell citizenship to any American child molester who wants it."

"Oh, ye of little faith," he said, smiling. "Just wait until Rocket is released. You'll see."

I don't know why I was wasting my breath, but I said, "Pat, did it ever occur to you that Rocket is in on the scam? Maybe he's being transferred in January and he's made up this release story to steal money from desperate suckers willing to part with thirty-five thousand dollars to get out of prison." The thought obviously had not crossed Pat's mind, and I made him promise me that he wouldn't give anybody any money. "Besides," I said, "You have a wife and nine kids and you get out in a year!"

In the end, Rocket wasn't a part of the scam. He was just a sucker willing to do anything to get out of prison. The prisoner running the scam gave him regular updates: "Your paperwork is being processed. Your passport has been approved. Your release date is six months from now. Your ticket has been issued. Your Bahamas residency permit has been approved. Congratulations!" The scammer went home a month before Rocket's "release." Even when the release date came and went, it took him another couple of months to realize that he had been ripped off and would get nothing for his $35,000. His letters to the Russian and Bahamian embassies went unanswered, and Rocket settled in to do the remainder of his twelve-year sentence.

Welcome to Prison

May 20, 2013
"Letter From Loretto"

Greetings from the Federal Correctional Institution at Loretto, Pennsylvania. I arrived here on February 28, 2013, to serve a thirty-month sentence for violating the Intelligence Identities Protection Act of 1982. At least that's what the government wants people to believe. In truth, this is my punishment for blowing the whistle on the CIA's illegal torture program and for telling the public that torture was official US government policy. But that's a different story. The purpose of this letter is to tell you about prison life.

At my formal sentencing hearing in January, the judge, the prosecutors, and my attorneys all agreed that I would serve my sentence in Loretto's Federal Work Camp. When I arrived, however, much to my surprise, the Corrections Officer (CO, or "hack") who processed me said that the Bureau of Prisons had deemed me a "threat to public safety," and so I would serve the entire sentence in the actual prison, rather than the camp.

Processing took about an hour and included fingerprinting, a mug shot (my third after the FBI and the Marshals Service), my fourth DNA sample, and a quite comprehensive strip search. I was given a pair of baggy brown pants, two brown shirts, two pairs of underwear, two pairs of socks, and a pair of cheap sandals. My own clothes were boxed and mailed home to my wife.

The CO then led me to a steel bunk in "Central Unit" and walked away. I didn't know what to do, so I took a nap.

My cell is more like a cubicle made out of concrete block. Built to hold four men, mine holds six. Most others hold eight. My cellmates include two Dominicans serving twenty-four- and twenty-year sentences for drugs, a Mexican serving fifteen years for drugs, a Puerto Rican serving seven-and-a-half years for a drug conspiracy, and the former auditor of Cuyahoga County, Ohio, who's doing a long sentence for corruption. They're all decent guys and we actually enjoy each other's company.

The prison population is much like you might expect. Loretto has 1,369 prisoners. (I never call myself an "inmate." I'm a prisoner.) About 50 percent are black, 30 percent are Hispanic, and 20 percent are white. Of the white prisoners, most are pedophiles with personal stories that would make you sick to your stomach. The rest of the white prisoners are here for drugs, except for a dozen or so who ran Ponzi schemes. Of the 1,369 prisoners, 40 have college degrees and 6 of us have master's degrees. The GED program is robust. (But when I volunteered to teach a class, my "counselor" shouted, "Dammit, Kiriakou! If I wanted you to teach a fucking class, I'd ask you to teach a fucking class!") I'm a janitor in the chapel.

The cafeteria, or "chow hall," was the most difficult experience of my first few days. Where should I sit? On my first day, two Aryans, completely covered in tattoos, walked up to me and asked, "Are you a pedophile?" Nope, I said. "Are you a fag?" Nope. "Do you have good paper?" I didn't know what this meant. It turned out that I had to get a copy of my formal sentencing documents to prove that I wasn't a child molester. I did that, and was welcomed by the Aryans, who aren't really Aryans but more accurately self-important hillbillies.

The cafeteria is very formally divided. There is a table for the whites with good paper, a section of a table for the Native Americans, a section of a table for people belonging to a certain Italian-American stereotypical "subculture," two tables for the Muslims, four tables for the pedophiles, and all the remaining tables for the blacks and Hispanics. We don't all eat at the same time, but each table is more-or-less reserved as I described.

Violence hasn't been much of a problem since I arrived. There have been maybe a half-dozen fights, almost always over what television show to watch. The choices are pretty much set in stone between ESPN, MTV, VH1, BET, and Univision. I haven't watched TV since I got here. It's just not worth the trouble. Otherwise, violence isn't a problem. Most of the guys in here have worked their way down to a low-security prison from a medium or a maximum, and they don't want to go back.

I've also had some luck in this regard. My reputation preceded me, and a rumor got started that I was a CIA hit man. The Aryans whispered that I was a "Muslim hunter," but the Muslims, on the strength of my Arabic language skills and a well-timed statement of support from Louis Farrakhan, have lauded me as a champion of Muslim human rights. Meanwhile, the Italians have taken a liking to me because I'm patriotic, as they are, and I have a visceral dislike of the FBI, which they do as well. I have good relations with the blacks because I've helped several of them write commutation appeals or letters to judges and I don't charge anything for it. And the Hispanics respect me because my cellmates, who represent a myriad of Latin drug gangs, have told them to. So far, so good.

The only thing close to a problem that I've had has been from the COs. When I first arrived, after about four days, I heard an announcement that I was told to dread: "Kiriakou—report to the lieutenant's office immediately." Very quickly, I gave my wife's phone number to a friend and asked him to call her if for some reason I was sent to the SHU (Special Housing Unit), more commonly known as "the hole," or solitary confinement. I hadn't done anything wrong, but this kind of thing happens all the time.

When I got to the lieutenant's office, I was ushered into the office of SIS, the Special Investigative Service. This is the prison version of every police department's detective bureau. I saw on a desk a copy of my book, The Reluctant Spy, *as well as DVD copies of all the documentaries I've been in. The CO showed me a picture of an Arab. "Do you know this guy?" he asked me. I responded that I had met him a day earlier, but* our conversation was limited to "nice to meet you." Well, the CO said, this was the uncle of the Times Square bomber, and after we had met, he called a number in Pakistan, reported the meeting, and was told to kill me. I told the CO that I could kill the guy with my thumb. He's about five foot four and 125 pounds, compared to my six foot one and 250 pounds. The CO said they were looking to ship him out, so I should stay away from him. But the more I thought about it, the more this made no sense. Why would the uncle of the Times Square bomber be in a low-security prison? He should be in a maximum security penitentiary. So I asked my Muslim friends to check him out. It turns out that he's an Iraqi Kurd from Buffalo, NY. He was the imam of a mosque there, which also happened to be the mosque where the "Lackawanna Seven" worshipped. (The Lackawanna Seven were charged with conspiracy to commit terrorism.) The FBI pressured him to testify against his parishioners. He refused and got five years for obstruction of justice. The ACLU and several religious freedom groups have rallied to his defense. He had nothing to do with terrorism.

In the meantime, SIS told him that I had made a call to Washington after we met, and that I had been instructed to kill him! We both laughed at the ham-handedness by which the SIS tried to get us to attack each other. If we had, we would have spent the rest of our sentences in the SHU—solitary. Instead, we're friendly, we exchange greetings in Arabic and English, and we chat.

The only other problem I've had with the COs was about two weeks after I arrived. I get a great deal of mail here in prison (and I answer every letter I get.) Monday through Friday, prisoners gather in front of the unit CO's office for mail call. One female CO butchers my name every time she says it. So when she does mail call, I hear "Kirkakow," "Kiriloo," "Teriyaki," and a million other variations. One day after mail call I passed her in the hall. She stopped me and said, "Are you the motherfucker whose name I can't pronounce?" I responded, "Ki-ri-AH-koo." She said, "How about if I just call you Fuckface?" I just walked away and a friend I was walking with said, "Classy." I said to him, "White trash is more like it." An hour later, four COs descended on both of our cells, trashing all of our worldly possessions in my first "shake-down." Lesson learned: COs can treat us like subhumans but we have to show them faux respect even when it's not earned.

Best regards from Loretto,
John

Rules to Live By

I REALIZED THE MOMENT that I was escorted into the prison that I would have to use my CIA training to keep myself safe there. To tell you the truth, and I'm not saying this to be dramatic, there are a lot of similarities between many of the CIA officers I worked with over the years and prisoners I encountered during my twenty-three months at Loretto. The CIA is full of aggressive alpha personalities. So is prison. The CIA is full of people constantly plotting against each other. So is prison. The CIA is full of people who are always jockeying for some better situation than the one they are currently in. So is prison.

I'm the first to admit that in prison I was a serious jerk. I was arrogant, manipulative, and opinionated. But I was also adaptable to changing situations, I could think quickly, and I possessed a certain degree of ruthlessness necessary for self-preservation. The CIA taught me well, and I used those CIA-taught survival skills to keep myself at the top of the prison heap, to stay out of trouble (usually), and to get what I wanted.

These skills were important to a successful CIA career, but they were certainly not unique to the CIA. Indeed, anybody can use them in daily life. Some are more important than others. Some are quite a bit easier than others.

Rule 1: the first and most important thing the CIA taught me in operational training at the Farm, its famed training facility in the Virginia countryside—and the first thing that I set out to do in prison—

was to *recruit spies to steal secrets, or to steal anything else I needed, frankly.* This was how success was determined in the CIA. That's how we got promoted. The cool gadgets, technology, and spy gear were all ancillary. The bottom line is that you must identify a target, identify his vulnerabilities, assess his access, and move in for the kill.

Every time James Bond goes into Q's workshop for the latest spy gear, every time the NSA rolls out another program to intercept communications, every time a trainee fresh from the Farm targets a potential source, he's doing it for one reason: to facilitate the stealing of secrets.

But what is a secret? A secret is any piece of information that is not publicly available. In the context of prison, most secrets are held by the administration and the COs. The only way a secret becomes valuable to an inmate is if that inmate can use it to his advantage. I'm not talking about rumors, which I'll discuss later, and which you can start for your own purposes. I'm talking about actionable information that you can use to your own benefit.

It's the same way with unavailable goods. You won't have access to everything you want and need, so you'll have to recruit people with access to get them for you.

There are four reasons why a person would go against his own best interests to steal secrets for you: revenge, greed, ideology, and excitement. The best, for your purposes, is ideology. Even though you may have nothing in common with your target, and even though your interests and backgrounds may be diametrically opposite, you must convince him that you are kindred spirits. If your target is a "true believer," he will do what you want. The ideologues are the easiest to manipulate. They would likely do what you want anyway. They just need a little guidance.

Generally speaking, one should never underestimate the collective stupidity and gullibility of your inmate peers (or, for that matter, of the prison staff). This makes your job of convincing people to do your bidding much easier. First, every successful operations officer must convince others that they are his best friend. That friendship should become deep, to the point that that person is willing to take a personal risk for you just because of that friendship.

Here's the way you would want such an approach to play out. Perhaps you're doing legal work, or you may be writing a book about surviving and thriving in prison. Let's say you find yourself in need of a few metal binder clips for documents. In prison, these are considered to be contraband. But you know that in the prison office complex supply room there are hundreds of binder clips, rubber bands, paper clips, pens, pencils (not the cheap ones from commissary), and even a copy machine. How do you get access to these goodies? One way is to get to know the orderly who cleans the office and has regular routine access to it. You have to ask yourself what makes this guy tick. What would convince him to risk a good job and the possibility of solitary confinement to steal some clips for you? Does he believe that all inmates should have clips? Would he be willing to steal clips for money to finance his gambling problem or to buy contraband cigarettes? Does he want revenge against the CO who called him a moron two hours ago? Or is he just an adrenaline junkie who's always looking for the next thrill?

A typical conversation might begin like this:

Revenge

You: "You know that asshole CO you work for? Did I tell you what he did to me? During a shakedown that bastard took all of my binder clips. Now my legal work is in chaos! It's like that jerk is trying to trample my constitutional right to defend myself!"

If you pitch it well, the target may say, "Yeah? I can get you some clips." If not, you could follow up with, "It's too bad that piece of shit doesn't trust you enough to give you access." In that case, you might expect to hear, "Wait a minute! I *do* have access!" The target thinks it was his idea in the first place.

Greed

Maybe the target doesn't care about the CO he works for one way or the other. Maybe he gets no money from home or, as I said, gambles or smokes. You can offer to pay him with a $1.35 bag of mackerel, the unit of currency in the prison system, or, if he really comes through for you, with a book of stamps, the unit of currency for gambling.

Ideology

Perhaps the target believes in the "us versus them" aspect of the prison experience. The "man" keeps us down and tries to control every aspect of our lives. Our first names are all "inmate" and the target resents it. He's willing to give you the clips because you're both inmates and you have to stick together against the cops. Maybe, in an earlier conversation, you gave the target the impression that you care about him, his family, or his problems.

Excitement

Experts estimate that as many as 80 percent of American prison inmates have at least some degree of mental illness, and most inmates have very low self-esteem. They want to be something they're not, to do something heroic or exciting. They're also impulsive. It's that impulsivity that will allow you to manipulate them. But be careful here, because impulsive thrill-seekers are the most difficult to control.

I became friendly—and later roommates—with Robert, the Australian inmate I mentioned, on my very first day in prison. Robert had been convicted of burning down a Department of Motor Vehicles office in Buffalo, New York, over a sales tax dispute. He was extremely gregarious, always wanting to be involved in everything. It also became clear to me quite quickly that he was a clinical sociopath. In fact, he would have checked every box on Dr. Robert Hare's "Psychopathy Checklist Revised (PCL-R)," which I'll discuss later. Among the many characteristics used by psychologists to identify sociopaths is pathological lying. Robert was a pathological liar.

A person with Robert's personality would rarely be motivated by greed or ideology. (Frankly, a person with Robert's personality would rarely be motivated by revenge, but he was an unusual case. That's another thing I'll discuss later.) He was an excitement junkie first and foremost. It was very easy to manipulate Robert; you just had to make him feel like he was "involved." You wanted to make him admire you and want to be like you because his self-centered personality demanded attention. Robert was only interested in other people for what they could do for him, whether because being associated with them enhanced his own status or gave him access to people who otherwise wouldn't have spoken to him, or so that he could mark them for his next scam. As long as you know what this kind of person is, you do not need to fear being his next victim, and you can use his sociopathy for your own benefit.

Whenever I needed something that was not freely available, or whenever I needed to have somebody "taken care of," I turned to Robert. Need sponges or rubber gloves? Robert would steal them because it was daring and exciting. Want food that was specific to the officer's mess? Just ask Robert. He enjoyed the thrill.

Soon after my arrival, the prison went a full week without any meat in our meals in the cafeteria. The problem was that many of the inmates in the kitchen who got no money from home stole the meat so they could then sell it to other inmates. As a result, the Chicken Pot Pie was actually Vegetable Pot Pie, and the Chicken Fried Rice was Vegetable Fried Rice. All of the meat that had been stolen was for sale in plastic bags in three or four cells. I understood, of course, that many inmates have a "hustle" by which they earn black market money. But we were entitled to 3.5 ounces of meat at lunch and dinner, and I wanted my fair share.

I immediately went to work on Robert. "This is an outrage!" I told him. "We're being ripped off and they're taking food out of our mouths!" Robert became so angry that he did exactly what I thought he would do. He dropped an anonymous note to the administration, telling them where the meat could be found and who was stealing it. The result was that almost the entire kitchen staff was fired and replaced, the meat sellers were shaken down and the meat confiscated, and the meals over the next few weeks were a bounty of meaty goodness. Coincidentally, two of the meat thieves lived next door to

Robert and routinely picked on him. As part of the shakedown they were sent to solitary and, eventually, to other prisons.

Robert often used to ask me, "Would I make a good CIA officer?" My answer was always a resounding "No!" It was because of his congenital inability to keep his mouth shut. I did tell him that he made a good asset, and in the real world, if he had had access to classified information, I would have recruited him. But he loved the clandestinity of doing "operations," and he would frequently do things on his own and report back to me. He "recruited" somebody in the prison laundry and, very proud of himself, came back to the cell with new sheets, pillowcases, socks, and T-shirts for all of us. Thanks to Robert's successful operation to "recruit a spy to steal laundry," I had enough underwear and socks to last a lifetime.

These examples may seem petty, and they are. It's because prison life is petty. If you need a pencil, a highlighter, even a rubber band, you have to steal it or get someone to steal it for you. You have to do whatever is in your power to make your life easier and more comfortable with as little risk as possible.

Power, or the lack thereof, is the problem. You have only a limited amount of control over your own personal situation. The trick is to enhance your limited control by leveraging the skills, the access, the weaknesses, and the motivations of others.

Rule 2: seek and utilize available cover (or blend in with your environment). I reminded myself in my first hour of prison to do exactly this. It's always best to operate under the radar. If there's a fight in the unit, get out. If there's trouble on the horizon, make yourself scarce. Stay away from people who can drag you down, and try not to come to the attention of the cops.

In the life of a field operative, this rule is straightforward: when the shit hits the fan, you take cover immediately to protect yourself and to make yourself a difficult target. In prison, this rule is just as important as it is in intelligence operations.

When a predator enters the scene in nature, the crickets stop chirping, birds stop singing, and smaller animals run for cover. It is a natural instinct to seek cover and go silent. As humans have evolved, we have lost this instinct. It is only when faced with a challenge unnatural to modern human existence that one must rely on one's training. I received this training at the Farm. I was taught to "duck and cover," to become invisible, and to get out of the way. If noticed, I was taught to employ misdirection to direct attention elsewhere while making a stealthy exit.

In 2011 in Pakistan, Ray Davis, who has been identified in the press as a CIA contractor, shot and killed two Pakistani nationals who were trying to rob him in Lahore. The men approached Davis with guns drawn while he was stuck in traffic. Davis fired through his windshield, killing one of the men. Davis then got out of the car and shot the second man in the back. Rather than seeking and utilizing available cover, or better yet "getting off the X" (CIA parlance for fleeing the scene), Davis got back in his car and called the American Consulate for help. A few minutes later, a consulate vehicle sped to the scene. But before getting to Davis, the consulate's SUV struck and killed an innocent Pakistani man riding a bicycle. Davis was left at the scene, standing like a deer in the headlights, as Pakistani police arrested him, saving him from a potentially murderous crowd. After arresting Davis, Pakistani authorities found at the scene a black mask, a hundred bullets, and a cell phone containing photos of Pakistani military installations.

A trained field officer would never have let this happen. The training a field officer receives at the Farm would have prepared them for this or any similar situation. A trained field officer would have immediately departed the scene and fled to a safe house or to a predetermined safe site after shooting the robbers. As humans have evolved and the modern world has taken much of the danger out of everyday life, fear as a survival instinct has all but disappeared.

A good example of seeking and utilizing available cover happened just after I arrived at Loretto. A fight broke out in my housing unit. After the initial yelling, screaming, and swinging of fists, an eerie calm settled on the unit, not unlike what would happen in the jungle when a predator arrives. Everybody was quiet.

The natural reaction of a wild animal would be to seek shelter as far from the problem as possible. To those who have spent most of their lives in prison, and who are used to the laws of the jungle, the reaction would also be to seek shelter, lest they come to the attention of the COs, who undoubtedly would arrive any minute to investigate after being tipped off by their many rats. But to a white-collar first-time offender, the situation would be calm, quiet, pleasant, even refreshing, much changed from the norm.

Randy, a newly-arrived mortgage fraudster, came strolling into the unit after lunch, not noticing that anything was amiss on this oddly-sedate afternoon. It never occurred to him to wonder why everybody was huddling in their cells, trying to make themselves invisible. The halls were empty and the nearby TV room was a ghost town.

Randy walked past one of the cells and noticed Jose, a Mexican convicted of drug crimes. Being the friendly guy he was, and not noticing Jose's puffy, bruised face, Randy gave him a thumbs-up and said, "Hey, Jose! What's up?" Jose looked up, presented a bloody fist, and, squinting out of his one good eye, replied, "I gave him what he came for!" Randy, confused, smiled at Jose, gave another thumbs-up, and said, "OK then!"

As he continued walking back to his cell, Randy was approached by Tyree, a six foot three, three-hundred-pounder. Tyree, who had overheard the conversation between Randy and Jose, and who had been Jose's antagonist, assumed a camaraderie between the two, an assumption over which he did not linger for more than a moment before pummeling Randy with both fists.

Had Randy, now lying bloody and still in the corridor, used the rule of seeking and utilizing available cover, he would not have been taken to solitary confinement with Jose and Tyree. Nothing he could say or do could affect the fact that he would now spend the next six months in solitary, pending the formal investigation that would eventually exonerate him.

This would never have happened to me, and indeed it didn't. First, I would have been attuned to my environment. It is absurd that a prison unit with 198 people in it would be quiet, other than at 3:00 a.m. (And even then it was chaos half the time.) I would have noticed that immediately, and I would have noticed that Jose had been beaten. Once I saw him bruised and battered, I would have immediately sought cover and put as much distance as possible between me and what was obviously a brewing problem. (Not everyone is as clueless as Randy. This was a very clear-cut example of what not to do. There are an infinite number of situations that could present a problem, almost all of them far more subtle and less obvious than the one I've given here. This actually happened, and that's why I'm writing about it.)

You have to blend in both literally and figuratively in prison. Randy should have sought cover literally. But to survive prison on a daily basis, to handle the daily challenges of prison life (which are nothing like life on the outside), you have to learn to blend into your environment. Remember, prison is a combination of seventh grade, *Lord of the Flies*, and a mental institution.

If you are out of the norm for this environment—educated, intelligent, well-read, well-spoken, well-traveled, or even sane—you will stand out like a sore thumb. This, like everything out of the norm, will initially lead to suspicion and mistrust. All the above traits are attributes, but you must learn quickly not to ram them down people's throats. In the prison environment, anything out of the ordinary is immediately assumed to be a threat. That's why it's so important to blend in and keep a low profile.

It's natural and easy for human beings to blend in in the real world because human beings tend to be homogeneous. They gravitate toward their own kind, whether socioeconomic, educational, religious, or even racial. In prison, you'll be judged immediately based on whether you're white, black, Asian, or Hispanic. It's something you simply can't get away from. For example, you could be an African-American Internet billionaire or a white hillbilly cooking meth in a shack in Kentucky, but you will be identified first and foremost by your inmate peers and by the prison staff by your race. In prison, stereotypes abound. It's just a fact of life. Take that knowledge and use it to blend in.

Rule 3: *admit nothing, deny everything, make counteraccusations.* This rule was actually something of a joke at the CIA. It was even emblazoned on T-shirts and coffee mugs in the CIA gift shop. In truth, though, this rule can do a lot for you, especially if you're dealing with a moron. Your refusal to admit anything, your quick denials of all accusations, and your incessant counteraccusations will often confuse and frustrate your accuser. And if you do it with a loud arrogance, it's even better.

You don't necessarily have to be a bad person with dishonorable intentions to tell a lie. Sometimes it's as simple as not wanting to disappoint someone you love, respect, or admire. As a child, it is the most natural thing in the world to deny spilling that glass of milk or taking that last cookie, and even to blame a sibling. It's not that you're a bad kid. It's just natural. There is a fine line between not wanting to disappoint and being malevolent, between influencing and manipulating, between being persuasive and conning somebody. It's all a matter of intent.

I encountered this behavior in a fellow prisoner almost as soon as I arrived at Loretto. Dave L. was convicted of running a Ponzi scheme, for which he received a twenty-year sentence. To hear him tell it, it was all a terrible mistake, a misunderstanding, a situation that got wildly out of control. He admitted nothing and denied everything. Dave maintained that he was the victim, not the more than five hundred people who lost nearly $20 million in his scam. Dave described himself as a successful money manager who was brought down by a vindictive assistant US attorney because he criticized her in a letter to his girlfriend that was intercepted by law enforcement authorities. In this letter, he bragged about "snookering" the prosecution and the court, and predicted that he would get away with his crime because of his self-described superior intellect. He made no apologies for his private jet, his condo on Central Park South, his second home in Paris, the luxury vacations, or the $5,000 racing bike. He said he earned all those things, and, if any crime had been committed, his punishment should have been a short stint in a minimum-security work camp. Indeed, he told me that he still had a considerable amount of money hidden, and that as soon as he got to a camp, he would flee via private jet to a hideout in the Caribbean, thus continuing to refuse to take responsibility for his criminal behavior.

As the prosecution of Dave L.'s case progressed, he chose to cooperate with authorities against his codefendant, not an unusual decision among people with Dave L.'s personality traits. When a fellow inmate found Dave L.'s case documents on the computer in the prison's law library, and saw the news that Dave L. had cooperated with authorities in an attempt to save himself, the inmate went to the white "shot-caller." The shot-caller confronted Dave L. with the document, but Dave simply shrugged and denied its authenticity. He then made counteraccusations against the prisoner who had told the shot-caller, an action completely consistent with a person who thinks nothing of others and only of himself. Whenever anybody asked Dave L. what the trouble had been about, he said that his accuser was a rat who had set him up to deflect attention from himself. He never admitted to testifying against his codefendant. He also didn't have to move to the "rat" table in the cafeteria.

In prison populations, according to psychologist Robert Hare, nearly 80 percent of people incarcerated in the United States suffer from antisocial personality disorder (ASPD). The *Diagnostic and Statistical Manual of Mental Disorders*, Fifth Edition (DSM-5) defines antisocial personality disorders as "a pervasive pattern of disregard for, and violation of, the rights of others that begins in childhood or early adolescence and continues into adulthood." To qualify for a diagnosis of ASPD, per the DSM, adults must present with at least three of the following seven criteria:

1. Failure to conform to social norms with respect to lawful behavior;
2. Deceitfulness;

3. Impulsivity;

4. Irritability and aggressiveness;

5. Reckless disregard for self and others;

6. Constant irresponsibility, as indicated by repeated failure to honor financial obligations; and

7. Lack of any remorse or rationalization of one's hurtful behavior.

It is entirely consistent that individuals with ASPD would put themselves first before anyone and anything else. It is entirely consistent that they would break the law, deceive the authorities, turn on their partners in crime, lack any remorse, rationalize their behavior, and accuse others of being the real wrongdoers. That was Dave L. You, however, can use this rule to your own advantage. Deflect accusations, make the discussion about the other guy. Protect yourself.

Rule 4: adapt to your current environment. This really goes without saying. Adapt and survive. Don't stand out where undue attention works to your disadvantage. Go along to get along. Your private shenanigans should be done in private.

Rule 5: everybody is working for somebody. You are the only person who has your best interests at heart. By all means, recruit spies to steal secrets, run your "operations," and do everything else to your own advantage. But remember that others are doing the same thing. Sometimes your interests will intersect, sometimes people will do your bidding because you've recruited them, and sometimes they'll be working actively against you. Keep in mind that the latter could very well be the case.

Two offhand comments, one by a CO and one by a fellow prisoner, illustrate this rule better than anything. I once heard an investigative CO brag to a fellow CO that he had so many informants among the prisoners that "the whole building would collapse if they all went out to the yard at the same time." One "made" member of a New York organized crime family told me once that if the prison fence were to fall down, 90 percent of the prisoners would hold it up, while the other 10 percent would run to tell the cops that the fence had fallen down. Don't trust anybody.

Rule 6: it's all about the relationship. A person's success rises and falls on the strength of his or her personal relationships. At the risk of sounding cynical, it's best for everybody to *think* they're your friend, or at least that you don't pose a threat to them. If you don't have to worry about these people, you can focus on your more important work. Take the time to cultivate these relationships, whether they're sincere or not. They will likely work to your benefit later. This can be as easy as a smile and a nod in the hallway, a "good morning" on the way to the cafeteria, or a "how's your son doing" in the TV room. It costs nothing, and it's worth the effort.

Rule 7: eliminate potential problems using dirty tricks. I acknowledge that this doesn't sound very nice. But prison isn't very nice. As in life, you will encounter people whom you just can't win over no matter how hard you try. Your charms will get you nowhere. At that point, you may have to get nasty.

Wallace was a prisoner during my stay in Loretto whom everybody hated, but whose company everybody nonetheless enjoyed. Good-looking, smart, and sophisticated in his dealings with others, he claimed to have had a child with an A-list Hollywood star, he had appeared numerous times in *People* magazine, and he loved the notoriety. He was well-read, spoke multiple languages, and was an accomplished con man.

Wallace was serving thirty-eight months for fraud. He just couldn't help himself. He loved the good life—the fancy restaurants, ocean-going yachts, exotic vacations, and handmade sports cars. He learned the trade from his con man father. Wallace subscribed to yachting magazines and to the *duPont Registry of Homes*, and he bragged to unsuspecting saps about which yachts in the magazine his family used to own and which mansions in exotic locales he intended to buy when he got out of prison.

The funny thing about Wallace was that he was also a coward and a crybaby. Every time he felt stressed, he would pretend to faint, whether it was in court, when he was caught cheating in a poker game, or when he thought he wasn't being treated with due respect in the medical unit. When he wasn't fainting, he was crying. He cried when his lawyer didn't answer the phone. He cried when he didn't get responses to his emails. He cried when he had a visitor or when he didn't have a visitor. We could even hear him crying in the shower.

For all the talk about his money and his Hollywood lifestyle, Wallace only had one visitor the entire time he was in prison. His mother would stay in a local fleabag motel four times a year and visit him on a Sunday morning. But the truth of the matter was that Wallace had stolen from so many people in such a wide variety of schemes that he had no friends. Nobody cared about him enough to come all the way to central Pennsylvania to see him. (His father couldn't come; he also faced fraud charges.) So because he had no friends on the outside, Wallace focused on making friends on the inside.

These friendships weren't based on mutual respect and admiration (besides the fact that no one should come to prison to make friends). Instead they were based on the question Wallace would ask himself whenever he met somebody new: "what can this person do for me?" He would actually wait for the Friday buses that brought new prisoners from other prisons, pick out those who looked weak, frightened, and alone, and begin ingratiating himself with them. It was even better if they were white-collar criminals with money. Wallace would show them around, "generously" give them shower shoes and basic toiletries, and gently start to make his pitch.

Wallace had a million different ideas about how to spend other people's money. They usually involved another prisoner's family making a wire transfer to one of Wallace's off-shore accounts, sometimes as a direct investment and sometimes for "legal services" Wallace pretended to provide. Halfway through his sentence, he owed thousands of dollars to dozens of people he had ripped off, and an equal number of people wanted to break every bone in his body. He did a good job of borrowing from Peter to pay Paul, and he owed every loan shark in the prison money.

At the same time, Wallace would come to my room almost every night, crying about how he was misunderstood, how he was just trying to be a nice guy and help people, and how he would soon win his appeal, go home, and live the good life again. He would cry at reports that this ex-girlfriend was dating this-or-that Hollywood star, and wail that this was all a big mistake and that he just wanted to go home. Then he would ask if he could borrow money.

About fourteen months before Wallace was due to be released, I had had enough. No matter what anybody said to him, he wouldn't stop being a pain in the ass. I was tired of his scams, his coldhearted thievery, and his constant crying about how he had been wronged. So my closest friend in prison, Mark, and I decided to take action.

One of my cellmates was due to be released in a matter of days. Every prisoner approaching release is given a form called a "merry-go-round" that has all the prison offices listed on it. The prisoner spends his last full day getting somebody in each office to initial the merry-go-round, then he takes the completed form with him to Receiving and Discharge to be released. I took my cellmate's merry-go-round, made a photocopy, whited out his name and registration number, and typed in Wallace's information. On a Friday, I waited until the staff left at 5:00 p.m., put the new merry-go-round on Wallace's bed along with a duffel bag Mark had asked Robert to "borrow" from laundry, and I waited.

At 5:15 p.m., Wallace strolled into the room after dinner, whistling. He picked up the merry-go-round and gasped. "Oh my God!" he shouted.

"What?"

"I'm going home! I must have won my appeal! I'm going home on Monday!"

"What are you talking about?!" Mark and I put on a good show, acting shocked and thrilled for him at the same time. He was in a frenzy. He ran to the case manager's office to ask for more information, but the case manager was gone for the day. He called his attorney in New York, but even attorneys head home at 5:00 p.m. on a Friday. He called the federal courthouse in New York. It was closed.

Finally, I got him to sit down for a minute. "Wallace, let us throw a party for you Sunday night. We want to help you celebrate!" He was thrilled. He drew up a guest list and we set out making pasta with marinara sauce, a tomato salad, and a cheesecake made with mozzarella cheese from the commissary and vanilla pudding stolen from the cafeteria. In the meantime, I said, he should get that merry-go-round signed before Monday morning.

A lot of the offices are open on the weekend: the chapel, Education, Recreation, even the lieutenant's office. The only person who would have known that the merry-go-round was a forgery was the case manager, and he was off until Monday. So Wallace got as many signatures as possible over the weekend. He also gave away all of his belongings, which he wouldn't need on the outside. On Monday morning I convinced him that the case manager's signature was unnecessary; after all, the case manager had sent him the release form in the first place!

After 6:00 a.m. breakfast, a half-dozen of us walked Wallace over to R&D to bid him farewell. True to form, he cried. He gave each of us a hug and promises of a Mediterranean yacht cruise if we ever ran into each other again.

The rest of the story we later got from the R&D CO. Wallace walked in and handed the CO his merry-go-round. "Who the hell are you?" the CO asked.

"I'm Wallace!"

"What are you doing here?"

"I'm going home!" The CO looked at the forged merry-go-round.

"Turn around. You're under arrest."

Wallace panicked. "What? Why?"

"You're under arrest for attempted escape." The CO radioed the lieutenant's office. Minutes later, two thuggish COs escorted Wallace to solitary confinement, where he spent the next few months, safely out of my hair. He was then transferred to another prison until his *real* release.

Was this a mean thing to do? You bet it was. But desperate times call for desperate measures. The cops couldn't prove where the forged merry-go-round had come from, so Wallace was never charged with attempted escape. There was no lasting punishment. He didn't even lose his good behavior time. At the end of the day it was a good little operation. An exhausting pain in the ass was no longer my problem. Wallace's inmate victims were happy that he had gotten what was coming to him. And I didn't have to listen to that infernal crying anymore.

Rule 8: don't be afraid to make a strategic retreat. There are some battles that you just can't win outright. When that happens, there's no shame in retreating to regroup and refine your strategy. Your enemies may misinterpret your move as weakness. They'll let their guard down and declare victory. In fact, victory is not theirs. It will be yours when you make your well-thought-out counterstrike. I would also add that this was a particularly effective technique to use with staff. They felt like they were in complete control, while you were reassessing your options. You could launch another attack from another angle later.

Rule 9: don't underestimate the power of another man's greed. I'm not necessarily talking about money here. You can use a man's greed for any material thing to your advantage. If you have access to contraband—food, cigarettes, porn, even highlighters or pens—you can use them to buy what you want on the black market or to bribe somebody for what you want. If you have regular access to contraband in prison, you can make "friends" who will do anything for you.

Rule 10: the human body can endure much more than the brain says it can. This is a rule that everybody can personalize. First, if you keep your body healthy, your mind will remain healthy, too, even in the stress of a prison environment. Exercise, go for long walks, do yoga or tai chi, make time for yourself. If your mind feels good, your body will, too.

Second, don't allow depression to sap your energy. That could result in a mental and physical spiral that will be difficult to dig your way out of. If you feel like you might be chronically depressed, get some help and get back on the treadmill. There's no shame in going on an antidepressant for a little while.

Third, and I don't mean to sound morbid here, but a punch in the face really doesn't hurt that much. The pain is temporary. And while nobody wants to fight (except the psychopaths and people with anger management or antisocial personality disorders), you can't back down from a challenge. If you do, you lose all credibility and you risk becoming a regular punching bag. So maybe you take one to the jaw. Your body can endure it even if your brain doesn't want to. What you should do next is to punch the guy back, harder than he punched you. It's worth it in the long run.

Rule 11: if stability is not to your benefit, chaos is your friend. I like this rule very much. While it's just plain fun to stir up trouble once in a while, chaos keeps your enemies off-balance, guessing about next moves and reacting to situations rather than being proactive. This was an important and valuable rule for me, especially in my dealings with a certain pedophile I'll tell you about later.

Rule 12: be the power behind the throne. There's a famous story that illustrates this point even better than I can. Nicolas Fouquet was the French Superintendent of Finance from 1653 to 1661 under King Louis XIV. This position granted him direct access to the French bankers that served, and loaned money to, the king. Fouquet married into a moneyed Spanish noble family and his personal wealth soon rivaled the monarch's. He reportedly was an obsequious minion of Louis' and served him well. However, he was corrupt and extremely extravagant in his personal tastes. Louis tired of Fouquet's brazen ambition to become head of government, and when Fouquet built a palace even grander than Versailles, Louis destroyed him. Fouquet was arrested in 1661 and charged, tried, and convicted of corruption. He died in prison in 1680. There is an important lesson here: keep a low profile, don't make waves, work in the shadows, and *never* outshine the boss.

Rule 13: listening is a better strategy than talking. This comes down to strategic elicitation. You don't necessarily ask direct questions; you elicit information during the course of a conversation. Most people love to talk, especially about themselves. Let them. Egg them on.

You'll be surprised how much information they give up without even realizing it. And remember, information is power. The more information you have, the more powerful you are. So listen as much as you can.

There are a few techniques involved in elicitation. At their most basic, they are to use naivete, ego, flattery, and deliberately misspeaking with your targets. Every case officer has to be at least somewhat well-informed on a very wide variety of issues from US and world politics, to the theater, sports, literature, economics, you name it. That way you can carry on at least a basic conversation with just about anyone you may encounter who might be interesting operationally. Naivete works well in a situation like this. Discussing an issue with a target, you might say, "My opinion is X, although I'm not sure I have a complete understanding of the issue." Most people, wanting to talk about themselves, to be helpful, and to show how smart they are, will then naturally expound on that issue. You've successfully elicited their opinion without even asking for it.

Ego and flattery are related and are my favorite methods. We're all arrogant in our own ways. Well, most people are arrogant. With this technique, you subtly inflate the target's ego, implying how much you admire them, how much you respect their opinion, and how important they are. Most professionals enjoy a good ego stroking. Again, they'll likely talk about themselves and their jobs and give you an entrée to follow-up elicitations or questions. In prison it's even easier. Since so many people suffer from low self-esteem, various personality disorders, and chronic depression, they will welcome a conversation. And I'm not just talking about staff. Prisoners will engage with you, too.

Deliberately misspeaking is the last of the most basic elicitation techniques. This is something you do so that the target jumps in to correct you and to expound on his passion on an issue. For example, "I heard that the Taliban is resurgent in Herat." The target will likely respond that, "Actually, Herat has many more Shia Muslims than Sunnis, and things have been peaceful there." I found this technique to be the least useful in prison because so many people are conspiracy theorists that, no matter how outrageous your misstatement, people will usually just nod their heads and agree with you.

One time, a prisoner tried to use this technique on me—unsuccessfully, I might add. Near the end of my sentence, Russia sent troops into Ukraine and captured the Crimean Peninsula. Meanwhile, half a world away, Malaysian Airlines flight MH17 disappeared somewhere over the Indian Ocean. As I had a reputation as a well-educated spook, one particularly annoying prisoner sought me out to talk about these recent current events. "Here's what I think happened," he said. "Russia invaded Ukraine to get a warm water seaport in the Black Sea. The United Nations was trying to get a secret envoy to Moscow to talk the Russians into withdrawing. The Russians sent up a drone from a secret base in India to shadow MH17 because they knew the envoy was on the plane. When they confirmed that he was a passenger, they neutralized the plane's autopilot, sent it toward Australia, then shot it down." I looked at him and said, "You need to be medicated."

Rule 14: find out what the target wants and use it to you advantage. Oftentimes, it can be to your benefit to help somebody get what he wants because it helps you get what *you* want. For example, let's say Butch wants a transfer to a prison in Indiana because it's closer to his family. Butch is a pain in the ass, so you definitely want him to go to Indiana, or to anywhere else, for that matter. A casual comment over the phone, which the cops are listening to, that Butch is running a poker game, stealing food from the cafeteria, or bullying a pedophile gets him sent to solitary for a month of "investigation." Then, being deemed a potential problem, he gets shipped to Indiana. Or somewhere else. You don't care where. But by now he's out of your hair.

Rule 15: hide in plain sight. This rule goes hand-in-hand with "be the power behind the throne." Yes, you want to run things. Yes, you want to have your way. But don't be so high profile that you make yourself a target. Keep your mouth shut and don't draw attention to yourself.

Rule 16: use the subtle art of misdirection. Like "admit nothing, deny everything, make counteraccusations," this rule is best used with cops when you don't want them to know your business. During questioning or in an "investigation," a subtle nudge in the wrong direction can confuse them, send them off on a tangent, and generally get them off your back. I'm not recommending that you lie. Just send them off in the wrong direction. I'll illustrate this later.

Rule 17: trust no one. I was lucky at Loretto. I made a few true friends on whom I could rely. Otherwise, assume that nobody is honest, nobody is your friend, and that you're on your own. It's the best way to stay out of trouble, not just with the degenerates you're surrounded by, but with the crooked bully cops, too. Rely on yourself, your instincts, your intelligence, and your wiliness.

Rule 18: never underestimate the power of rumor. This is one of my favorite rules. Rumors in prison are treated as fact. Want to ruin somebody? Start a rumor that he was caught getting a blowjob behind the gym. Of course, the rumor has to be believable.

As an example, here's something I did: a guy with a very common name, I'll call him Bob Jones, sat at my table in the cafeteria. Jones spoke constantly about the government conspiracy to withhold the cure for cancer, how NASA faked the moon landing, and how George W. Bush colluded with "Jews" to bring down the World Trade Center. He accused me repeatedly of being a part of these conspiracies because of my years with the CIA. Normally, I wouldn't have cared about such silliness, but a lot of people in prison are conspiracy theorists, and I had had enough trouble convincing these idiots that, as a former CIA officer, I had *not* been a cop. I couldn't stand to hear one more word out of this guy's mouth. And, frankly, his incessant conspiratorial yammering was putting me in danger from the Aryans.

I went to the law library and found a case from the 1970s belonging to a guy with the same name. The 1970s Bob Jones had beaten and raped a male prison guard in Ohio. I took those case papers and cut and pasted them onto the pain-in-the-ass Bob Jones' case papers, then discreetly circulated them to the white "shot-callers" who ran the cafeteria table and who decided who got to sit there. Some doubted the new paperwork, but some believed it, and I was able to get rid of Bob Jones. He ended up sitting at one of the many pedophile tables, and he never figured out what had happened.

Rule 19: always maintain a plausible cover for action. In other words, have a believable excuse for doing what you're doing in case somebody asks you. Are you looking up other people's cases in the law library? Say you're working on your appeal. Did you get called down to the lieutenant's office as part of an investigation? Tell people that you got into a beef with a cop and you were filing a formal complaint against him. Always have a story. That way it keeps the heat off of you and keeps away prying eyes.

Rule 20: know your enemy. Understand your enemy's motivations. Know his friends. Discern his network of support. Don't act against him unless you know you'll be successful. Use the rest of these rules to get yourself to that point. Good luck.

Friends, Enemies, and the Weirdos and Lunatics In-between

BEFORE I HAD GOTTEN to prison, people had told me—and I had intended—to keep my circle of friends small. Prison, after all, is not the place one goes to forge long-lasting relationships. On my second day, Dave Phillips approached me in the cafeteria and introduced himself. We shook hands and he said that he and Art Rachel had been waiting for me to arrive. We went to Art's housing unit, where Art welcomed me and said that I shouldn't be worried about a thing. My reputation as a highly-trained CIA officer, he said, had preceded me, and he added that I wouldn't have any problems. I felt at ease immediately.

I liked Dave and Art from the very start, and I knew we would be friends. There was also something about Dave that was familiar to me. Finally, after a couple of days I asked him a question: "Were you in Pakistan in two thousand and two?" He paused, surprised, and said, "You were the guy in the office, weren't you?" I said that I was, and that I remembered him coming to work one day in Pakistani clothes, but with a baseball cap. My colleagues and I had made fun of him all day. "What are you doing here?" I asked.

Dave said that after a long CIA career that took him all over the world, he returned to the US and went to work for a defense contractor. His job was to win new business in the intelligence community for his employer, which he did successfully, including getting his company accepted as one of the CIA's preferred and vetted bidders.

When asked to help on a contract the firm was having trouble with, he agreed. The facility security officer (FSO) had told him that he had been added as a member of the contract team. He logged onto the secure "Intelink" database, managed by the Office of the Director of National Intelligence (DNI), to begin his background reading for the contract. But as it turned out, Dave's firm had neglected to add him to the contract. The Justice Department charged him with unauthorized access of a secure database in hindrance of national security, a felony. Dave was initially offered a plea that included a fifteen-month prison sentence. He declined, intending to clear his name at trial.

The feds then did what they always do: they dove into Dave's background looking for anything they could find against him. Dave said that a few years earlier his wife wanted to buy a car. She and Dave went to the local dealership and picked one out. The dealership, however, didn't have the color she wanted, so the dealer ordered one from the factory. This was in late spring. Dave's wife, meanwhile, a British citizen, flew to London to get their house there in order. The dealership called Dave to say that the car had arrived shortly after his wife had left for the UK.

The next day Dave went to the dealership to pick up the car. As he was signing the papers, the dealer asked if his wife had come too. Dave explained that his wife was in London, so the dealer told him to just sign her name next to his own. Dave signed, took the keys, and drove home. As a result, the Justice Department charged Dave with two counts of mail fraud for taking delivery of the car, two counts of wire fraud for receiving a $2,000 manufacturer's rebate that came with the car, and one count of aggravated identity theft for signing his wife's name. These were all felonies and were in addition to the charge of accessing the database. Together they carried a sentence of fifty-four years.

When Dave continued to resist taking a plea, the government got even nastier. They seized everything of value that he owned: property, money, art, electronics, furniture, even his clothes. He was forced to claim indigence to qualify for a public defender to fight the charges. The government then went one step further and charged him with perjury for claiming poverty, as he sat in jail with the government holding everything he owned.

With Dave facing fifty-four years and relying on an inadequate public defender, the government came back with another offer. It was for nine and a quarter years and, if he did not accept it within forty-eight hours, the Justice Department was prepared to subpoena and then indict his eighty-nine-year-old grandmother and his sixteen-year-old daughter because they had been home when he accessed the database and when he brought home the car. Dave no longer had a choice. The risks were too high. He signed the plea, even though he had maintained his innocence.

Art Rachel was a career criminal. In his mid-seventies by the time I met him, his first arrest, and first escape, were at the age of fourteen when he was sent to reform school for truancy. In the late 1950s and 1960s, Art did ten years at the federal penitentiary at Leavenworth (where his cellmate was legendary New York mob boss Vito Genovese) for bank robbery. In the 1970s, Art did additional hard time at the federal penitentiary at Terre Haute, Indiana, for counterfeiting bearer bonds. (Art is an accomplished artist.) The bonds were so well done that they were never spotted as fakes. Art was arrested after his sister's friend was caught with marijuana and she ratted him out in exchange for no jail time.

In the early 1980s, Art and a friend pulled off what was, at the time, the greatest jewel heist in British history when they stole the fifty-four-carat "Marlborough Diamond" from London's famed Graff's Jewelers. Art was caught at Chicago's O'Hare Airport, having fled London, and was extradited back to the UK, where he was sentenced to another fifteen years. The diamond was never recovered. I once asked Art what he did with it. He just smiled and said, "I lived a lot of good years on that rock."

Art was doing another eight years at Loretto for conspiring to rob the home of the deceased boss of the Chicago "Syndicate," while the family was at the boss's funeral. He didn't realize that the FBI had been tipped to the plot and had wired his van for sound.

I introduced myself to Frank Russo a couple days after I arrived at Loretto. Frank, sixty-five, was the former auditor general of Cuyahoga County, Ohio, which includes Cleveland and all its environs. Frank was the number two in Cuyahoga County, and as auditor, his picture was on every gas pump in greater Cleveland. He was widely considered to be a strong future candidate for governor of Ohio. Unfortunately, he got involved in a bribery and kickback scandal that involved more than seventy people and led to a twenty-two-year prison sentence. I liked Frank from the moment I met him.

Indeed, Frank was the most widely-liked person in the entire prison. A natural-born politician, he had a way of putting people at ease and making them feel liked. Unlike most politicians I've known, Frank couldn't remember *anybody's* name, but that was more endearing than anything. That way, everybody become "buddy" or "pal" or "big guy." Frank had testified against some of his codefendants, and he was acutely aware that he was known on the compound as a "rat." I told those who didn't like him (mostly Italians in on organized crime charges) that he was misunderstood; everybody had testified against everybody in his case. The Italians ended up either befriending him or just ignoring him.

Frank had a terrible first day at Loretto. When he arrived in November 2012 it was nearly lunchtime. He got his uniform and went to the cafeteria, where he was immediately confronted by an Aryan. "Are you a chomo?!" the Aryan shouted.

Frank had never heard of the term "chomo" before, and he thought it was a name.

"No. I'm Russo," he said. "Chomo wasn't on my bus."

"Are you crackin' wise with me?" the Aryan asked incredulously.

"No," Frank said innocently. "I'm Russo. Maybe Chomo's coming on the next bus."

"Fuck you!" the Aryan shouted, turning heads. Frank thought, *Oh, no. I'm sixty-five years old, I've been in prison for one hour, and*

I'm going to have to fight. The Aryan, though, puzzled, just walked away. Somebody pulled Frank aside to tell him what a chomo was.

I moved into Dave's room three months after I got to Loretto, and Frank moved into the room a month or so later. This made life much, much easier for all of us. Housing is a critical issue in prison. If you don't like your cellmates you're in for a tough time. Once Dave, Frank, and I were together, that left three other spots in the room. One was occupied by "Beard," a forty-year-old African-American, lifelong drug dealer, and one of the easiest people I could have hoped to live with. I liked and respected Beard, and I frequently turned to him for advice on the prison "experience." The fifth spot was taken by "Steve," a fifty-five-year-old, long-haired, toothless child molester from Indiana. We didn't talk to Steve, and Steve didn't talk to us, which was better for everybody. Our sixth spot was vacant.

A week or so after Dave, Frank, and I moved in together, I noticed a young-looking kid who had just self-surrendered. He looked to be about twenty (he was actually thirty), blond haired, blue eyed, and he was sitting on his bunk near the front of the unit, scared to death and near tears. I felt a little sorry for him, but I didn't engage him in conversation. As the months passed, I learned that his name was Erik, and that he had been sentenced to five years for possessing child pornography. His case, though, wasn't quite as simple as that. Erik was diagnosed as a child with attention-deficit/hyperactivity disorder, autism, and Asperger's syndrome. He worked in a tool and die shop and lived in his parents' basement. He also had a serious adult pornography addiction.

What earnings Erik didn't spend on his Ford Mustang, his motorcycle, his dog, and video games, he spent on pornography. He subscribed to every fetish site he came across and actively traded adult porn with people he met in porn-oriented chat rooms. He readily told me that he was a virgin and that he had never actually seen a real-life woman naked.

One day, early in the morning, the FBI entered Erik's parents' house in force, arrested Erik, and confiscated all of his computers and electronics. It turned out that several of the photos Erik had received in a trade were of girls who were sixteen years old. The photos had been electronically tagged by the FBI, and the trail led to Erik. In court, the judge recommended to both sides that, rather than being incarcerated, Erik be sent to a psychiatric facility for intensive therapy. The prosecution objected and demanded that Erik serve the mandatory minimum of five years. The judge's hands were tied, and Erik arrived at Loretto in April 2013.

I don't know what made me feel sorry for Erik. I guess I just never considered him to be a chomo, all of whom I loathed. But he was so out of place in prison that it was pathetic. And at five foot eight and 130 pounds, he had no way to defend himself.

One day in the summer of 2013, Dave noticed a notorious member of the Bloods street gang walk quickly and stealthily into Erik's room. Dave walked up to the room, peered in, and saw the gangbanger, Red, caressing a sleeping Erik. Red had a reputation as a sexual predator who, in the penitentiary earlier in his sentence, had been accused of raping young, thin, defenseless white guys. Dave came back to our room immediately and told me what he had seen. "What do you think we should do?" he asked. We huddled and came up with a plan.

We were not rats, but wrong is wrong, and Erik was in danger. Dave wrote an anonymous note to the Special Investigative Service telling them what he had seen. I went to the unit manager with the same story. Within minutes, Erik was called to the lieutenant's office. Thinking he had done something wrong, he immediately burst into tears. He told the cops that he didn't think that anybody had touched him, but he admitted that he was a deep sleeper. He said Red had been coming into his room a lot lately with gifts like chocolates, cookies, even a pillow. This was classic grooming behavior common among prison sexual predators, and Red was taken to solitary an hour later. Two months later he was shipped to a medium-security prison. On the way out, one of our friends overheard him say, "Somebody must have seen me go into that kid's room."

The day after Red was locked up Dave and I went to the unit manager. We asked him to move Erik into our room. "We'll watch out for him," we said. "And we'll put out word that people should leave him alone." A day later, with the paperwork completed, Erik became our sixth roommate.

Another inmate who became a good friend—my best friend—was Mark Lanzilotti. Mark was a forty-five-year-old Italian-American from the south side of Philadelphia. He grew up there and in the working-class suburbs of New Jersey. A few years after graduating from high school, his mother's boyfriend introduced him to the world of methamphetamine manufacturing. The boyfriend taught Mark, who had never used drugs, how to manufacture high-quality meth, which the boyfriend then sold to members of Philadelphia's Bruno/ Scarfo organized crime family. Mark decided after six months that this wasn't the life for him, and he became the only person in the eight-man operation to leave the conspiracy. He then opened a car-detailing business, which became successful and employed six people.

Six months after Mark walked away from drugmaking, DEA, FBI, and ATF agents arrested the conspirators—but not the boyfriend or Mark—and charged them with multiple counts of conspiring to manufacture and distribute meth. As the conspirators negotiated plea deals for themselves, they began informing on each other, and on Mark. He was arrested and charged a year later.

The boyfriend hired an attorney for Mark with the proviso that he not testify against any of his codefendants. If he decided to testify, the boyfriend said, Mark was on his own. Besides, the attorney told him, "I don't represent rats." The truth is that the boyfriend was the conspiracy's leader, and he couldn't risk Mark talking. The only way to ensure that was to demand that Mark go to trial.

All of the coconspirators received five-and-a-half-year sentences. They all testified against Mark. But his attorney never told him that the government had offered him a non-cooperation deal of ten years. Twice. So against his better judgment, Mark went to trial. Not surprisingly, he was quickly found guilty. With sentencing enhancements for failure to accept responsibility, having a "leadership" role in the conspiracy, as the rats had testified, and an upgrade for the total amount of meth, Mark received three life sentences without parole. On appeal, the sentence was reduced to thirty years.

I owed Mark a real debt of gratitude even before I met him. He had followed my case in the newspapers and he had read that I was going to be sent to Loretto. Anticipating that many of the prison's Italians would not understand me or my case, he took it upon himself to go to each and every Italian, from associate to solider to captain to boss, to explains the difference between the CIA and the FBI ("CIA people are heroes; FBI people are cops and rats") and the difference between a whistleblower and a rat ("whistleblowers are trying to help the country; rats are snitching for personal gain"). When I finally arrived, the Italians welcomed me with open arms. I sat at their table in the cafeteria, I was invited to their dinners and parties, and we socialized in the rec yard. I had Mark to thank for all of that.

Mark was also one of the best cooks I've ever encountered, in or out of prison. He made elaborate Italian meals with pasta, chicken, sausage, cheese, and vegetables stolen from the cafeteria and prepared in a garbage pail with a live electrical wire thrown into the water. I told him once, "I don't know what your plans are when you get home, but I would pay twenty-five dollars for this in a restaurant." He was that good.

The last of my circle of close friends was Clint Goswick, whom I met when I began working in the prison chapel. Clint owned a successful heating and air-conditioning business in northern Texas. He had led an exemplary life, was and remains a strong Christian, and had never been in trouble. After a very difficult divorce, Clint decided to start dating again. At forty-two, he met a twenty-two-year-old woman who was just getting out of an abusive relationship. An earlier ex-boyfriend had been a meth cook who later killed himself playing Russian roulette. After Clint's relationship with the woman ran its course, she began dating another meth cook who had been recently released from prison.

Three years later, the woman and her boyfriend were arrested for manufacturing meth. Clint's phone number was still in her cell phone, and Clint's father had once called the woman looking for Clint, so his home phone number was in her records, too. Under questioning, Clint told the FBI that when he and the woman were dating, he had hosted a cookout at his home, and she had invited several friends. This, according to the FBI, constituted a drug conspiracy. In truth, Clint had never met or heard of most of the other conspirators. He had never used, manufactured, possessed, or distributed drugs. Clint was charged in the conspiracy and he pled not guilty.

Outraged that he would go to trial, prosecutors added a gun charge, even though Clint had no gun. (In a conspiracy, every defendant is deemed to be guilty of every other defendant's crime, so if one defendant had a gun, they all had a gun.) His attorney told him to take a plea, but Clint believed in the justice system, and went to trial in 2006. Four of the other defendants agreed as part of their deals to testify that Clint owned "the party house." The jury made its decision after a three-day trial. Guilty. Because Clint had protested his innocence and had gone to trial, prosecutors asked for as much time as possible. The judge sentenced Clint to twenty-two years, seven months.

As I've already mentioned, one of the first people I met at Loretto was Robert. Robert was one of the most continually fascinating people I knew, and that was saying a lot. Robert was a sixty-two-year-old man who behaved like an adolescent—not child-like, but child-ish. Born in Israel of an Armenian mother and a British father, he grew up in Australia. In his twenties he married an Australian woman, had a son and a daughter, and divorced. Marriages to a Swiss citizen, a Canadian, and an American got him Canadian and American citizenship, in addition to Australian and British, and he settled in Buffalo, New York.

Robert was without a doubt the most antisocial and sociopathic person I had ever met. And remember, my former profession brought me into contact with people with sociopathic tendencies on a daily basis.

Robert claimed wildly successful careers as a nightclub owner, a DJ, a border patrolman, a bush pilot, the owner of the largest video store chain in Australia (and Canada and the US), a used car dealer, a radio host, and a voice-over artist. He also claimed to have dated Australian international tennis champion Yvonne Goolagong, to whom Robert also attributed the title of "Miss Universe." I told him that Yvonne Goolagong was never Miss Universe, an argument that went on for some months until Robert admitted that she wasn't Miss Universe. Oh, and it wasn't Yvonne Goolagong he was dating. It was somebody who reminded him of Yvonne Goolagong.

There was probably a grain of truth to many of these boasts. I think Robert probably had worked in a nightclub, DJed an occasional party, rode along once with a border patrolman, owned a video store, was on the radio, and did an occasional commercial. But in the end he was merely a fantasist, a modern-day Walter Mitty.

Robert had what he described as a very successful used car dealership at a major intersection in suburban Buffalo. He claimed that a group of rival businessmen, crooked cops, and organized crime figures conspired to put him out of business by denying approval for his signage, putting a hold on his business license, and even trying to steal the very land the business sat on. Robert's appeals to the police, the FBI, and municipal authorities were ignored. But he bobbed and weaved and kept his business open.

One thing Robert didn't do, as he negotiated these travails, was to pay sales tax to the State of New York, which resulted in the state suspending his dealer's license. Robert never accepted responsibility for his failure to pay taxes. Instead, he blamed his enemies in the police force, the Mafia, and the Buffalo business community, which brings us to a fateful day just before Christmas 2006.

Robert went to the local Department of Motor Vehicles because he had not received his "dealer" license plates for the New Year. The clerk there told him he could not have the dealer plates until he paid his sales taxes. He spoke to the manager and demanded the plates, only to be told that he simply would not be allowed to have them until he paid his tax bill. The situation escalated to the point that the manager finally had to inform Robert that the police were on their way. Fleeing toward the front door, he turned as he exited and shouted, "I'm going to burn this place to the ground! Merry Christmas!"

He returned to his dealership fuming. Remember, in Robert's mind nothing was his fault, and by God, someone was going to pay. He called two small-time Russian hoodlums he knew to the dealership and hatched a plan for revenge against his perceived tormentor, the manager of the DMV. Robert claimed not to have been present late that night when the Russians threw Molotov cocktails into the DMV manager's office and among the fleet of DMV cars. The Russians then went to the manager's home, where they broke into his car, doused the interior with gasoline, and set it alight. The fire soon snuffed itself out because the arsonists failed to crack a window to allow oxygen on which the flames could feed.

It was not long before arson investigators honed in on Robert. The Russians had been apprehended and were cooperating freely with the authorities. Robert was quickly fingered as the ringleader and mastermind of the arson plot. He fled to Canada to a rural cabin owned by his then-wife (his fourth) to await the outcome of the investigation. When it became clear that the trouble was not going to blow over and US and Canadian officials were drawing up extradition papers, Robert again fled, this time to Australia, where he appealed for Australian citizenship and moved in with a Vietnamese woman. A year passed, during which Robert enjoyed the hospitality of his new girlfriend while systematically transferring all the funds from his stateside business (including the money from the dealership) and joint marital and personal bank accounts to Australia, effectively leaving his wife back in Buffalo a pauper. As an aside, Robert's wife, some seven years after the events of 2006–07, was living in rented accommodations after losing her home to foreclosure (she owned her home prior to her marriage to Robert) and was working selling beer and condiments at Buffalo Bills football games, her life ruined. New York state tax officials sued both Robert and his wife and got judgments for sales taxes, penalties, and interest. Robert did manage to talk his wife into cosigning loan papers. She is on the hook for the tax bill, too.

The US authorities, meanwhile, followed Robert's trail to Australia and soon had obtained an extradition warrant for his arrest. The Australian police arrested Robert and he was held pending an extradition hearing. While Robert claims to have not opposed extradition, he did manage to stay in Australia for well over a year until US marshals flew in to pick him up to return him to the US.

Robert was eventually sentenced to five years in federal prison for arson and sent to Loretto. He was precluded from serving his sentence at a minimum-security prison camp because arson is considered a crime of violence, therefore making him ineligible for such a designation. This really bothered Robert, who spent almost the entirety of his remaining sentence fighting to get to a camp.

There were a couple of other guys with whom I would hang out. "Pete" was a senior captain in New York's Bonnano crime family. He had been in prison for about a decade and was always the voice of reason when it came to dealing with just about anybody. I trusted and liked him very much. A few months after my arrival at Loretto, Pete and I went for a walk around the prison yard. I was very depressed, and Pete asked how long my sentence was. "Thirty months," I said, "and it feels like thirty years." Pete laughed. "Compared to most guys here," he said, "it'll feel like thirty minutes. Snap out of it!" He was right, of course, and his common sense advice was consistently helpful to me.

Joey "the Kid" Cassolo, from Connecticut, was doing five years on an organized crime charge. Joey wasn't the smartest guy in the world, but he had a good heart, he was honest, and he was immensely proud of his daughters. I enjoyed his company. "Doc" Grivas was a doctor from Staten Island who ran a Medicare/Medicaid kickback scheme. He became the de facto physician for the housing unit, whether the cops liked it or not. Paulie Apostolopoulos was Mark's roommate and was my only Greek-American compatriot in prison. There was no reason for Paulie to be in prison. He should have been home with his five daughters. But that's the curse of mandatory minimum drug sentences in our country.

There were many more weirdos, lunatics, and freaks than there were good guys. That's what made prison such a challenging experience. And it was against these dangerous characters that I had to use my CIA training. There were two people, especially, whom I loathed from the minute I met them. And I knew that, eventually, I would have to take some action against them.

Clyde Ware was a nut who tried to insert himself into my circle from the minute I arrived. I resisted successfully, but was able to use his lunacy and his quickness to use violence when I needed it. I met him in our housing unit during my second or third week in prison. Sixty-five years old, bald, fat, and tall with a mouth full of remnants of blackened and rotted teeth, Ware, who went by the name "Truck" because of his past as a long-distance truck driver, came up to me and in his normal booming voice said, "Were you CIA?" Yes. "I hate those motherfuckers! They abandoned me in Da Nang!"

This was not a conversation I wanted to have, so I said, "Wow. Tough break," and started to walk away.

"Wait a minute!" Truck shouted. "I ain't no chomo!"

"Excellent," I said, and I escaped him.

A few days later, Truck pulled me aside to say that he had done some "contract work" for the CIA. "Really?" I said, unimpressed. "What kind of work?"

"I ran guns from Mexico to the Angolan rebels in a shrimp boat back in the seventies." This was absurd on so many levels, the most obvious of which is that no shrimp boat in the world can go from Mexico to Angola; it can't hold enough fuel, and it would capsize in the first big wave. It was such an inane assertion that I just looked at him, speechless.

"You think I'm a chomo, don't you?" he finally said.

I told him that I didn't know him, I had no idea what his crime was, I didn't care, and I knew he was never involved with the CIA.

"I still have friends there," I told him. "And besides, if you aren't a chomo, why do you sit at the chomo table in the cafeteria?"

If I had known him better I wouldn't have said any of this. He had a reputation for violence, not just in his crime, but in the prison, as well. For his part, I think he was probably afraid of whatever self-defense training I may have had. Instead of lashing out, he bellowed, "Just read my paperwork!" I decided that I would.

As I said, Truck was a long-haul truck driver, mostly in the western US. He had a real penchant for prostitutes, and the younger, the better. The thing was, he didn't like to pay the prostitutes once he was done. Instead, he would beat them unconscious. Some he would just rape without making any pretense of paying. Two of the prostitutes he raped were fourteen years old. Technically, at least in prison parlance, that made him a chomo. But the twist in Truck's case wasn't that he was raping underage prostitutes. It was that along that same truck route, at the same truck stops and diners, and at the same time that Truck was raping and beating prostitutes, a serial killer was murdering prostitutes, and the cops thought it was Truck.

This was in the 1970s, when Truck was supposedly running guns to the Angolan rebels. In fact, he was simply a sexual predator in Colorado at that time. This was an age before DNA testing, but there were enough living victims that Truck was identified, arrested, convicted, and imprisoned on multiple rape charges, including two counts of rape of a minor. He did twenty years in Colorado and then was released.

The cops in Colorado, though, didn't want him to get away with murder, so they kept up the pressure once he was released. Unannounced home visits by his parole officer was one of the parole stipulations. So the PO would show up at all hours of the day and night. This so enraged Truck that he ended up making a threat against the PO, who issued a probation violation and called the police to search the house. Inside was a treasure trove of weapons, and Truck was quickly and successfully prosecuted on multiple federal charges of being a felon in possession of a gun. He got another twenty years. And although the authorities could never get him on the murder charges, they did put him away for a total of forty years. Interestingly, there were no more truck stop murders in Colorado while Truck was incarcerated.

Truck was proud of having worked his way down from a penitentiary to a low-security prison. He knew he would eventually die in prison, but he liked being a big tough guy in a small pond. I don't know why, but Truck openly and actively sought my approval. This was not a guy that I wanted to know, so I kept a distance, although I was never openly rude to him. If he came up to say, "There's a new radio station on fourteen-hundred AM that plays classic rock," I would answer, "Great, Truck. I'll check it out." If he said, "We're having lasagna tomorrow night," I would say, "It's usually not bad." This kept me on his good side. And in the back of my mind, I knew that I could use him for my own ends. I began thinking of my CIA rules.

Truck was known (and in some cases hated and feared) around the unit not only for his past but also for his volatile temper. He gave one of his cellmates a serious beating over whether to have the overhead light on or off. Nobody reported him because they were afraid he would beat them to death. Two months later he beat another cellmate senseless for talking loudly while Truck was napping. Everybody had to walk on eggshells around him.

One day I was in the TV room when I heard a rat named Larry Raviv mention my name. (I had been called to the lieutenant's office earlier in the day to sign an acceptance form for a journalist's interview request.) I was sitting next to Truck when Raviv, not seeing me, said, "They called Kiriakou down there because he's a rat and a cop." Truck looked at me and said, "Did you hear that motherfucker?" The rules flashed through my mind: the CIA had taught me to "adapt to my current environment; to rely on relationships; to eliminate potential problems using dirty tricks; that if stability was not to my benefit, chaos was my friend; and to let others do my dirty work."

I told Truck, "Ha! Two hours ago he was telling a group of guys that you're a chomo." Truck calmly got up, walked over to Raviv, and beat him to a bloody pulp in front of fifty witnesses.

Truck and Raviv were both taken to the SHU—Truck for punishment, and Raviv for his own protection. Raviv got out a few days later, swollen, bruised, and humbled. Truck received an additional assault charge and was sent back to a medium-security prison. Raviv, a couple days later, came up to me to apologize. I calmly said, "If I ever hear my name come out of your mouth again, you're dead. Understand?" He understood. Truck had done all the heavy lifting for me.

Raviv was the kind of sociopath who did not endear himself to unsuspecting people. He was a mean, dangerous nut with a bad temper, but nothing to back it up. Robert the Australian first introduced me to Raviv when Raviv arrived by bus from a medium-security prison, where he was serving twenty years. When he got down to ten, he came to Loretto.

Robert, as usual, told everybody that Raviv, a sixty-year-old dead ringer for the Cat in the Hat, was "good," meaning that Robert had seen his paperwork and that Raviv was neither a child molester nor a rat. When Robert brought him around, my first question was, "What are you in for, Larry?"

"Murder for hire" was the response. Ouch.

"What do you mean?"

"I hired a guy to kill my business partner. He deserved it. He was a rat."

"Well," I said, making a mental note to check the guy out, "welcome to Loretto."

Raviv's case papers in the law library were horrific. He was in business for many years with an old friend. He also had a serious gambling problem and owed an organized crime figure more than $100,000 in gambling debts. So what was his plan to get out of this jam? He took out a $100,000 life insurance policy on his friend, and then hired a hit man to murder him.

Raviv flew the hit man from New Orleans to Pittsburgh, picked him up at the airport, gave him a loaded gun, drove him to the friend's house, and sat in the driveway while the hit man went into the house and committed the murder. Once the friend was dead, Raviv took the gun, drove the hit man back to the airport, and dropped him off. He then called the insurance company to report that his friend was dead.

It was only a matter of hours before the cops picked up both Raviv and the hit man. What was surprising, at least to me, was that the hit man said nothing, but Raviv immediately confessed and blamed everything on the hit man. He agreed to rat the guy out in exchange for twenty years. The hit man was looking at the death penalty. Before they could go to trial, however, the hit man died in jail of a heart attack. The feds had to abide by the deal they had made with Raviv, and he ended up with twenty.

I decided to confront Raviv with this information. I said I wanted nothing to do with him. I didn't like his crime or his response to it. I didn't associate with murderers or with rats. Raviv was enraged. Who was I to judge him? he asked. He began arguing his case to me, and it was chilling. "My partner was old. He probably would have died soon anyway." "What else was I supposed to do? I owed the Mafia money." "I'm not heartless. I was going to send his daughter a check to help pay for the funeral." I was disgusted by this display, and I told Raviv to buzz off. I wanted nothing to do with him.

I also told Robert at this point that if he ever again tried to introduce me to somebody who turned out to be a rat, a chomo, or a murderer, I would gouge his eyes out with a spoon.

I must have hurt Raviv's pride because he immediately began telling people that I was a low-level Mafia nobody and that he had to put me in my place when I tried to shake him down. (Throughout my stay at Loretto, I was friendly with Pete, the captain in the New York–based Bonanno crime family. We had similar interests, shared books, and watched TV together.) Raviv reacted by having a friend mail him articles about Pete's case, which he taped to the wall in the telephone room, with Pete's name highlighted and the word "RAT" written across the top. Of course, I told Pete that it was Raviv's handiwork.

Pete showed genuine restraint. He got a couple members of his crew together, approached Raviv, and helpfully told him that they didn't want any trouble. It would be "unfortunate" if something should happen to Raviv based on a "misunderstanding," right? Raviv started to deny having anything to do with the article, but Pete put up his hands, "No need for words. Just keep your mouth shut."

"Yes, sir."

But Raviv hadn't gotten the message. He walked up to me at the end of the day and said, "I'm not afraid of you and your goomba friends."

I responded with a smile, putting my hand on Raviv's shoulder. "Larry. You misunderstand me. I would never be so crude as to come after you in public. But what I will say is this: if you ever fuck with me or mention my name to anybody, in any context, you won't live to see the next day." Still smiling, I walked away. Raviv collapsed in a chair, trembling. He never spoke another word about me or about the Italians, until, of course, the run-in with Truck, when he didn't realize I was nearby.

An Open Letter to Edward Snowden

I HAD ONLY BEEN in prison a few months when Edward Snowden revealed to the world evidence that the National Security Agency had violated US law and its own charter by collecting telephone metadata and emails from American citizens. I thought this was an outrageous affront to American civil liberties, and I followed the case closely.

I could hardly believe my ears when the Snowden news broke. One could not underestimate the importance of what Snowden had done. NSA's charter—and US law—forbade the NSA from spying on Americans, not only American citizens but US "persons." That is, the law also protected foreign nationals living in the US as resident aliens, or green card holders.

The more information that was published, the more I thought that Snowden had performed a great national service. Plainly said, Americans would have had no idea that their government was spying on them had Snowden not gone public. I will admit that I thought there were some things he shouldn't have said. For example, the NSA is supposed to spy on foreign leaders. I want them to do that. If spying on foreign leaders helps us to formulate our own policy or to get a leg up in trade negotiations, then great. But overall, Snowden revealed government illegality on a massive scale.

There was even more to think about in the immediate aftermath of the Snowden disclosures. The most important thing was "what would happen to Edward Snowden?" I knew from my own experience that the government would seek to try Snowden in the Eastern District of Virginia (EDVA), the so-called Espionage Court. This is despite the fact that Snowden was living and working in Hawaii at the time of his disclosures and NSA is located in rural Maryland, not in the Eastern District of Virginia.

That's where my case was heard, and I knew firsthand that Snowden wouldn't have a prayer there. The Justice Department will frequently "shop" for a friendly court, and on national security matters none is friendlier than EDVA. Besides judges who come down hard on leaks no matter what the motivation, juries can be largely made up of current or retired CIA, FBI, and Defense Department officers. A whistleblower like Snowden wouldn't have a chance.

When I read in *The New York Times* a week or so later that Snowden had said that Tom Drake and I had inspired him to come forward, I sent him a detailed private letter. He had to look out for himself. Nobody else would.

This was the open letter:

Dear Ed:

Thank you for your revelations of government wrongdoing over the past week. You have done the country a great public service. I know that it feels like the weight of the world is on your shoulders right now, but as Americans begin to realize that we are devolving into a police state, with the loss of civil liberties that entails, they will see your actions for what they are: heroic. Remember the immortal words of Abraham Lincoln: "America will never be destroyed from the outside. If we falter and lose our freedoms, it will be because we destroyed ourselves." That is what's happening to our country now. Your whistleblowing will help to save us.

I wanted to offer you the benefit of my own whistleblowing experience and aftermath so that you don't make the same mistakes that I made.

First, find the best national security attorneys money can buy. I was blessed to be represented by legal titans and, although I was forced to take a plea in the end, the shortness of my sentence is a testament to their expertise.

Second, establish a website so that your supporters can follow your case, get your side of the story, and, most importantly, make donations to support your defense.

Third, you're going to need the support of prominent Americans and groups who can explain to the public why what you did is so important. Although most members of Congress are mindless lemmings following our national security leadership over a cliff, there are several clear thinkers on the Hill who could be important sources of support. Cultivate them. Reach out to the American Civil Liberties Union, the Government Accountability Project, and others like them who value our individual freedoms and who can advise you.

Finally, and this is the most important advice that I can offer, DO NOT, under any circumstances, cooperate with the FBI. FBI agents will lie, trick, and deceive you. They will twist your words and play on your patriotism to entrap you. They will pretend to be people they are not— supporters, well-wishers, and friends—all the while wearing wires to record your out-of-context statements to use against you. The FBI is the enemy; it's a part of the problem, not the solution.

I wish you the very best of luck. I hope you can get to Iceland quickly and safely. There you will find a people and a government who care about the freedoms that we hold dear and for which our forefathers and veterans fought and died.

Sincerely,
John Kiriakou

The *Huffington Post* picked up my open letter, and from there it went viral, appearing in stories on all the major broadcast networks, as well as on CNN, Fox News, MSNBC, BBC, and Al Jazeera. It hit the newspapers a day later, including *The New York Times, Washington Post, Wall Street Journal,* and *USA Today.* By the end of the week it was in the magazines, including *The Economist, Esquire, GQ, Time,* and even *Playboy.* I even received a friendly, supportive, and grateful letter from Ed Snowden's father. I would certainly remain relevant on this issue.

The Big Challenge, Part I

BECOMING JEWISH IN PRISON was a very popular thing for prisoners to do, not because anybody was necessarily in search of spiritual enlightenment, but because Jews got higher-quality kosher meals, as well as candies that nobody else got. The scam worked like this: you approach the chaplain and say that one of your grandparents was Jewish and that you'd like to explore your Jewish heritage. The chaplain asks if you intend to become kosher, you say yes, and he schedules a short "test" for you. You do some rudimentary reading into Judaism, then you take your test. "Who was Abraham? What is Moses known for? What does kosher mean?" Answer those questions correctly and you're a Jew!

So what did being Jewish get you in prison? Several desirable things were yours for the asking. First, you got the kosher meal three times a day rather than the inedible slop that everybody else got. Breakfast was oatmeal, wheat bread, butter, jam, and fresh fruit, while everybody else got loose grits, a small piece of cheap yellow cake, and a hideous piece of fruit that would be thrown away in a store. Lunch was often fish—tuna or sardines, for example—while the rest of us ate sloppy Joes or three different starches. Dinner was usually a meat—chicken, a sirloin burger, or sliced turkey—along with beans, a vegetable, and a dinner roll. The rest of us ate cheap Mexican. The Bureau of Prisons spends about $0.85 per meal per prisoner. But kosher meals cost $4.00, and it showed.

Besides daily meals, Jews got extra treats. Around the High Holy Days every Jew in the prison got a box of matzo every week, a large heavy bar of Israeli chocolate, a fistful of hard candies, and the most coveted treat in prison—a canister of chocolate macaroons. Many fake Jews immediately set out to sell their treats. The matzo went for three bags of mackerel (about four dollars.) The candy bar and macaroons each went for a book of stamps ($7.00 if used to gamble or $9.80 if bought legitimately.) It was a ready-made source of income, especially if you got no money from home or if you liked to gamble. Not bad for doing nothing.

None of the fake Jews went to Friday services in the chapel. An outside rabbi came in occassionally to lead services, and a couple times a year he'd look at the list of Jews, note the people he'd never met, and declare that they were not Jews. When that happened, they would lose the meals, the treats, and the catered dinners on the High Holy Days. Then they had to start the whole process all over again.

In the chapel, Orthodox, Conservative, and Reformed Jews were all represented. (There is a separate prison in Connecticut for ultra-Orthodox and Hasidic Jews.) The outside rabbi was Orthodox, but he didn't normally come on Fridays, and services were led by an inmate "faith coordinator." This caused unending problems.

The Jewish faith coordinator at Loretto was a seventy-year-old child molester. A former resident of Chicago, he had arranged over the Internet to "buy" an eleven-year-old girl from the child's drug-addicted mother. He repeatedly emailed the mother, who was in Atlanta, admonishing her to make sure the girl did everything he would tell her to do once he got to Georgia, and added that he wanted to be her "naughty grandpa." As it turned out, there was no eleven-year-old girl, and the drug-addicted mother was a male FBI agent. The soon-to-be prison faith coordinator got fifteen years. He'll probably die in prison, where he rediscovered his faith and set himself up as the go-to guy for Judaism.

Two years into the position, another devout Jew arrived to challenge "Chicago" for his position. A forty-eight-year-old

Philadelphia attorney and wealthy philanthropist named Kenneth Schaeffer arrived at Loretto in 2013 and immediately got involved with the chapel's Jewish group. A gay child molester who raped a Russian boy as many as four times a week for six years, Schaeffer was convicted of violating the Mann Act for bringing the child to the United States and raping him here, and was sentenced to fifteen years in prison.

As sedate an inmate as Chicago was, that's how pushy and aggressive Schaeffer was. He immediately lined up all the Jewish pedophiles, organized a coup, and tried to replace Chicago as the Jewish faith coordinator.

All of this backbiting and political infighting infuriated the non-pedophile Jews. Two who were especially strident in their opposition to having either Chicago or Schaeffer as their faith leaders came to me for advice. I told them what I had learned in my years in intelligence operations: "If stability is not to your benefit, chaos is your friend."

I first met Kenneth Schaeffer, although he was calling himself "Kevin," in April 2013. It was Robert, yet again, who brought another unvetted person to meet me. Schaeffer was looking to move from the overpopulated Central 2 down to Central 1 and he knew that there was an empty bed in my room. (This was just before Erik moved in.)

Schaeffer made a good first impression, prison-wise. He used polysyllabic words and spoke in a manner I could understand. He didn't finish each sentence with "you know what I'm saying?" I learned in my later research that Schaeffer had earned a Bachelor's degree at the University of Chicago and a law degree at Harvard. He was a successful attorney specializing in mergers and acquisitions, and was based in London. I was excited that someone wanted to move into the unit with whom I might be able to speak.

Still, in prison, you always have to be careful who you're dealing with, especially in a prison which by all accounts was at least 25 percent pedophiles, including a clear majority of whites. I asked Schaeffer what he was in for. His response was "it's complicated," at which I rolled my eyes. Wrong answer.

Let me take a moment to talk about what it's like to have a pedophile or child molester living in your room. They associate exclusively with other pedophiles, so there's a constant stream of perverts coming into and out of your room, even when you tell them repeatedly that chomos are not allowed visitors; they talk about their cases incessantly in an effort to relive the thrill of their crimes; they trade seminude photos of "barely legal" eighteen-year-olds; they cut out and trade photos of children from the Toys "R" Us catalogue, *Parenting* magazine, *Disney Magazine*—any magazine with young children. Some even subscribe to *Teen People* or *Seventeen Magazine* and tape up pictures of shirtless boys or bikini-clad girls in their lockers. You can imagine what it's like having this happen where you live—it's obviously not something you would want.

Hearing pedophiles ceaselessly regurgitate their cases—"the kid came on to me," "she said it felt good," "she wanted me to do it" even though she was five years old—led me to consult with a former colleague. Before prison, I was an adjunct professor at a university in Virginia. I reached out to the dean of the psychology program there to ask what to do when encountering pedophiles. The answer, in the short, was to "run screaming from the room." Pedophiles, the dean said, talk about their cases because they get sexual gratification from reliving them. The decision to not talk to pedophiles was thus an easy one for me.

Back to Schaeffer. When he said his case was "complicated," I told him that I had a right to know with whom I was dealing, especially if he had any thoughts of moving into my room. He paused for a moment and said that he had misused client funds that had been placed in an escrow account. This simply didn't ring true to me. Why was he in prison and not in a minimum-security work camp? And more importantly, why was he serving fifteen years, rather than just getting a slap on the wrist? I decided to go to the law library and look him up. I thought there was some funny business going on, but I was stunned to read the sickness and depravity involved in his case. Here's what I learned.

On October 1, 2010, Schaeffer was convicted by a jury of "traveling in foreign commerce with the intent to engage in sex with a minor between the ages of twelve and sixteen," and "transporting a person in foreign commerce with the intent that such person engage in criminal sexual conduct."

"The charges against Schaeffer, who, in 2001, was thirty-six years old, stem from his travel on August 22, 2001, from Russia to the United States in the company of [John Doe], a fifteen-year-old Russian boy. At the time of his travel, Schaeffer had housed [Doe] in a Moscow apartment for three years and, during the year immediately preceding the flight, had regularly raped the child.

"Schaeffer first met [Doe] in 1998 when [Doe] was twelve years old. [Doe] had recently been forced to leave a prestigious ballet-training program in Russia at the Moscow Academy of Ballet, also known as the Bolshoi Academy, after his parents became unable to pay his dormitory fees. [Doe's] parents wanted their son to continue his ballet training and considered sending him to a ballet school in St. Petersburg, where he had a scholarship. In the summer of 1998, however, two of [Doe's] former Academy instructors, Nikolai Dokukin and Tatiana Dokukina, raised the possibility of securing payment for [Doe's] education at the Academy from Schaeffer, a ballet aficionado, who had told the Dokukins he was interested in creating a charitable organization to provide scholarships to talented arts students in Russia.

"At the time, Schaeffer was working in Moscow as an attorney and had become acquainted with the Dokukins because of his interest in ballet. After meeting the Dokukins, Schaeffer became involved at the Academy, donating furniture to the Academy, paying for ballet footwear for the students, and providing grants to the instructors. He also visited ballet classes at the Academy and videotaped the students, telling Dokukina he planned to send the videos to his friend, Olga Kostritzky, an instructor at the School of American Ballet. Within a month of meeting Schaeffer, Dokukina told him about [Doe's] financial troubles and asked if he would be willing to sponsor [Doe's] ballet education. Schaeffer indicated he might be interested, but told Dokukina he wished to meet [Doe] and see a demonstration of his ballet ability before agreeing to sponsor him.

"Schaeffer and the Dokukins went to [Doe's] house and asked him to perform a number of ballet exercises. Schaeffer videotaped this demonstration, during which [Doe] was dressed only in a pair of black underpants. During the demonstration, Schaeffer told [Doe's] parents, 'If you show this recording, they will grab him for ballet and throw you into the bargain. They'll be asking 'where did you dig up this treasure?'" according to court records. Dokukina testified that having such a tape would provide [Doe] with a 'huge chance to be admitted to [a ballet] school.'

"[Doe's] parents were interested in having Schaeffer finance their son's education and agreed to additional meetings with Schaeffer. During one of these meetings [Doe's] father asked Schaeffer for a loan so that he could repay the debt he owed to the Academy for [Doe's] delinquent dorm fees. Schaeffer agreed, loaning Doe's father 4,300 rubles, approximately $470 at the time. A notary public in Russia drafted a loan agreement, which was signed by Schaeffer and [Doe's] parents, requiring the [Does] to repay the loan over four months, with the final payment due December 31, 1998.

"At another meeting, Schaeffer told [Doe's] father that after [Doe] reenrolled at the Academy he would not live in the dormitory, but would instead live with Schaeffer. Schaeffer explained he could provide better accommodations because [Doe] would have his own room in Schaeffer's apartment, would get better rest and better food, and would have access to a personal ballet instructor. Although this arrangement made [Doe's] father uncomfortable, he felt he had to agree to it to ensure his son was able to reenroll at the Academy. Before [Doe] moved in, the [Doe] family visited Schaeffer's apartment, a two-room apartment with one small bedroom and a larger main room. Schaeffer told the [Does] he would sleep in the bedroom and [Doe] would sleep on a pullout couch in the main room. The [Does] were satisfied that this was an appropriate sleeping arrangement for their son.

"When the new school term started, [Doe] began living with Schaeffer from Monday to Friday, returning to his parents' home on weekends, holidays, and in the summer. Schaeffer discouraged [Doe's] father from visiting him during the week, telling him [Doe] had everything he needed. While at Schaeffer's, apartment, [Doe] was taken care of primarily by a woman who lived across the hall from Schaeffer, Ludmila Kozyreva. Kozyreva woke [Doe] up, prepared his breakfast, helped him get ready for school in the morning, watched him after school, and prepared his dinner. Because the [Does] did not know Schaeffer well, [Doe's] father advised his son to tell Kozyreva if he was ever sexually molested by Schaeffer. During the time [Doe] lived with Schaeffer, Schaeffer paid for his food and some of his clothing and purchased other items for [Doe], including a PlayStation videogame console and a bicycle. Schaeffer also paid for Dokukin to provide private dance lessons to [Doe] in Schaeffer's apartment, and bought [Doe] a cellular phone.

In 2001, when [Doe] was fifteen years old, Schaeffer encouraged [Doe] to apply to summer ballet programs in the United States and elsewhere, and offered to take [Doe] to Philadelphia so he could study at the Rock School. [Doe] testified that in the year before he and Schaeffer traveled to the United States, Schaeffer had been engaging in oral and anal sex with him approximately three to four times a week, with the encounters typically taking place at night in Schaeffer's bedroom. Schaeffer told [Doe] to keep these encounters secret because people would not understand their relationship, and Schaeffer would go to jail. Schaeffer worried that the effects of his molestation of [Doe] would be discovered by a nurse at the Bolshoi Academy, and told [Doe] if the nurse asked about injuries to his rectum, he should say he was using a hemorrhoid stick. When the nurse did attempt to examine [Doe], Schaeffer called the school to complain about her, and she was eventually fired. Schaeffer also told [Doe] that if Schaeffer was gone, [Doe] 'wouldn't be able to fulfill his dreams as a ballet dancer and would stay in Russia,' according to court records.

"[Doe] also testified that Schaeffer had previously told him their relationship was similar to the relationship of the famous Russian ballet dancer Vaslav Nijinsky and his mentor and director, Sergei Diaghilev. When [Doe] was thirteen, Schaeffer showed him *Nijinsky*, a film that depicts Diaghilev and Nijinksy as lovers, and suggests that Nijinsky was emotionally destroyed after he ended his relationship with Diaghilev to pursue a heterosexual marriage. After the film, Schaeffer told [Doe] that Nijinsky made a mistake by leaving Diaghilev, and warned him not to make the same mistake. Schaeffer also told [Doe] that relationships with girls were 'disgusting,' and [Doe] should avoid girls because they would take advantage of him. That same year, Schaeffer gave [Doe] a birthday card inscribed with the message, '[Johnny], until trillion thirty years. Your friend, Ken,' and told [Doe] they should be together 'until trillion thirteen [*sic*] years.' Before they traveled to the United States, [Doe] thought of Schaeffer as his friend and role model. In an essay he wrote as part of a school application, [Doe] said Schaeffer made him very happy by reenrolling him in the Academy and by helping him with any problems he had, and described Schaeffer as 'a friend' and 'second father.'

"Schaeffer helped [Doe] complete his application for the Rock School, which admitted [Doe] to its summer program and awarded him a scholarship, which paid for [Doe's] travel to and from Philadelphia. After his acceptance to the summer program, [Doe] and his parents went to the US Embassy in Moscow to apply for a travel visa. In the application, [Doe's] parents authorized Schaeffer to take [Doe] to the United States from July 4, 2001, until August 31, 2001. When Schaeffer and [Doe] traveled to Philadelphia, [Doe] stayed with Schaeffer's parents at their home in Berwyn, a suburb of Philadelphia. Schaeffer did not stay at the Berwyn home for the summer because he was traveling for work, although he visited [Doe] there occasionally. While Schaeffer and [Doe] were in the United States, they did not engage in any sexual activity, though Schaeffer held [Doe's] hand, hugged him, and kissed him once, according to court testimony.

"On August 22, 2001, Schaeffer and [Doe] flew from Philadelphia to Moscow. After arriving in Moscow, [Doe] went to his parents' house and stayed with them for a week before he returned to school. When [Doe] returned to school and moved back into Schaeffer's apartment, Schaeffer's molestation of [Doe] resumed, and continued to occur two or three times per week."

In 2002, after spending the summer at Schaeffer's Pennsylvania home, Schaeffer and Doe moved to Cambridge, Massachusetts, and remained there until 2004, when Doe completed high school. Doe testified that he and Schaeffer had sex in Massachusetts during this period. Doe also testified that he and Schaeffer took a vacation to Montana in 2003, where they also had sex.

Over Christmas in 2006, Doe attempted suicide in the United States and was hospitalized. Shorty thereafter, he moved in with Jane Doe and her family. Around this time period, Schaeffer's mother, Marjorie Schaeffer, arranged a meeting with Doe and asked him to sign a release, which stated as follows:

"Bernard Schaeffer (Schaeffer's father), Marjorie Schaeffer, and Kenneth Schaeffer (the "Hosts") have acted as host family and legal guardians for John Doe (the "Guest"), a citizen of the Russian Federation, from the year 1998 until the year 2007. During this time, the Guest also received assistance and support from The Apogee Foundation (owned by the Schaeffer family), a New York not-for-profit corporation ("Apogee"). This reconciliation dated January 12, 2007, establishes that the Guest is now ceasing to be hosted by the Hosts and will no longer have his financial status guaranteed by the Hosts or by Apogee. The Parties each acknowledge and agree that no harm has come to the Guest at any time by virtue of his relationship and activities with the Hosts or with Apogee, and the Guest forever releases, acquits, and discharges the Hosts and all relatives of the Hosts, as well as Apogee, of all causes of action, claims, and liabilities of any kind. Doe, Marjorie Schaeffer, Bernard Schaeffer, and Kenneth

Schaeffer, on his own behalf and on behalf of the Apogee Foundation, signed this release."

Marjorie Schaeffer went to Doe's hospital room after his suicide attempt and demanded that he sign the release. He did not, and Marjorie Schaeffer forged his signature. It was later thrown out by the court.

Doe told the court that because of his relationship with Kenneth Schaeffer, he had to seek mental health treatment, focusing on dealing emotionally with the abuse. Doe maintained that he suffered from depression and alcoholism, and was often withdrawn from his peers. He claimed to have difficulty performing at work, making friends, and maintaining relationships. Indeed, he was fired from his job with the Boston Ballet because of poor performance.

"[Doe] never told his parents that he had been sexually abused by Schaeffer. After he began living with Schaeffer, however, his personality changed. His father noticed that he was more withdrawn and silent, and seemed to be keeping something to himself. [Doe] eventually moved to the United States in 2008 told his girlfriend, whom he has since married, about Schaeffer's sexual molestation, revealing that Schaeffer had sexually abused him while they lived together in Russia.

"On August 12, 2008, [Doe] filed a civil lawsuit against the Schaeffers and the Apogee Foundation, bringing claims stemming from Schaeffer's sexual abuse. After [Doe] filed his lawsuit, he was contacted by the FBI, which launched a criminal investigation into Schaeffer's conduct with [Doe]. On January 14, 2010, Schaeffer was charged in a two-count indictment with 1) traveling in foreign commerce for the purpose of engaging in sex with a minor, and 2) transporting a person in foreign commerce with the intent that such person engage in criminal sexual conduct." Schaeffer's defense against the charges was novel. First, he denied that any sexual contact with Doe ever took place. His attorneys argued that "there is a very real risk that such evidence (of sexual abuse) could lead the jury to make its decision on an improper basis. Namely, the jury would be so overwhelmed by the victim's detailed descriptions of sexual abuse that it would find Schaeffer guilty based on repulsion to the alleged acts and antipathy toward child sex abusers, instead of weighing whether, on August 22, 2001, Schaeffer *intended* to engage in sexual conduct with the victim.

This distinction is crucial because the acts of sexual abuse allegedly committed by Schaeffer from 1998 to August 2001 do not form the basis for charges against Schaeffer. Instead, Schaeffer is charged with a crime of intent, and the jury will be charged with determining not whether he actually engaged in abusive sexual practices, but whether he intended to engage in such practices on August 22, 2001. Therefore, exhaustive evidence of Schaeffer's prior and subsequent sexual misconduct would exceed the probative value of showing his intent on August 22, 2001, and would be unduly prejudicial.

Finally, it is evident that a litany of abuse will invariably disgust and inflame the jury. Although evidence of prior sexual misconduct is relevant and probative, exhaustive evidence of such misconduct is unduly prejudicial.

Schaeffer was found guilty on both counts, although his conviction on the second count was eventually overturned. He was sentenced to fifteen years in prison.

I approached Schaeffer armed with my newfound knowledge and asked him why he had lied to me. I said I had a right to know about the person who wanted to live with me. His first response was that the person in the court papers wasn't him, and he insisted emphatically that he wasn't a pedophile. He said, "I don't know this Kenneth guy. My name is Kevin." I told him that over the previous several days I had heard him paged to the mail room as "Kenneth" Schaeffer several times, and for two of those times I had been behind him, as I had been called to the mailroom too. (The CIA had taught me to be constantly aware of my surroundings. You never know when the smallest detail of something you observe could become crucial.)

Faced with his duplicity, Schaeffer got nasty. His response to me set the stage for the remainder of our relationship. He spat,

"Don't you fuck with me! I'm more dangerous than you think." I was amused. I looked at five-foot-six Kenneth, with his potbelly. With all the training the CIA had provided me, I was a formidable physical presence in this dispute, and Schaeffer wouldn't have lasted ten seconds against me. I walked away shaking my head.

Over the next couple of weeks, Schaeffer approached every person with an empty bed in his room, telling all of them that he was a crooked attorney. But by then, I had a reputation as someone who knew his way around the law library, and countless people approached me, wanting me to "check out names" for them. This proved to be a double-edged sword. The prisoners who had something to hide—and you can't believe how many people had something to hide—were very wary of me. The "good guys," though, were eager to use my "skills." To be clear, the "skills" I'm talking about here consist of typing a name into a search box on the Lexis-Nexis database. It was as simple as that.

Anyway, the guys Schaeffer approached about moving into their rooms made a beeline for me to ask for the real story. My responses were unvarnished. I even allowed them to copy what I had printed on Schaeffer's case from the law library. Eventually, Schaeffer went to the unit counselor, who put him in a dorm-type room in my unit, the least-desirable place one could live, although still in my unit.

It was about this time that Schaeffer began his counteroffensive against me, not having any idea how ill-prepared and outgunned he was. Schaeffer was a very arrogant little man and was used to being the smartest person in the room. He was also used to getting his way. But he had badly misjudged the situation. I would have been happy to leave him alone. I wasn't looking for trouble. He just wouldn't stop picking at the scab. He realized that, to go up against me, he would need allies.

It wasn't long before Schaeffer ingratiated himself with a small group of African-American prisoners, convincing them that he was not a pedophile and plying them with copies of the *Robb Report*, the *duPont Registry*, and stories about his $300,000 watch, his houses, luxury cars, and international vacations. To say these dolts bought his stories hook, line, and sinker would be an understatement. They wanted to be associated with success and to bask in the glow of his wealthy past life. (Besides Schaeffer, who is very wealthy, the only people in prison who read the *Robb Report* or the *duPont Registry* were the people furthest away from the bright center of luxury consumerism. There will never be any Lamborghinis or McLarens for them.)

At this point, I started getting dirty looks from some of the African-Americans and one or two Spanish-speaking prisoners. I shrugged it off. It was nothing I couldn't live with, and I assumed this would be the status quo. Schaeffer had found his little crew, and I figured a "Pax Loretto" would ensue. A weekend visit by my family changed everything.

The atmosphere of détente was short-lived. That weekend, my wife and three youngest children (my eight-year-old son, six-year-old daughter, and one-year-old son) came to visit. We sat in the very first row of chairs in the visiting room, next to Schaeffer and his parents. About twenty minutes into the visit, when my wife and kids had gone to the vending room, CO Duran motioned for me to get up. He whispered that he was moving my family and the large family of another prisoner to the opposite side of the room. I told him that my family had plenty of room, so if he was trying to give us more space, it wasn't necessary. "Well," he said, "I *need* for you to move. I think there's a problem." He nodded at Schaeffer. "We're not supposed to call them out like this, but that pedophile keeps eyeing your son." He nodded in the direction of my eight-year-old. We moved.

This was highly unusual. The visitor's room was filled with pedophiles on any given visiting day. Families are almost never moved because of them. (COs will routinely warn pedophiles to "take the child off your lap!") But Duran saw something. He saw Schaeffer licking his chops at the sight of my son and another little boy, and he acted to stop it. After the incident, during the many times I was in the visiting room with my family, and Marjorie Schaeffer was visiting Kenneth, she glared at me, as if to project the blame for her son's sickness and perversion on others, almost making it out to be my fault for bringing an object of her son's desire into the room.

I think Schaeffer's problem was a simple one. Oftentimes, Type A personalities don't get along well with other Type A personalities. My training at the CIA prepared me to get along with other Alpha types. Frankly, the CIA's clandestine operatives are all Type A personalities. Consequently, I was, and am, perfectly comfortable dealing with other strong personalities. Schaeffer, unfortunately, was not. This was never a problem I had with Kenneth Schaeffer. If I had had trouble dealing with strong personalities, I would have had trouble getting along with 90 percent of the people in prison. This was a one-sided problem on the part of Schaeffer and it became a one-sided feud. Some people just need a boogeyman. Schaeffer decided I was his.

Immediately after the visiting room incident, I became the focus of Schaeffer's ire. He did what he was raised to do: he bought allies and demonized those people he couldn't buy.

Schaeffer's first strike came when he addressed the prison's Jewish congregation during Friday evening Shabbat services, stating that he had uncovered "an insidious anti-Jewish faction within the prison." I was the one who organized and ran this cabal. Schaeffer said that I was a "virulent anti-Semite and a danger to all Jews." He went on to say that I had even recruited members of the prison staff.

Later in that same service, the Jewish faith coordinator, Chicago, got into an unrelated argument with Schaeffer over what course the Jewish services should take. Schaeffer called for Chicago's ouster and more conservative services. When he was rebuffed, he threw a chair and had to be separated from another inmate by chapel orderlies.

Over the course of the next week, another Jewish inmate, Corey Lyman, with whom I was friendly, and Chicago approached me to say that Schaeffer had made wild accusations of anti-Semitism against me, saying I was leading a vast "underground conspiracy intent on hurting Jews." (As an aside, Chicago told me that when Schaeffer first arrived at Loretto Chicago had encountered him on the walking track. He welcomed Schaeffer, said he was the Jewish faith coordinator for prisoners, and invited him to services. Schaeffer looked around as though he feared someone had heard that he was Jewish, and said, "I have to be very careful because it's very anti-Semitic around here." Chicago responded that he had been at Loretto for two years and had never experienced any anti-Semitism. He asked Schaeffer rhetorically, "You've experienced anti-Semitism in your first week?" Schaeffer was silent.)

At the next Shabbat service, which Schaeffer boycotted, Chicago stood and spoke for me. He said he knew me. I had once advised him on how to confront a bully, and he could state unequivocally that I was not an anti-Semite. A day later word got back to Schaeffer that Chicago had spoken out on my behalf. Schaeffer immediately began a counteroffensive, telling other members of the congregation that Chicago was "a pawn in the anti-Jewish faction. He's nothing more than a stooge and a collaborator." Lyman kept me updated throughout the weekend.

A few words about Lyman: Lyman, like Schaeffer, was a lawyer who had gone bad, although he was not a pedophile. He took an instant liking to me, and I set out to "recruit" him as a source of information, and as an "access agent," thinking that I might need a presence in the Jewish congregation if Schaeffer decided to move against me there. Lyman, who was new to the prison and had very few friends, welcomed the attention and was an easy target for recruitment, and I moved him in that direction. This was not entirely cynical on my part. I liked him very much, he hated Schaeffer's entitled attitude, and he enjoyed my company. So I got to work.

I hatched a plan to divide the pedophile vote and to elect a non-pedophile as the Jewish faith coordinator. After surreptitiously making a copy of all the registered Jews in the prison, I divided the names between those who were pedophiles and those who were not. One of the non-pedophile Jews began engaging with other non-pedophile Jews to ask for their support. Meanwhile, the other non-pedophile Jews began lobbying the pedophile Jews to support either Chicago or Schaeffer, thus splitting the pedophile vote. After weeks of "campaigning," an election was held, and the non-pedophile won. Loretto's Jews were then led by a convicted methamphetamine manufacturer and drug smuggler, thanks to a valuable CIA life lesson. And there were still chocolates and treats for everybody.

I engaged Lyman in a conversation about the types of losers and criminals you meet in prison, "people who aren't like us," and created a camaraderie where none existed before. I dangled my disgust with pedophiles before Lyman, knowing that he would jump at the opportunity to express his own disgust with Schaeffer's crime, as well as the disruption Schaeffer was causing in the Jewish community. Although Lyman had heard the rumors regarding Schaeffer's crime, I enlightened him with the full details.

The recruitment bore immediate fruit. It was Lyman who first came to me to report that Schaeffer had denounced me to the Jews. Indeed, Schaeffer had gone directly to Lyman, among others, to say that Chicago was a stooge and collaborator. With this source of information, I was able to stay one step ahead of Schaeffer. The next challenge came quickly in the form of two rather large African-Americans.

As I was waiting to get into the visitor's room one afternoon, I was approached by two African-Americans, whom I vaguely remembered having helped write some commutation request letters a couple months earlier. The letters had taken only five minutes and required only a working knowledge of the English language, but it meant the world to these guys. The conversation went like this:

MAN #1: Yo, John. We need to talk to you.

JOHN: (*Momentarily not having any idea who these guys were.*) Hey! What's up? Good to see you again!

MAN #1: Do you know the little white guy, Schaeffer?

JOHN: I know him. I don't like him.

MAN #2: He asked us to do something pretty fucked up.

JOHN: Yeah? Like what?

MAN #2: He wants us to lay you out.

MAN #1: Really fuck you up.

JOHN: Why on Earth would he want to do that?

MAN #2: He said you were going to plant a shank under his bed, then tell the cops we did it.

JOHN: That's absurd.

MAN #1: That's why we came to you. You've been good to us. That's why we wanted to give you a heads up. We told him we weren't interested, but you should still watch your back.

JOHN: Thanks, guys. I really appreciate it.

It was this conversation that made me realize that I had to be proactive, rather than reactive. I had to use my training to create an operational plan that would result either in Schaeffer being shipped to another prison or at least being moved to another housing unit. Prior to this, I had been easy on Schaeffer. But this was serious. There was a potential for violence. Schaeffer had tried to hurt me and it was time to take off the gloves.

I first made an assessment of Schaeffer's state of mind. He was not a person who could stand any viewpoint not in sync with his own, and if the facts didn't suit his idea of himself, he would spread disinformation and discredit or eliminate those with differing opinions. I decided that I had to fight fire with fire; if he was going to make up stories to hurt me, I would use disinformation the same way. I sat down and started to plot.

The oldest trick in the book in prison is that when a new prisoner comes in and is deemed by others to be weak and ripe for exploitation, he is immediately targeted by stronger, tougher, meaner prisoners. It's even better if the weak individual happens to have money. The game is to convince the weak inmate that someone is after him—he's in physical danger. He needn't worry, however, because the stronger, tougher, meaner prisoner would protect him for a monthly fee, anywhere from $100 to $500 in commissary, or money wired to his account by the weak inmate's family. Most of the time this is a tag-team effort, with an associate of the man making the approach acting the part of the bully. But sometimes, the "savior" will use one or more individuals with whom the weak inmate already has had problems. This is what happened with Schaeffer. I became the boogeyman, the threat from which Schaeffer needed to be protected. So all of a sudden, not only was I the person who would not permit Schaeffer to be who he was pretending to be, but now he had a group of bodyguards convincing him that I was a threat to his safety. I knew that eventually, if I did not act to defend myself, I would be the one to get in trouble. I was determined for this not to happen.

To get in front of this problem I was going to have to establish a more compelling and unassailable position. I was going to have to portray myself as the victim. To accomplish this, I was going to elicit information from people close to Schaeffer and plant disinformation that would get back to him. I would do this in two ways. First, I would speak directly to people who I knew would repeat what I said to Schaeffer. Second, I would speak within earshot of people who I knew were close to Schaeffer, and who I knew would run to him with the information. (This is often the best way to pass disinformation because the listener is usually not suspicious that the speaker is trying to influence him, and believes that he very cleverly came upon this information on his own.) One example of this would be to stage a situation where you know you are being overheard and you begin a conversation with "don't tell anybody, but…" or "listen to what I just heard, but keep it to yourself…" or anything to make a person's ears prick up.

There were several different "camps" on the Schaeffer issue. Most people wanted nothing to with him. He was, after all, a child rapist. Most of the Jews hated him because he was so pushy and tried to take over and run the Jewish services. Most whites, blacks, and Hispanics hated him because he was so arrogant and because he absolutely denied his crime. The only people who had anything to do with him were the blacks taking his money for "protection," the prisoners who thought that his connections and money could somehow help them when they got out, and the prisoners who were too stupid to believe that he had committed his crime, even when faced with documentary proof.

I knew I couldn't achieve my goals simply by manipulating inmates. My goals could only be achieved by actions taken by staff, and to do that, I was going to have to convince them to act on my behalf. To add credibility to any operation, the premise had to be believable, and it wouldn't have been credible for me to approach a staff member and rant, rant, rant about how much I hated Schaeffer and then expect something to be done. I had to map out a plan, sow seeds about Schaeffer with the right staff, count on Schaeffer to continue to be his own worst enemy by pissing everybody off, and wait for the information to take hold.

The first thing I did was to put out word that there was a conspiracy afoot and that I was the victim. I mentioned this discretely to rats and blabbermouths, and I allowed others of the same ilk to "overhear" me expressing trepidation about being a potential target of violence. Soon, "requests to staff," also known as "cop-outs," flowed from all corners to SIS. As I had expected, rats reported to the authorities that I was in danger, and it was Schaeffer who was doing the planning against me. So as not to be sent into protective custody, I laughed it off and said I had no fear. I could defend myself against Schaeffer with my pinky finger.

Weeks passed, and not a day went by that I didn't stoke the fire I had started. I went just as often to see the unit manager, who became an ally. The fact was that the staff didn't want Schaeffer on the compound any more than I did. As time went on, I saw the unit manager more and more often, and when rats reported to the Special Investigative Service that I was in danger, things came to a head.

Late one evening a different black prisoner came up to me to say that Schaeffer had offered him one hundred dollars "to fuck up Kiriakou." The prisoner told Schaeffer, "No way. Fight your own battles." He said he had no beef with me and didn't want to get involved. Schaeffer disingenuously responded that I was planning to plant a shank under his mattress and blame the black prisoner, the same story he had tried with others earlier. The prisoner, recognizing the absurdity of the statement, walked away, found me, and told me everything. I made a mental note that the pressure seemed to be getting to Schaeffer. He seemed to be getting more and more desperate to beat me to the punch.

A few days later, Ali, the black "shot-caller"—the prisoner who represented black interests and worked with the leaders of other races to keep the peace, and with whom I had a warm and open relationship—approached me to say that another prisoner, "Blaze," said Schaeffer had asked him to "lay Kiriakou out." Blaze told the same "shank under the mattress" story I had heard twice previously. A day later, an organized crime figure with sources among the COs told me that he had heard that Schaeffer had sent SIS six "cop-outs" alleging that I was going to hurt him. Finally, Lyman said that Schaeffer had stood up in the Jewish congregation to shout that I was a danger to all Jews and that I had threatened him with "railcars and ovens." He was coming unhinged. Perfect.

I decided to call a meeting with both the black and white shot-callers. I should also note Ali's involvement in this. I liked Ali and occasionally hung out with him. I even designed his website. But why would the black shot-caller, who spends his days mediating between the Crips and the Bloods, care one whit about a gay white pedophile? Well, it was clear to me from the beginning that Ali was the primary person on Schaeffer's payroll. I decided to use that to my advantage.

I asked Dave to sit in on the meeting and to play the "good cop." For my part, I had to rely on the acting skills the CIA had drilled into me.

The meeting took place two nights later in our cell. Dave started things off. I was silent. "Schaeffer's constant efforts to hire black guys to give John a beating have to stop. He keeps upping the ante, and the only one who's going to get hurt is Schaeffer himself. We wanted to try to defuse the situation by bringing the shot-callers together." Heads nodded and assurances were given. Then it was my turn.

"May I say something?" I shook with faux anger. "If I have to hear one more fucking time that I'm going to be 'laid out,' or if I have to hear one more fucking time that I'm an anti-Semite, there's going to be blood on the floor! And it's going to be Schaeffer's! Do I make myself clear?! I'll kill the motherfucker myself!"

There was a moment of shocked silence before the white shot-caller said, "We'll take care of it, buddy." Ali nodded in agreement.

The shot-callers must have gone to Schaeffer immediately, because my next conversation was with a Jewish Mexican illegal immigrant. He asked for a meeting with me and said disingenuously that a group of Mexicans were "going to fuck you up" for bullying Schaeffer. This Mexican must have thought I was stupid. He must have thought that I, a chapel employee, had never seen them in the chapel together acting like long lost friends. I thought I'd teach the Mexican a lesson, too. I went to my closest friends, the Italians, and asked them to weigh in with the Mexicans. The Mexican shot-caller was furious that one of this people would make an unsubstantiated threat against me on behalf of a pedophile. He apologized and asked me to just forget about it.

Schaeffer made one last, desperate, attempt to punish me. He went to the chaplain to ask that I be fired for "bullying" him, and he repeated the ridiculous "railcars and ovens" story. I told the chaplain that I thought Schaeffer was insane, that he was peddling this story unsuccessfully all around the compound, and that the entire Jewish congregation would verify my side of the story. That was good enough for the chaplain. Now it was time to hit Schaeffer where it would hurt the most—in his wallet. It was time to write a letter to John Doe's attorney.

Dave and I went to the law library and looked up John Doe's civil case against Schaeffer. The documents listed Doe's attorney as Kenneth Harriman of Philadelphia. It turned out that Harriman was one of the most highly respected, able, and accomplished litigators in the city. Dave wrote the first letter on September 6, 2013:

Dear Mr. Harriman,

I am currently incarcerated at FCI Loretto with Kenneth Schaeffer. In fact, we are in the same unit. Several months ago an incident occurred that I thought should be brought to your attention. This incident took place in the visiting room when a friend and former colleague, John Kiriakou, was having a visit with his family. John's wife and his three young children (including his eight-year-old son) were visiting from the Washington, DC area. Kenneth Schaeffer was visiting with his parents at the same time. During the course of the visit, a Corrections Officer approached John and another inmate who was sitting near John (and who also had a young son visiting) and said he needed to move both families to another part of the visiting room. John told the officer that he and his family were comfortable and did not need more room. The officer responded that there was a problem with another of the inmates and discreetly indicated that the problem was with Kenneth Schaeffer. When asked to explain, the officer said Schaeffer had been observed ogling John's son and the son of the other inmate. John had noticed the intense looks Schaeffer was giving his son, but he did not make an immediate connection for two reasons. First, the visit room is a busy and frenetic place. Second, when Kenneth Schaeffer first introduced himself to us several days earlier, he indicated that he was incarcerated for a fraud conviction. So initially no flags were raised. As a side note, Schaeffer tells people his name is "Kevin," not Kenneth.

John wrote about the visiting room ordeal in the third installment of his "Letters from Loretto" series that has been published by firedoglake.com and picked up by news sites such as CNN, The Huffington Post, MSNBC, Esquire, The Economist, Playboy, and others. He is willing to give a sworn statement or help in any other way, as am I. We both have lived in the same 150-man unit as Kenneth Schaeffer for many months, and we have been subjected to his profligate lying and deceptions. We may be able to shed additional light into his character of late. The only thing I personally am unable to do is to speak to the aforementioned incident in the visiting room, as I was not there. But John is more than willing to speak, and he looks forward to hearing back from you. We offer our help for no other reason than it is the right thing to do.

John Kiriakou's inmate number is 79637-083 and he can be reached at the same address as I. When writing to either of us, please follow the enclosed instructions for sending legal mail. The staff will use any excuse to open mail from lawyers.

Thank you for your time. We hope our efforts help in some small way so that your client finds the justice he seeks and deserves.

Yours Sincerely,
David Phillips

Two weeks passed with no response, so I wrote a short follow-up:

Dear Mr. Harriman,

My name is John Kiriakou, a CIA anti-torture whistleblower incarcerated in the Federal Correctional Institution at Loretto, Pennsylvania. My friend and cellmate, David Phillips, wrote to you two weeks ago to tell you about an incident that my family had with Kenneth Schaeffer in the visiting room here. I wrote about the incident in a blog entitled "The New Normal" at firedoglake.com. It received widespread press coverage.

I seek absolutely nothing from you. I am sickened by Kenneth Schaeffer's crime, and I am personally offended that he would openly leer at my son. I want nothing but to keep him behind bars. Please let me know if I can help you in any way.

Sincerely,
John Kiriakou

Two weeks later I received a letter from Harriman. It said simply, "Please call me immediately," followed by a phone number.

I did call him immediately. Harriman answered his own phone and said he had been looking forward to hearing from me. He said that he would arrange an immediate legal visit and would fly his own plane to meet with me as soon as the visit was approved. True to his word, two weeks later, Harriman flew his twin-engine Cessna to nearby Johnstown, Pennsylvania, rented a car, and arrived for the meeting. Elegant, silver-haired, and dressed in a $2,000 Italian suit and custom-made shirt with gold cufflinks, Harriman introduced himself. I thought that he would want me to repeat the visiting room story. But instead, he wanted to do the talking. He was as excited as I was.

Harriman asked if I was aware of the circumstances of Schaeffer's arrest. I said I had not heard any of the details. He continued that, after Schaeffer's abuse of John Doe had ended, he returned to Moscow, where his only client was a billionaire Russian oligarch. Soon after arriving in Russia, however, Schaeffer heard, probably from his parents, that he had been indicted in Philadelphia on two felony counts of violating the Mann Act. His response was to flee immediately to Israel, knowing that the Israeli government does not extradite Jews to any country, no matter the crime. At the same time, several million dollars of Schaeffer's money disappeared from Russia. Did Schaeffer hide it in Israel? Did he leave it in Russia? Did he transfer it to London, Cyprus, or maybe Lichtenstein? If John Doe was going to get any justice, Harriman would first have to find the money.

Harriman continued that Schaeffer was safely ensconced in Israel when, one day, he saw an ad for a children's ballet performance set to take place in Cyprus. Unable to control himself, he bought a ticket and flew to Cyprus, where he was immediately arrested at Nicosia Airport on an Interpol fugitive warrant, and extradited to the US.

Schaeffer was forced to return to Philadelphia to face the criminal charges. John Doe's civil suit was different, though, and Doe had engaged Harriman to handle it. Within weeks the attorney began running into roadblocks. Schaeffer's family enlisted the support of Pennsylvania's then-senior US senator, Arlen Specter. Three judges, friends of Schaeffer's parents, recused themselves. And the judge who finally agreed to preside over the civil trial assigned all his other cases to other judges so he could focus solely on Schaeffer. It turned out that this judge had also had a social relationship with Schaeffer's parents. The deck was stacked, but Harriman pushed forward with the case.

In my short interaction with Harriman, I found that he was a renaissance man—highly educated, highly skilled, and multitalented. He was also very successful financially and he owned a house along Philadelphia's Main Line, not far from Schaeffer's parents. As a hobby, Harriman was an amateur astronomer, and he had a sophisticated and expensive Meade telescope. He told me the following story as an indication of the Schaeffer family's power, as an example of what he was up against.

Harriman's home is located across the street from one of the most prestigious Jewish high schools in suburban Philadelphia. Around ten one evening, Harriman and his telescope were in the front yard; Harriman was looking at Jupiter and its moons when a bus full of high school students pulled up to the school at the end of a day-long field trip. Several of the students saw Harriman and his telescope and asked if they could take a look. Soon the entire class was lined up to take their first look at the planet. Once everyone had seen it, they thanked Harriman and went back across the street to meet their parents and to go home.

The next day Harriman received a phone call from the school's principal, who thanked him for the kindness of the impromptu astronomy lesson. The kids had been raving about it, he said, and several had even expressed an interest in studying astronomy. The principal continued that the senior class was planning a trip to Israel, and they wanted to invite Harriman to go as their guest, all expenses paid. Harriman said that he had never been to Israel, had always wanted to go, and was delighted to accept. A few weeks later, he was on a plane for Tel Aviv.

Harriman said that Israel was the "trip of a lifetime." He saw all the holy sites, the museums, Jerusalem, Bethlehem, and Nazareth. Toward the end of the week, one of the teacher-chaperones told Harriman that they had scheduled a courtesy call for him with the Israeli deputy minister of education. Harriman said he was happy to make the call. A few days later he went to the Ministry and was ushered into the deputy minister's office. The deputy minister was warm and engaging. "Thank you so much for introducing the students to astronomy," he began. "They told me how much fun they had looking through your telescope. It's important for students to have a strong background in science. You've encouraged them to seek this, and it will help them in college and in life. You've done them a great service. By the way, can't you make this Schaeffer case go away?" Harriman was dumbfounded. "That," he said, "is what I'm up against."

Harriman's request to me was simple: help me find the money. As it so happens, I know a former CIA officer and a former KGB officer who have a consulting firm together in Washington that specializes in tracking laundered money around the world. I made an introduction, and they began their investigation. "In the meantime," Harriman said, "What can I do to help you?"

The truth is that there was nothing I needed, although I appreciated the offer. I suggested a follow-up meeting, along with Dave, so that we could lay out a more comprehensive plan. I reminded Harriman that my goal was to hit Schaeffer in his wallet and to help John Doe find justice. He agreed to set up another legal visit in the coming weeks, we shook hands, and he departed.

In the meantime, several prisoners approached Dave and me to say that Schaeffer was in the market for a shank. I had no idea if he was going to use it to stab me, or if he wanted to hire somebody to plant it in my room. I didn't care which, and I didn't want to take another chance. I frankly didn't trust the two bumbling fools in SIS, so I went back to the unit manager. I told him what I had heard and I said that if something wasn't done about Schaeffer—soon—there was going to be trouble, somebody was going to get hurt, it wouldn't be me, and it would be the fault of the prison administration. I was tired of getting the brush off. The unit manager called SIS, demanded an investigation, and told me to sit tight.

A few minutes later I heard Schaeffer paged to the SIS office. I was glad to hear it, but the proof was in the pudding. An hour later I was called to SIS, too. The CO offered me a seat. He started by saying, "Well, your friend's in the SHU."

"What friend?" I asked.

"Schaeffer," he said. "I sent him to the SHU, pending investigation."

"It's about time," I snapped. "I've always said you guys were lazy, but Schaeffer was going to get himself hurt. The SHU is the safest place for him."

The CO, unfazed by my swipe, responded, "He fainted when I told him. I had to call medical to carry him down there. He cried like a baby." Much to my surprise, the CO continued, "Look, if you want to keep this guy locked up, I have to have corroboration. Give me some names." I was furious. He was asking me to rat, which I refused to do.

"You want me to do your job for you?" I shouted. "You know exactly who you need to talk to." I walked out.

Schaeffer's lockup was a reprieve for me, but it was too early to celebrate. SIS began paging a parade of my friends and contacts: the white shot-callers Big John, Bryce the Aryan, and Bam; Mark Lanzilotti; Clint Goswick; and several of the Jewish prisoners who argued with Schaeffer in the chapel. A few days later the warden stopped me in the hall and said, "You know I'm going to have to cut this guy loose, right?"

I said, "Warden, SIS better do the right thing here. They know this guy is a problem."

"We'll see what happens," was all he said.

By a few hours later, I was more concerned about the fallout of the SIS questioning than I was about Schaeffer. The white shot-callers were livid at being called to SIS. Despite our protestations, they blamed Dave, who loved to stir the pot and was an easy target for them. Big John was the angriest. "You're gonna pay for this, Dave! You fucking rat!" The Jews all told different stories, depending on where they were in the congregation. The Orthodox supported Schaeffer, the Reformed supported me, and the conservatives didn't want to get involved. Mark and Clint were dismissed because we were friends and SIS said they were biased. Schaeffer was released from the SHU the next day at 11:00 a.m., just in time for lunch. He had been locked up for only five days.

Attorney Harriman wrote to me in the midst of the investigation to say that he was flying back out and that he had gotten approval to meet with both Dave and me together. This was highly unusual, perhaps unprecedented, and I wondered if the prison administration did it as a consolation prize for releasing Schaeffer from the SHU. Two days later, a Friday, Harriman flew to Johnstown, and then drove to Loretto.

The visiting room CO called my name first. "Kiriakou to visitation." I was patted down in the anteroom, then went into the visitation room, where I gave my ID to the CO before meeting Harriman in a windowed area for a private meeting at the back of the room. But as soon as I walked through the anteroom door, I saw them—Schaeffer, his mother, and his father. They were deep in a whispered conversation and they didn't notice me. I said hello to Harriman and pointed them out. A minute later, the CO paged Dave. He, too, came in through the anteroom. The gazes of all three Schaeffers locked on him.

Watching Marjorie Schaeffer physically rise from her seat, mouth agape, eyes locked on Dave as he walked to the meeting room, made my day. Harriman said he had not been in the same room with the Schaeffers since a contentious deposition more than a year earlier. Seeing us all together ruined the Schaeffers' visit, and they stared at us for the next two hours. We got a kick out of it, and certainly Harriman enjoyed himself. What I didn't realize at the time was that it probably pushed Schaeffer over the edge. Things would soon get worse.

The next day I ran into Nacho, a Mexican gangbanger, in the hall. I openly loathed this filthy midget rat. He stopped me and asked for a minute, so I said I was willing to listen. "Please leave Schaeffer alone," he said. "He's shaking. He doesn't want trouble with you. Please just let it go." I shot back, "He has a funny way of showing it. He's tried to hire half the black guys on the compound to give me a beating. He's the one who started this, Nacho. I'm willing to give him space, but as God is my witness, if he tries anything again, I'll kill him and make it look like an accident." Nacho nodded and walked off. This conversation convinced me that, as was the case with Ali, Nacho was on Schaeffer's payroll for "protection."

Dave and I discussed the Nacho conversation over lunch. We decided to give Schaeffer a week. If he backed off, fine. If not, he was going down. In the meantime, we would continue our cooperation with Harriman. I could have just declared victory, but what I really wanted now was for Schaeffer to either go to the SHU for a long stretch or go to another prison. He would soon change the scope of my problem with him.

The next evening Dave and I were outside walking the track when one of the recreation COs, McCarthy, stopped us. I liked McCarthy. We both did. He was the only member of the staff with whom, in another life, I would have had a beer. In his early thirties, physically fit and a new father, he was always friendly, engaging, and honest. I always said that the idiots on staff could learn a lot from this guy.

McCarthy pulled me aside and said, "Kiriakou, I just found an anonymous note under my office door. It said that a guy named Schaeffer had a shank in his room that he was going to use to stab you."

I laughed, "I could crush that guy like a bug. What did you do?"

"I turned it over to the lieutenant," McCarthy said. "He's investigating right now."

"Who's the lieutenant tonight?"

"Gramble," he said.

I laughed again. "I'd be surprised if it wasn't Gramble who gave Schaeffer the shank!" I went back inside and waited for everything to play out.

I waited and waited and waited. Nothing happened. One of Schaeffer's cellmates at this point was Art. The next morning I asked him if there had been an incident in his room the night before. He said, "Actually, the cops came in last night and shook us down. Gramble was the lead."

"Did they find anything?" I asked.

"I don't know," Art said. "They did the shakedown and walked out."

By the next morning, news of the anonymous note and the shakedown had spread like wildfire. At least half a dozen people told me that they heard I was in danger. This put me in a tricky position. If I had gone to the cops with any concern about my physical safety, they would have put me in the SHU "for my own protection." What was the alternative? Stabbing Schaeffer wasn't an option, at least not realistically. I called Harriman for advice.

Harriman said that something was certainly "up." When he visited several days earlier, he noticed that a prominent attorney from Philadelphia, from a firm that represented the Catholic Archdiocese of Philadelphia's pedophile priests, had signed in for a visit "in the administrative office" the previous Tuesday. Legal visits with prisoners are allowed only on Fridays, Saturdays, and Sundays. "This had to be a meeting with the warden," he said. "Why? Why are they protecting Schaeffer?" He advised me to write a "strong, sharp" letter to the warden.

"Tell him that Lieutenant Gramble covered up the confiscation of the shank, and tell him we know about the Tuesday meeting. Tell him you're willing to go to the press. Tell him you want immediate action."

I began the three-page letter with, "Warden: in the unlikely event that you are unaware of the past three days' events..." The letter was sharp to the point of being accusatory. I handed it to him directly at lunch and I took a seat where I could watch him read it. Halfway into the first page, I saw him mouth the words "oh, shit" and hand the letter to his executive assistant, who was standing next to him. His response was, "Oh, no," and he handed the letter to the assistant warden, standing next to him, turned, walked out of the cafeteria, and went across the hall to the SIS office. A minute later, the PA system barked, "Inmate Schaeffer to the lieutenant's office immediately." Fifteen minutes later, as I left the cafeteria, I saw a weeping Schaeffer being led to the SHU in handcuffs. Again.

Dave and I went back to our room, got changed, and headed toward the rec yard. In front of the SIS office, waiting to go out, were all three of Schaeffer's cellmates: Art, Al the arsonist, and a young pedophile. We wished Art luck and went outside for a walk. An hour later, on our way back in, another prisoner ran up to us saying, "Did you hear? The cops locked up the whole room for investigation. Art's in the SHU!" We told the guy to not panic. Art would probably be in the SHU for a few days, and then they'd let him out. He hadn't done anything wrong. Besides, he's a tough guy. He's been in prison for forty years. He knows how to handle himself.

In the meantime, more rumors began to spread. There were two shanks, not one. They were meant for me, not for Dave. Lieutenant Gramble had been suspended. I thought it best to keep my head down and my mouth shut, and to see how things played out in the coming days.

The next day, the day after Schaeffer's cell was taken to the SHU, I was sound asleep at 1:00 p.m. when Dave woke me up in a panic. "I just got called to the lieutenant's office," he said. "You know what to do if I don't come back." (We had planned in advance for if either of us was ever taken to the SHU; one would secure the other's personal property and call home to pass the news.) Only fifteen minutes after Dave was called down, a lunatic who goes nightly to the zombie pill line came to my cell to say, "Your...buddy...just got...taken...to the SHU... He says...goodbye."

Frank and I looked at each other, stunned. We knew we had about five minutes to take all of Dave's books, legal work, and personal papers out of his locker before the cops came and loaded everything into green military-style duffel bags. Dave wouldn't get his property back until he was released from the SHU or arrived at his final destination. That could be a year from now, depending on whether he was put into diesel therapy or on Con Air and flown around the country. I sent all his books to his grandmother and everything else to his attorney. A prison administrator told me later in the day, "You two will never see each other again."

A day later it was my turn to be called to the lieutenant's office. From there I was sent directly to SIS. Graham offered me a seat and said bluntly, "The only reason you're not in the SHU is that we couldn't find any video of you going into Schaeffer's room."

"Well," I said, "that plus the fact that that I haven't done anything wrong."

"Here's our theory," Graham said. "Your buddy Dave made the shanks and got Art to plant them in Schaeffer's property."

Recalling the CIA's rule of "admit nothing, deny everything, make counteraccusations," I responded, "Are you insane?" Graham's face was blank, but he didn't speak, so I continued. "Dave could have killed Schaeffer with his pinky finger. Did you forget that he's a fourth-degree black belt in Tai Bo Jiu Jitsu? And you want me to believe that he talked a seventy-five-year-old man with forty years of prison experience into getting onto his hands and knees to do Dave's dirty work? Even I gave you more credit than that!"

"So what was Phillips doing in Schaeffer's room?" he asked.

I said flatly, "I get stacks of magazines every week. You know that because you monitor my mail. When I finish the magazines I give them to Art. Dave took them to his room because Art's an old man. It's as simple as that."

"Before you go," Graham said, "You should know that a four-year-old could have made those shanks. They were toothbrush handles with razor blades glued to the end. There were for slashing, but they wouldn't have done much damage to anything."

"All the more reason to conclude that Schaeffer made them," I said, but I could see that Graham was already bored with the entire saga. "If Dave had made them they would have been professional killing weapons," I said. Graham stood to signal to me that the conversation was over.

"Either way, I have to separate all of you. You're lucky. You get to stay here."

"Whatever," I said as I turned and walked out the door.

Two months later, Schaeffer was sent to a low-security prison in Fort Dix, New Jersey, where he could start his whole scam all over again: tell everybody he's a crooked attorney, then when they find out he's a child molester, claim anti-Semitism, then hire black guys to protect himself. Two weeks after Schaeffer left, Dave was sent to a low-security prison in Elkton, Ohio. Art got his wish of being closer to his sister and was put on Con Air for eventual incarceration at a low-security prison in central California. I remained at Loretto. I never saw Dave or Art again.

Did Dave make the shanks? Did he plant them? Did Art? Was this all meant to push Schaeffer over the edge? Or was this the culmination of Schaeffer's plot against me? My lips are sealed. I will say this, though: Schaeffer had no idea with whom he was dealing. If he had known about the "rules," he would have walked away from me at the very beginning.

Nobody saw Lieutenant Gramble for weeks. Some prisoners even took to calling him Sergeant Gramble. Rumors were rampant that he had been suspended because he had been caught punching a timecard for another lieutenant who was only pretending to work, that the other lieutenant was punching Gramble's timecard, that Gramble had sexually harassed a staff member in the medical unit, or that he had sexually harassed a prisoner's wife in the visitation room. I kept my mouth shut, and I think the warden probably appreciated it. Gramble eventually came back to work, with his lieutenant's bars, but first as a "recreation lieutenant," a new position with no interaction with prisoners, and then on the midnight shift, with supervisory authority over the janitors. The prison was a better place for it. At least temporarily.

The Stress of a
Hostile System

I BELIEVE FIRMLY THAT medical care is the most important challenge any prisoner faces in the American penal system. Indeed, poor medical care has led to riots in higher-security prisons, and in the short time that I was in Loretto, four prisoners died of preventable illnesses and incidents. I had only been at Loretto for a week when I had my first exposure to Health Services, which the medical unit has the nerve to call itself.

First some background: prison officials are compelled by law to provide prisoners with adequate medical care. In order to prove that these officials treated them with "deliberate indifference"—that is, that they provided substandard medical care in defiance of the law—prisoners must prove that the medical provider knew of the seriousness of their illness but failed to take "reasonable steps to abate the risk."[2]

Health officers' knowledge can be proven with both circumstantial and direct evidence. This can include the fact that the prisoner had gone to sick call to report the problem, whether the medical condition significantly affected daily activities, or whether there was "chronic and substantial pain."[3]

The courts have found that a "serious medical need" is present whenever the failure to treat a prisoner's condition "could result in

---

2   Farmer v. Brennan 511 US 837, 847 (1994).

3   Brock v. Wright, 315 F.3d 158, 162 (2d Cir. 2003)

further significant injury or the unnecessary and wanton infliction of pain if not treated."[4] The courts have held further that significant injury, pain, or loss of function can constitute "serious medical needs" even if they are not life-threatening.[5] Pain can constitute a "serious medical need" even if the failure to treat it does not make the condition worse.

The bottom line is this: if a prisoner is ill or injured, prison medical officials must provide adequate and appropriate treatment. I've heard prison officials complain that there are malingerers among the prison population, especially those prisoners who simply don't want to work that day. But we're talking here about prisoners who are obviously sick or injured and who are willing to pay the two-dollar medical co-pay designed to keep the malingerers out of the medical unit's sick call line.

June 21, 2013
"Letter from Loretto"

Hello again from the Federal Correctional Institution at Loretto, Pennsylvania. First, I wanted to thank everybody for the interest in my first letter. We had more than one million hits! Second, thank you for the more than two hundred letters I've received since the last letter was published. I'm answering each of them, but sending them out is a slow process because I have to use mailing labels and we're only allowed to print five per day. Third, thank you very much for your very generous contributions to my family. I've told several of you that I could only make it through this nightmare because of friends and supporters like you, and I mean it.

Health care is a major topic of debate in the national press, especially now that the Affordable Care Act (Obamacare) is law. Health care is

---

4   Gayton v. McCoy, 593 F.3d 610, 620 (7th Cir 2010); Atkinson v. Taylor, 316 F.3d 257, 266 (3rd Cir. 2003); Clement v. Gomez, 298 F.3d 898, 904 (9th Cir. 2002); Harrison v. Barkley, 219 F.3d 132, 136 (2nd Cir. 2000).

5   See "Know Your Rights: Medical, Dental, and Mental Health Care: ACLU National Prison Project," July 2012, page 3.

also a major topic of conversation and debate here at Loretto, although we prisoners don't have much authority to change the status quo.

Loretto is considered to be a Level 2 medical facility; that is, it is supposed to be equipped with a medical unit that can handle prisoners with chronic problems like diabetes, emphysema, and other issues. In fact, the medical unit is well equipped and has its own x-ray facilities, a dental clinic, and a lab. There is an osteopath in charge and several physicians' assistants (PA) from the US Public Health Service on staff.

But that's not to say that all is well in Loretto's medical unit. Just before I arrived here, prisoner Cameron Douglas, the son of actor Michael Douglas, had a mishap while playing handball. He injured his leg and went to the medical unit, where he was told he had a sprained knee and was given ibuprofen. After suffering with intense pain for two weeks, complaining all the while, he finally could not get out of bed, and the warden ordered that he be taken to a local hospital. An x-ray showed that Douglas had a broken femur, a condition that, if left untreated, could lead to death. The hospital also found a large blood clot in the leg, as well as a broken finger. Douglas underwent surgery to repair the broken bones and to relieve the dangerous clot. The Douglas family has filed a lawsuit against the Bureau of Prisons which is still pending.

I've had my own personal experience with the medical unit. Two weeks after my arrival, I dislocated my left pinkie finger while exercising. I popped it back into place, but having broken bones in the past, I knew the finger was also broken, so I went over to Medical. "Sick call" appointments are only accepted between 6:00 a.m. and 6:15 a.m., but I went directly to the evening pill line attendant and told him that I had an emergency. He wrapped the finger and told me to see the PA in the morning. I returned to Medical in the morning with my entire left hand swollen, my finger doubled in size, and I told my PA that I was certain it was broken. No, the PA said, it's just jammed. He put it in a splint, despite my request for an x-ray. He told me to come back in a week and he gave me some ibuprofen.

Even with the ibuprofen, the swelling and pain did not improve. Again I asked for an x-ray. Finally, ten days after the injury, the PA agreed to it. The x-ray found that a tendon had snapped off at the center knuckle, pulling a chunk of bone off with it. Broken. Just like I had said. The PA rewrapped it in another splint and said he would make arrangements to send me to an orthopedic specialist nearby. In the meantime, he said, keep it wrapped.

Eight days later and eighteen days after the injury, I heard that dreaded announcement: "Kiriakou—report to the lieutenant's office." I walked to the office and was told that I was going for an outside medical consultation. First I was escorted to the medical unit, where I was strip-searched and given brown pants, a brown T-shirt, a pair of underwear, a pair of socks, and a pair of slippers. The CO took my clothes and watch and put them in a plastic bag that he locked in the unit. I was then handcuffed and shackled around my ankles. A chain was placed around my waist, which connected to my handcuffs and my leg irons. Then a black steel box about the size of a computer hard drive was locked over the handcuffs so the lock could not be picked. (Remember, I'm a dangerous criminal.) If I had been in a camp, where I was supposed to be, an inmate driver would have simply dropped me off at the doctor's office and then picked me up afterward. But a nameless, faceless bureaucrat in the Bureau of Prisons decided that I am a "threat to public safety."

Now completely shackled, the CO handed me a form and told me to sign it. It was a list of "rules" for the trip to the doctor, including that I promise not to escape and that if I do try to escape, I understand that I'll be shot. One rule in particular caught my eye. It said that for the duration of the trip I was to call everybody "sir." I said I wouldn't sign. I wouldn't try to escape, but respect is earned. I am old enough to be the CO's father, yet he calls me "Kiriakou." I said I would call him CO, but not "sir." Well, he said, he simply wouldn't take me to the doctor. Fine, I said. We stared at each other for a moment, then the CO said, "OK. Forget it." So I took shackled baby steps to a waiting van with two COs in it, and they drove me to a nearby doctor's office.

At the office, the doctor looked at my x-rays and examined my finger. "It's broken," he said. "It's already started to heal. There's no point in rebreaking it and setting it because the resulting arthritis will make it even more painful." He said to try to bend it, squeeze a small ball and come back in two weeks.

Two weeks later, after complaining that I had not been able to see my PA since my visit to the doctor, the PA called me into his office. He said to just do what the doctor had told me to do, but the prison would not pay for the follow-up ordered by the specialist. It was an unnecessary expense, the PA said.

I have essentially lost the use of my finger. It is swollen, painful, misshapen, and discolored. My father-in-law, who happens to be a prominent physician, examined my finger last month during a visit. His verdict? "You're screwed. They should have treated this the day it happened. You'll never recover full use of the finger and now arthritis will set in." Thanks a lot. I'm lucky it wasn't my leg that was broken, like Cameron Douglas.

Until next time,
John

The Big Challenge, Part II

I HAD PROMISED MY attorney, Jesselyn Radack, that I would write an open letter to my supporters once I settled in at Loretto, and I sat down to do that six weeks after my arrival. That first letter would set the tone for the rest of my stay in prison. It was the guards and the administration that would be reactive. Not me. It was they who would have to make sure that they understood their own regulations. I wasn't going to back down in the face of official bullying. My sentence was short. I could take whatever they threw at me.

I mentioned earlier how two SIS COs tried to trick me into fighting an Iraqi Kurdish prisoner. This was unethical and patently illegal. The COs, Graham and Yardley, probably weren't bad guys, personally. They were just stupid. They didn't know how to deal with people, which is a serious disadvantage when the success of your job rests on your ability to recruit spies. Graham was the more senior and the more hapless of the two. For all his sources that he claimed to have all around the prison, he apparently didn't know that his CO wife was getting boned by a Puerto Rican prisoner until she was caught and fired. Also, the inflatable rat that he kept on his desk didn't do much to show his respect for any misguided prisoner who may have wanted to volunteer information. (Most people, I think, would say, "I risk my personal safety to come in here to give you information, and you just consider me a rat? Fuck you!")

On another occasion, I was visiting a friend in his housing unit when the red ceiling light went on, mandating that all prisoners return to their cubes, and that the gate be locked. This was highly unusual, and it caused me to be locked in a unit where I technically didn't belong. A lieutenant arrived and ordered all prisoners who did not live in the unit to go to the front. All of us, about two dozen in total, had their ID cards confiscated, were strip-searched, and sent back to our own units. (The reason for the strip search was that there had apparently been a fight, and the COs were looking for injuries.) The next day, I was called into SIS. Yardley was there. "So, do you want to tell me about that fight last night?"

"There was a fight? Where?" I responded.

"Very funny," Yardley said.

I retorted, "What, you want me to do your job for you now, too?"

Yardley gave me my ID back. "Get the fuck out of my office!"

The only other encounter I had with either Graham or Yardley, other than a nod in the hallway, was in the visitation room. All inmates are strip-searched after each visit, and on one particular Sunday Graham was doing the searches. I entered the search room and said, "So you have butthole duty today. Your parents must be so proud!"

Graham sighed and said, "You exhaust me. I give up. Truce?"

"Sure. Truce."

But a truce wasn't going to be possible with another foul-mouthed CO I had mentioned in my first Letter from Loretto. This was "Sarge," the CO who had called me "Fuckface" and who had trashed my room.

"Sarge" was by far the meanest, angriest, and unhappiest CO I encountered. A woman who embodied the phrase "rode hard and put away wet," she once may have been attractive. But nineteen years as a CO, an inability to get along with her colleagues, a filthy mouth, lots of poorly done tattoos, and an epic mean streak made her an even uglier person than her physical features let on.

I frankly had no idea that COs weren't allowed to speak to us like she had, so I never reported it to anyone. But what happened next was so much more satisfying.

I didn't realize it at the time, but I had accused Sarge of a regulatory violation that could have (and probably should have) resulted in a two-week suspension without pay. As a result of the letter, I was called to the SIS office and asked to swear out a complaint against her. I did, and several days later the warden transferred her out of my unit and reassigned her to a position driving a car around the outside of the compound while the yard was open for exercise. She remained in this exile for six months and she never forgave me. I didn't care.

A year later she returned as the afternoon shift CO in my housing unit. She called me into the CO office, a sort of glass bubble, and spat, "Don't you dare fucking speak to me. Turn your head when you see me." I responded similarly. "Stay the fuck away from me," I told her. "Mess with me and you'll regret it for a very long time."

I worked hard to keep my temper on an even keel, but this woman was a potentially serious problem. After all, I was under her complete control. She could trump up any charge at all and send me to solitary. She could accuse me of a crime. She could do anything she wanted. But in the end, she left me alone. She would not even speak my name for the rest of my time at Loretto. Even at mail call, when I received mail she just tossed it aside and I picked it up after everybody else had received their mail. That arrangement was fine with me.

The reaction in the press to this letter was astounding. I wrote another Letter from Loretto, this one about the COs in the Special Investigative Service. But I eventually destroyed it because I feared retaliation. And then I had a bit of good luck.

My cousin Kip Reese was a regular visitor and is a dear friend of mine. He came to visit shortly after my first Letter from Loretto was published. As he was waiting to be processed for the visit one Sunday morning, he heard this exchange between two COs.

FIRST CO: "Who is that guy here to see?"

SECOND CO: "Kiriakou."

FIRST CO: "The CIA guy? Why isn't he in solitary?"

SECOND CO: "I asked the warden that. He said they couldn't lock him up because he hadn't used anybody's name [in the Letter from Loretto.] Otherwise, they would have put him in the SHU."

Kip told me about this conversation as soon as I saw him in the visiting room thirty minutes later. This was a very valuable piece of intelligence. I could essentially write whatever I wanted—this was my constitutional right, after all—so long as I didn't mention any prison employees by name.

Rather than self-censor, which I had done by destroying my would-be second letter, I would write freely. It was in that visit that I decided to make Letters from Loretto a series, and to focus on the problems that I saw in our prison system firsthand. It would help me to remain relevant in the press and in the national debate over prison reform, it would give me something to do to pass the time, and it would eventually result in a book. This one.

Another prize of a CO was Horseface, a middle-aged blonde version of the Wicked Witch of the West. Her long face and pointed chin made her look like the daughter of Dudley Dooright, but I preferred the "Horseface" moniker. ("A horse walks into a bar. The bartender says, 'Why the long face?'") Horseface's job was to sit on a stool in the cafeteria to make sure no prisoner got an extra portion and that the kitchen employees didn't steal the food—well, didn't steal too much of the food.

One Sunday morning, I rolled out of bed just as the call for "chow" was made. I went to the cafeteria disheveled and still half asleep. After picking up my tray I passed Horseface, who said, "Excuse me! Are you grown?"

I looked at her with confusion and said, "Pardon?"

"Are you grown?"

Still confused, I said, "I'm not understanding you."

"Are you a grown man?" she said, her voice rising.

I had had enough, "Look, why don't you just say what you want to say?"

"Tuck your damn shirt in!" she shouted. I tucked my shirt in and moved on.

At lunch, Horseface was again in the cafeteria, sitting with a young male CO who always gave everybody a fair shake. As I passed the two, I whinnied like a horse and kept walking. Horseface turned to the young CO and said, "Why the fuck do people keep doing that? That's the fourth time today that's happened! What is that supposed to mean?" The young CO looked at me, winked, and smiled. Sometimes there really is satisfaction in passive-aggression.

Sarge and Horseface hated each other. (Sarge and almost everybody hated each other.) The two of them once got into a fistfight in the parking lot over a man, something that I learned was not such an unusual occurrence at Loretto. One female lieutenant, the rumor went, had children by three different COs and was collecting child support for all three while living in the luxury of her doublewide trailer. The CO wife of another CO got herself transferred to the satellite work camp so she could have sex with her CO boyfriend while her husband worked his shift in the main prison. It was Peyton Place, just at a lower socioeconomic level.

It wasn't just the COs' prurient antics that amused me. Their flat-out stupidity was fun to watch, too. The prison chapel is a place where just about everybody could practice their faith: Catholics, Protestants, Jews, Muslims, Wiccans, Rastafarians, Santerians, Mormons, and a bunch of smaller groups I had never heard of until I got there. All faith groups held their "feasts" in the chapel on the appointed days. These celebrations were a way to reflect, spend time with friends, and forget for an hour or two that they were in prison.

For Muslims, the most important feast of the year is the Eid al-Adha, which marks the end of the Hajj, the Muslim pilgrimage to Mecca. The chaplain had made all the arrangements for the 2013 Eid—tables, chairs, and food—and took the rest of the day off. At sunset, sixty-one Muslims descended on the chapel for their feast. The CO in charge of the chapel that night, however, Big Dummy, said that he hadn't "heard nothin' about no Mooslims," and he refused to open the chapel. Chapel inmate employees told him that the chaplain had made all the arrangements and that his was the holiest day in Islam. "Fuck the Mooslims!" he responded. That night sixty-one Muslims filed sixty-one formal complaints against Big Dummy. The next day the chaplain was back at work, the feast was back on, and Big Dummy was at the door telling each inmate, "As-salāmu 'alaykum. I'm sorry."

Lieutenant Gramble was by far the biggest jackass in the entire prison, and I knew immediately that I was going to have ongoing problems with him. When I first arrived I was told to avoid him. Tall, thin, with a shaved head and a perpetual grimace, his jutting chin made him look more like Dudley Dooright than anybody else I'd ever seen, including Horseface. Gramble was a bully, a provocateur, and a foul-mouthed sadist. He was nothing but trouble, and it was best to stay away from him.

I heard lots of rumors about Gramble. I don't know which were true and which were the products of prisoners' imaginations, but they all sounded plausible to me, especially as I saw more and more of him in action. For example, he had worked in, and been forced out of, several other prisons. He had sexually harassed a wide variety of women in and out of the prison. I personally heard him berate an inmate for standing in the hall between moves as a "stupid motherfucking cocksucker." Although this behaviour is against BOP regulations, there wasn't much that anybody could do. The cops all covered for each other anyway.

On Thanksgiving night 2013 I called my wife to see how the day had gone. During the course of the conversation, I recounted to her an experience I had had in the commissary a day earlier, where one of the COs had berated me for asking for more Cup-a-Soups than I was apparently entitled to. I told my wife that these COs are all tough guys when a prisoner can't respond to them and when they're sitting behind two inches of glass. I wondered aloud how tough they might be if I ran into one of them on the street. And during the course of the call, I said one of them was a "nimrod."

Well, as it turned out, Gramble would spend his free time in his tiny office listening to recordings of my phone calls. I knew this, of course, because on my first day in prison I was forced to sign a form acknowledging that I would be monitored electronically. So I frequently used my calls to plant messages among the staff: "if CO X doesn't get off my back I'm going to write an article about him and humiliate him in print," or "an idiot in my room, whom I hate, stole one hundred dollars worth of chicken and has it in a cooler under his bed. I hope I don't get in trouble for it." The idiot COs thought they were gathering "intelligence," when, in fact, they were hearing only what I wanted them to hear.

So on Thanksgiving night, my wife and I hung up at 7:30 p.m. and I went back to my room. Count was at 9:30 p.m., and nobody *ever* missed count for any reason. You can imagine my surprise when at 9:20 p.m. a prison-wide announcement came over the PA system, an angry-voiced Gramble shouting, "Kiriakou! Lieutenant's office! Immediately!" Everybody looked at me wide-eyed. I stuck out my hand. "Guys, it's been great knowing you. Help yourselves to whatever you want from my locker. Dave, call Heather and tell her I'm in solitary." As I left the unit, one of the few good COs said, "Good luck, buddy."

I walked downstairs to the lieutenant's office and knocked on the door. Gramble looked up and I walked in. "Did you want to see me?"

"I did. Can we talk man to man?" This was prison code for "I'm going to scream and swear at you and I don't want you to report me for it." Of course, it also meant that I could scream and swear at him and there was nothing he could do about it. I knew from this first question that I had him.

He began with "are you an educated man?" I responded quickly with "I don't answer rhetorical questions and I'm not going to play games with you. Why don't you just say what you want to say."

He exploded. "Do you think I'm a fucking nimrod?! Do you?! Who the fuck do you think you are?!"

I shot back, "I don't know if you're a nimrod. You might be. I haven't formed an opinion yet. But I am surprised that a private conversation with my wife that had nothing to do with you so offended your delicate sensibilities." Things just got worse from there.

Gramble told me to "stand at attention when a lieutenant is talking to you!" I told him to go fuck himself. In my book he was a nothing, a nobody, a medium-sized fish in a very small pond. He countered, "You think you're so tough. I'm the one who grew up tough! I got my GED in a youth correctional facility in Philadelphia!"

I said, "Congratulations. Your parents must be so proud."

He was enraged. He continued. "You think you're the only one who served your country around here? I did a tour in Afghanistan!" I thanked him for his service, which just pissed him off even more.

Getting back to his odd point, he said that he had better never hear me criticize another CO in a call to my wife again. I said he needed to bone up on the BOP's regulations and on the Constitution. When I walked through those prison doors, I didn't give up my right to freedom of speech. I could tell my wife anything I wanted, so long as it' was not a threat, not in furtherance of a crime, and not for the purpose of running a business. "I read the regs," I said. "You should, too."

Gramble exploded again, saying that I needed to learn my place and start "acting like an inmate." "What's that supposed to mean?" I asked. "Should I get a tattoo on my face? Should I steal food from the cafeteria? If you mean I should wring my hands and say 'yes, sir,' 'no, sir,' that's never going to happen. Never. You're not going to institutionalize me. And in the meantime, if I have to follow the rules, you have to follow the rules."

At that, I heard the announcement for count time, and Gramble's phone rang. It was the unit CO asking if he should count me, or if I would be counted in solitary. "Count him!" Gramble snapped, and hung up the phone. Our conversation was over, and I had won, at least this time. "Just go back to your fucking unit," he said. I turned and walked out.

The unit CO unlocked the gate, smiled, and said, "I can't believe you survived Gramble. Nobody survives Gramble."

"He underestimated me," I said. "And he's not as tough as he thinks he is. He also has a serious self-esteem problem."

My problems with Gramble were not over, but they were manageable. I had humbled him, and he decided to pretty much leave me alone. Pretty much. A month or so later, the chaplain mentioned to me that I was "wildly unpopular" in the prison. Shocked, I said "among prisoners?" No, he said. Among staff. "Ah," I laughed. "You've spoken to Lieutenant Gramble. You had me worried there for a minute, Chaplain." He said that Gramble had come down to the chapel to ask if I arrived on time for all my shifts. He was looking for a reason, any reason, to send me to solitary. The chaplain said I was an exemplary employee.

Five months later I decided to apply for a no-show job as a hallway orderly. I filled out the form, bribed the head orderly with three books of stamps, and waited for approval. Finally, the head orderly, a seventy-five-year-old bank robber (and a poor one, at that) came up to me to say that I had been rejected for the job. "Why?" I asked. "Well, Lieutenant Gramble is in charge of the hallways. I think he really hates you." He handed me my three books of stamps and my application, which Gramble had crumpled into a ball. I decided to go public and have some fun.

On March 31, 2014, I wrote a Letter from Loretto. It was ostensibly about life in the chapel. I wrote about how nice the chaplains were, how good the job was, and how I enjoyed the quiet there, but that I hated the fact that the chapel was a hangout for pedophiles. I segued into Gramble's denial of my job request, I made a copy of the crumpled-up application, and I recounted the Thanksgiving conversation. I knew that SIS had a Google Alert on me, and that they would read the letter as soon as it was published. They did. They launched an "investigation," and I didn't see Gramble for the next six weeks. It was six weeks of glorious peace. Gramble wasn't done with me, nor I with him. But he never again so much as made eye contact with me. And that's exactly how I liked it.

Just a few weeks before my release, I was called into the unit manager's office. He asked me to raise my right hand. "Do you swear that the information you are about to give is true and complete to the best of your knowledge and belief?" I did. We sat down, and he said, "Tell me about Gramble, slowly, while I type it. It'll be your affidavit for the formal complaint." He had made my day. Sweet revenge.

Although Gramble, Sarge, and the others were no Einsteins, some COs had even fewer brains. Drunk with power and with the idea that they could abuse people who had no recourse, they picked on prisoners for kicks. One of the things they liked to do was, during scheduled moves, open only one of the double doors into the main hallway. So instead of an easy flow of 1,400 prisoners from one part of the prison to the other, there were constant traffic jams. The prison wasn't big physically; there was only one hallway. So everybody was jammed up at the doors at the same time. Why do this? Because the COs want there to be a fight. They can break it up, look like tough guys, send somebody to solitary, and maybe even get a performance bonus. I wanted to take a swing at them every time I saw them standing at the locked door laughing as people struggled to get through.

One particular bully enjoyed the locked door game even more than the others. One day Dave and I were trying to get to the cafeteria for lunch, but we were delayed at the locked door, manned by CO Harrah. Dave politely said, "Do you mind unlocking the other door so we're not all jammed up here?"

Harrah's response was "Get over here, fella." I thought, *Oh, crap. We're going to miss lunch now.* But I decided to wait with Dave in case he needed a witness. After every person finally made it through the door, Harrah got in Dave's face. "Who the fuck do you think you are, challenging me?"

Dave, much nicer than I would have been, said, "I'm not challenging you at all. I'm just saying that it would be easier for everybody if both doors were unlocked."

Harrah replied, "You're being insolent." That was another CO code word. Insolence can mean anything they want it to, and it's grounds to be sent to solitary. But Dave remained calm, and I was standing there as a witness, so Harrah said, "Get the fuck out of here." We walked to the cafeteria, but not after Harrah had placed himself prominently on my shit list.

Harrah didn't have anything personal against Dave. He was an equal-opportunity douchebag. He was the midnight-shift CO in our unit one night. All other COs kept the gate unlocked, so when breakfast was called at 6:00 a.m., we just walked down there. For whatever power-trip reason, Harrah had the gate locked. One of the Mexican guys knocked on his door and asked Harrah to unlock the gate so that as soon as the call was made people could get to the cafeteria ahead of several other units that were farther away than ours. Harrah, in typical fashion, said, "I don't take my fucking orders from you." A minute later, the call to chow came. Harrah sat there with his feet on his desk, laughing, while every other unit went to breakfast. Finally, five minutes later he unlocked the gate. I heard several Mexicans talk briefly about stabbing him, but nothing ever came of it. I concluded that he was just a twenty-something punk who had never accomplished anything in his life, and he was trying to prove to himself how important and how badass he was.

Of course, my own run-in with Harrah was inevitable. I'm a hothead and, try as I might, I knew I would eventually lose my temper with him. It finally happened in June 2014, just after Dave was sent to the SHU. I was paged over the loudspeaker to go to the visiting room for a meeting with my attorneys. When you have a visit, you go to a door that leads to the small strip-search room and you activate a flashing light to alert the visiting room CO that you've arrived. I activated the light at 10:00 a.m. (The wait time was usually a few seconds to a few minutes.) After forty-five infuriating minutes, Harrah came out. I said, "What's the delay? I've been out here for forty-five minutes." He looked at me with indignation. "I don't fucking answer to you!" He said he would let me in when he was damn good and ready to let me in. Meanwhile, my attorneys had been waiting for me for an hour.

I thought, *Well, here we go. This was a long time coming.* I said to Harrah, "What's your problem, kid?" I used the word "kid" on purpose, of course. I knew it would enrage him, and I knew I was pushing the envelope.

"Insolence!" he shouted. "That's all I have to say is 'insolence' and you go to the SHU!"

I laughed. "You think I'm afraid of your SHU? You think solitary is worse than Yemen? Worse than Pakistan? Worse than Afghanistan? Don't make me laugh. Besides, you send me to solitary and it'll be on CNN by tomorrow. Do you really want to go down that road?"

Harrah was on his heels, stunned. He tried to recover. "This is *my* house, motherfucker. In *my* house you do what I say."

I shot back, "This may be your house, but this is *my* neighborhood." This statement was patently ridiculous. It just came out. I still don't even know what I meant by it, but, I thought, *In for a penny, in for a pound*, so I continued. "Do you really want to fuck with me? Really? Do you know what I can do to you? I'm not some piece of trash doing twenty years. I'm out in seven months. And I know where you live." I had no idea where he lived.

We stared at each other for a moment, and he said, "Go to your visit." I never had another problem with him.

It's not that all COs picked on me. They didn't. As I've said, most ignored me and some were actually nice. Many were just frustrating, the kind of people you would observe and just shake your head. These were people like Sarge and Horseface who got into a fistfight over a man who had come to prison to do some contract work. (Sarge won. She was much rougher and scrappier than Horseface.) They were people like the CO who had a prisoner read out the names at mail call, either because he simply couldn't read or because he was so severely dyslexic that it was too emotionally painful for him to try to do it in front of a hundred people. They were people like the CO who, during count time had to count on his fingers, still lost count, then had to do the whole thing over again—three times. They were people like the two COs who played chicken on the perimeter road around the prison yard. One raced his new Ford F-150 pickup head-on into the other, who was driving a prison-owned Jeep. They crashed into each other, destroying both vehicles. In any other government agency they would have been fired—maybe even prosecuted. But not in the BOP.

July 10, 2013
"Letter from Loretto"

Hello again from the Federal Correctional Institution at Loretto, Pennsylvania. I'm now nearing five months' incarceration against a thirty-month sentence for blowing the whistle on the CIA's illegal torture program. With good time, I have around sixteen months to go.

When you first come to prison, you almost immediately develop a new sense of "normal." What is normal on the outside—a rude clerk at 7-Eleven, a telemarketer calling your home at dinnertime—is no longer my world. My new normal is that the guy I may sit across from in the cafeteria is here for murdering a policeman. Normal is that the guy in the next bunk is the former methamphetamine king of Kentucky, and will likely die here. Normal is that nearly 30 percent of the now 1,325 prisoners at Loretto are pedophiles and child rapists.

I mentioned in a previous letter that I work now in the chapel. This is a highly sought-after and peaceful job. I like the chapel and the staff is terrific. The chapel, like the library, is seen as something of a safe haven for pedophiles. They aren't hassled there and they can sit and read for long periods. There is one informal rule in the chapel, however. No talking about your case.

One evening a particularly loud pedophile was complaining outside the chapel office that he was in the process of suing his mother, brother, and wife, who had completely disowned him after he was caught having sex with his fifteen-year-old daughter. ("But she wanted to," he protested. "She enjoyed it.") I walked over to him and reminded him that he was not allowed to talk about his case in the chapel. His response left me speechless: "But Jesus loved the little children." I just went back to my seat.

One elderly pedophile in my housing unit was caught on the old NBC television show To Catch a Predator. He thought he was going to have sex with a thirteen-year-old. Instead, the cops grabbed him. In the trunk of his car they found handcuffs, a hammer, a bag of lime, and a body bag. You can imagine his intentions.

I won't bore you with stories of how photos of my cellmate's five-year-old grandchild were stolen from his locker or how some pedophiles subscribe to teen magazines so they can cut out pictures of Selena Gomez and hang them in their lockers.

The purpose of these horrible accounts is not to disgust. Instead, it's to point out several problems, only one of which is unique to Loretto. First, if pedophiles are not permitted within one thousand feet of a school, why are they permitted within five feet of my children? Why isn't there a section of the visiting room where pedophiles can have their visits but that is separated by a partition? It couldn't possibly be expensive and it would serve to protect our children. (Of course, if I had been sent to a camp, as was recommended by both the judge and the prosecutor in my case, it would be a different story. Pedophiles are not permitted in camps. Remember, though, that a Bureau of Prisons bureaucrat deemed me a "threat to public safety.")

Second, despite what you may have read over the years, there is no such thing as "treatment" or "rehabilitation" in prison. It just doesn't exist. There's no counseling or medication for pedophiles. Once their sentences have been served, they're free to leave and to live in society again. Sure, they'll have years and years of probation, but that won't do anything to curb their urges. It's a proven fact that many of them will re-offend.

Finally, since I got here, I've come to realize how little the federal government does to protect our children from predators. Perhaps, it's time to consider the issue of civil confinement. That is where the government moves a pedophile to a secure location on the prison grounds after he has completed his sentence. He is not necessarily subject to "counts" or "ten-minute moves" like everybody else in prison, but he is not free to reenter society and to re-offend. This system works in Virginia and in other states, and it helps greatly to protect our children.

Thank you for the hundreds of letters of support and encouragement since my last letter. They've really kept my spirits up.

All the best,
John

July 24, 2013

"Letter from Loretto"

Hello again from the Federal Correctional Institution at Loretto, Pennsylvania.

I've learned over the past months that one's prison sentence is not the totality of his punishment. I took a plea in January 2013 to one count of violating the Intelligence Identities Protection Act. In addition to having to spend thirty months in prison, I will have to meet a probation officer monthly for three years after my release. I also lost my pension after nineteen years of proud federal service. My legal bills totaled nearly $1 million, and I sold most of my personal possessions to pay at least some of that million dollars.

But my punishment didn't end there. Last week my wife received a sharply worded letter from our insurance company, USAA—the United States Assurance Association. I have had my insurance with USAA—both auto and homeowner's—since 1993. They were a terrific provider during that time. The letter we received cut right to the point: USAA doesn't insure felons, and they were canceling our insurance effective immediately. I told my wife not to panic; call them in the morning and put the insurance in her name. She did that, only to be told that USAA doesn't insure "felonious families." Thank goodness she was able to find another, more reputable company with which to do business.

When I mentioned this travesty to my friend Dave, about whom I've written, he told me to soon expect the other shoe to drop. When he was arrested—even before he was convicted—his bank, Wells Fargo, closed his accounts and sent him a check along with a letter saying that they do not allow felons to bank with them. He had to find a small local bank that was willing to allow him the luxury of a checking account.

Similarly, immediately after my arrest, both Cardinal Bank and United Bank refused to allow my "John Kiriakou Legal Defense Trust" to open an account. A vice president at United Bank said, "We simply don't want to do business with you."

In addition, I learned recently that I could no longer travel freely to countries like Canada, the UK, and France. These and many other countries share law enforcement databases with the US, and they do not allow felons in their countries without a special visa. So when I want or need to travel abroad in the future, I will have to go to these countries' embassies, file a visa request form, and submit to an interview about my "crime."

Update: Many of you have asked for an update on the event that I reported in my first letter. In that letter, I wrote about two Special Investigative Service officers who tried to bait me into taking some sort of action against a Muslim prisoner. After the letter was published, I was assured by both the warden and by a CO lieutenant that an investigation would be conducted. It turned out that the investigation was of me. My email was put on a four-day delay, both incoming and outgoing, my incoming and outgoing snail mail was stripped open and read, and none of my witnesses were interviewed. I wasn't surprised by any of this. This is exactly what happens to all whistleblowers.

Thanks for reading,
John

The Guardian:
Obama's Abuse of the Espionage Act is Modern-Day McCarthyism

by John Kiriakou

SHAME ON THIS PRESIDENT for persecuting whistleblowers. The conviction of Bradley [now Chelsea] Manning under the 1917 Espionage Act, and the US Justice Department's decision to file espionage charges against NSA whistleblower Edward Snowden under the same act, are yet further examples of the Obama administration's policy of using an iron fist against human rights and civil liberties activists.

President Obama has been unprecedented in his use of the Espionage Act to prosecute those whose whistleblowing he wants to curtail. The purpose of an Espionage Act prosecution, however, is not to punish a person for spying for the enemy, selling secrets for personal gain, or trying to undermine our way of life. It is to ruin the whistleblower personally, professionally, and financially. It is meant to send a message to anybody else considering speaking truth to power: challenge us and we will destroy you.

Only ten people in American history have been charged with espionage for leaking classified information, seven of them under Barack Obama. The effect of the charge on a person's life— being viewed as a traitor, being shunned by family and friends, incurring massive legal bills—is all a part of the plan to force the whistleblower into personal ruin, to weaken him to the point where he will plead guilty to just about anything to make the case go away. I know. The three espionage charges against me made me one of "the Obama Seven".

In early 2012, I was arrested and charged with three counts of espionage and one count of violating the Intelligence Identities

Protection Act (IIPA). (I was only the second person in US history to be charged with violating the IIPA, a law that was written to be used against rogues like Philip Agee.)

Two of my espionage charges were the result of a conversation I had with a *New York Times* reporter about torture. I gave him no classified information—only the business card of a former CIA colleague who had never been undercover. The other espionage charge was for giving the same unclassified business card to a reporter for ABC News. All three espionage charges were eventually dropped.

So, why charge me in the first place?

It was my punishment for blowing the whistle on the CIA's torture program and for confirming to the press, despite government protestations to the contrary, that the US government was, indeed, in the business of torture.

At the CIA, employees are trained to believe that nearly every moral issue is a shade of grey. But this is simply not true. Some issues are black and white—and torture is one of them. Many of us believed that the torture policy was solely a Bush-era perversion. But many of these perversions, or at least efforts to cover them up or justify them, have continued under President Obama.

Obama and his attorney general, Eric Holder, declared a war on whistleblowers virtually as soon as they assumed office. Some of the investigations began during the Bush administration, as was the case with NSA whistleblower Thomas Drake, but Espionage Act cases have been prosecuted only under Obama. The president has chosen to ignore the legal definition of whistleblower—any person who brings to light evidence of waste, fraud, abuse, or illegality—and has prosecuted truthtellers.

This policy decision smacks of modern-day McCarthyism. Washington has always needed an "ism" to fight against, an idea against which it could rally its citizens like lemmings. First, it was anarchism, then socialism, then communism. Now, it's terrorism. Any whistleblower who goes public in the name of protecting human rights or civil liberties is accused of helping the terrorists.

That the whistleblower has the support of groups like Amnesty International, Human Rights Watch, or the American Civil Liberties Union matters not a whit. The administration simply presses forward with wild accusations against the whistleblower: "He's aiding the enemy!" "He put our soldiers' lives in danger!" "He has blood on his hands!" Then, when it comes time for trial, the espionage charges invariably are either dropped or thrown out.

The administration and its national security sycophants in both parties in Congress argue that governmental actions exposed by the whistleblower are legal. The Justice Department approved the torture, after all, and the US Supreme Court said that the NSA's eavesdropping program was constitutional. But this is the same Justice Department that harassed, surveilled, wiretapped, and threatened Martin Luther King Jr., and that recently allowed weapons to be sold to Mexican drug gangs in the "Fast and Furious" scandal. Just because they're in power doesn't mean they're right.

Yet another problem with the Espionage Act is that it has never been applied uniformly. Immediately after its passage in 1917, American socialist leader Eugene V. Debs was arrested and imprisoned under the Espionage Act—simply for criticizing the US decision to enter the First World War. He ran for president from his prison cell.

Nearly a century later, when the deputy director for national intelligence revealed the amount of the highly-classified intelligence budget in an ill-conceived speech, she was not even sent a letter of reprimand—despite the fact the Russians, Chinese, and others had sought the figure for decades. When former defense secretary and CIA director Leon Panetta boastfully revealed the identity of the Seal Team member who killed Osama bin Laden in a speech to an audience that included uncleared individuals, the Pentagon and the CIA simply called the disclosure "inadvertent".

There was no espionage charge for Panetta. But there was a $3 million book deal.

The Obama administration's espionage prosecutions are political actions for political reasons, and are carried out by political appointees. The only way to end this or any administration's abuse of the Espionage Act is to rewrite the law. It is so antiquated that it doesn't even mention classified information; the classification system hadn't yet been invented. The law was written a century ago to prosecute German saboteurs. Its only update came in 1950, at the height of the Julius and Ethel Rosenberg case. The law is still so broad and vague that many legal scholars argue that it is unconstitutional.

The only hope of ending this travesty of justice is to scrap the Espionage Act and to enact new legislation that would protect whistleblowers while allowing the government to prosecute traitors and spies. This would require congressional leadership, however, and that is something that is very difficult to come by. Giants like the late Senators Daniel Patrick Moynihan and Frank Church, and the late Representative Otis Pike, who boldly took on and reformed the intelligence community in the 1970s, are long-gone. Until someone on Capitol Hill begins to understand the concept of justice for national security whistleblowers, very little is likely to change.

The press also has a role to play, one that, so far, it has largely ignored. That role is to report on and investigate the whistleblower's revelations of illegality, not on the kind of car they drive, the brand of eyeglasses they wear, where they went to college, or what their next-door neighbor has to say about their childhood.

The attacks on our civil liberties that the whistleblower reports are far too important to move off-message into trivialities. After all, the government is spying on all of us. That should be the story.

The Threats Begin

B Y THE MIDDLE OF 2013, Letters from Loretto were driving the prison administrators crazy. They wanted to silence me—after all, they had said so—but they couldn't do it legally. So they tried a little trick.

As a former CIA officer, anytime I write anything having to do with the CIA, intelligence, or foreign or defense policy, I have to send it to the CIA's Publications Review Board for approval before I can send it to anybody else. I do that. But Letters from Loretto had nothing to do with the CIA, so I didn't send PRB a copy. I did, however, send one of my attorneys a copy, and I used the prison's "Legal Mail" system to do so. When a letter is stamped "Legal Mail," prison authorities are forbidden from opening it.

But that wasn't the issue. I was sending Letters from Loretto directly to firedoglake.com publisher Jane Hamsher through the prison's "Special Mail" system. Special Mail is the same as Legal Mail, in that it cannot be opened; it is meant to send private correspondence to members of the media, to Congress, or to other elected officials.

In addition, some of my friends and visitors just happened to be journalists. They visited me as friends, not in their official capacities, and they never wrote articles about our visits. They just came to say hello and to see how I was doing.

On July 18, 2013, my unit manager called me into his office. The unit manager is responsible for the housing unit in which I lived, Central 1, as well as Central 2, South 3, Southeast, and the Dormitory.

He had jurisdiction over about six hundred prisoners. The unit manager handed me a memo and told me that I had to sign it. It said:

"This memo is for clarification on legal mail and visiting procedures. As you are aware, Program Statement 5265.14, Correspondence, outlines the criteria for legal and special mail procedures. Correspondence intended for publishing does not meet legal mail requirements as described. Any use of legal mail procedures to circumvent mail monitoring will result in disciplinary action. Furthermore, any member of the media who wishes to interview you must make their request and follow the guidelines of Program Statement 1480.05, News Media Contacts. Social visits from news media are to be of a social nature, not used to circumvent the requirements of news media policy. Refusal to abide by this will result in disciplinary action."

I was stunned by the utter stupidity of this memo, which I was forced to sign. I had followed BOP regulations to the letter. It was the unit manager who did not know his own regulations. I knew I would have to sign the memo, so I decided to add some commentary. I pointed out that what I had sent was "Special Mail, not Legal Mail." I added that "You have no idea what it was meant for," and that "there is no reason to threaten me." I looked the unit manager in the eye and said, "You really ought to learn what your own regulations say. You embarrass yourself when you write things like this." But that wasn't the end of it.

A month later, on August 30, 2013, I was called to the lieutenant's office to meet with the Special Investigative Service lieutenant. She had her own threat to make. She handed me a memo and said that if I didn't sign it, I would be taken to solitary confinement immediately. The memo said:

"As you are aware, you have an obligation to the Central Intelligence Agency (CIA) to submit any draft writing you would like published to the CIA's Publication [sic] Review Board (PRB), prior to public dissemination. Should you need to submit an item to the

PRB while housed at FCI Loretto, the following procedures should be utilized:

"Place your written document in an addressed envelope and seal it. It should not be stamped.

"Hand deliver your sealed envelope to one of the following three staff members:

(Redacted) SIS Lieutenant

(Redacted) SIS Technician

(Redacted) SIS Technician

"Failure to follow these procedures will result in disciplinary action."

There were several problems with this ridiculous, amateurish, and bullying demand. First, unless my writing was about the CIA, intelligence, or foreign or defense policy, as I noted above, it was not subject to PRB review.

Second, let's say that I had actually written something classified. The act of then handing the article or document to SIS would have opened me up to an espionage charge. That's right. The Espionage Act says that any person is guilty of that terrible crime if he "knowingly provides national defense information to any person not entitled to receive it." The penalty is between five and twenty years imprisonment. No thanks.

Third, the memo's demand was unconstitutional and unenforceable. I chose to ignore it. There were no consequences.

BOP Breaks a Promise

FOLLOWING MY JULY 24 letter, I dropped out of public sight at the request of a relatively friendly prison administrator. He told me that his leadership was apoplectic about the popularity and wide distribution of my earlier Letters from Loretto, and he asked me to stop writing them. His exact words were, "What's it going to take to get you to stop writing these letters?" My response was, "What's it going to take for you to send me home to my family?"

I was heartened by his response. "What do you want?" I told him that I wanted nine months of halfway house. The law says that every prisoner is entitled to up to twelve months of halfway house time. I wasn't even asking for the maximum. Just give me nine months—in writing—and I'd stop writing these letters. "Done," he said. But he also wanted me to drop two complaints against staff that I had lodged and he wanted me to turn down any future press requests.

I told him that he was asking for a lot. And I added that, "Against my better judgment, I'm going to trust you. Put me in for nine months' halfway house and I'll stop writing." He did, and I stopped.

Of course, he was lying. This is another theme in prison. Everybody is lying—the warden, the unit manager, the counselor, the case manager, everybody. And what are you going to do about it? Nothing. You have no recourse. You can't call them liars to their faces because you'll be sent to solitary for "insolence." At least I had Letters from Loretto through which to vent.

What happened was that this administrator never had any intention of putting me in for nine months. The warden recommended "151–180 days." I ran into him in the cafeteria and I said, "The deal is off." He protested that he had done his best, but that nobody ever gets nine months. "That's nonsense," I said. I knew a CIA officer who had been caught up in a bribery scandal. His sentence was only twenty-two months and he got nine months of halfway house. The wife of Rep. John Conyers (D-MI) got twelve months of halfway house with a thirty-month sentence. I knew for a fact that nine months was possible. He just shrugged his shoulders.

I went back to my cell to write my next Letter from Loretto, which I intended to be a thank-you note to those who had helped me and a direct challenge to the warden.

January 20, 2014

Hello, everybody. I'm sorry I've been out of touch so long. After my last letter, I thought I had come to an understanding with the prison administration: stop writing "Letters from Loretto" and be put in for nine months of halfway house. Nine months would have seen me leave here on August 1, 2014. So I stopped writing. I withdrew two formal complaints against staff, and I turned down all press interviews. In the end, I was put in for six months of halfway house, not nine. And I was warned that the six months could be reduced to three or to nothing. Rather than twiddle my thumbs and hope for the best, I decided to start writing again. God bless the Constitution and its First Amendment.

This letter is not a blow-by-blow of my negotiations for halfway house time. That's a future letter. Instead, it's a note of thanks to the people who worked so hard to help me get that time. They put their reputations on the line for me, and I will be forever indebted.

First, thank you to Bruce and Elizabeth Riedel and to Rep. Jim Moran (D-VA). Bruce and Elizabeth worked closely with Congressman Moran on a letter to Bureau of Prisons Director Charles Samuels asking for "at least nine months' halfway house," and saying, "I believe Mr. Kiriakou is a patriotic American. I ask that you grant him at least nine months' halfway house time so that he may resume his rightful place as a productive member of society and as a father to his five children, three of whom are under the age of nine." Congressman Moran pointed out that, "It is my understanding that twelve months of halfway house time is well within BOP guidelines."

Thank you to Dr. Iris Diamond and to Billy Halgat, who contacted Rep. Lloyd Doggett (D-TX) on my behalf. Congressman Doggett wrote a letter to Director Samuels also asking for nine months' halfway house. He also made a personal inquiry to the prison asking about my well-being.

Thank you to Jeremy Karaken and to former governor Gary Johnson (R-NM). Governor Johnson, the 2012 Libertarian Party nominee for president, wrote to Director Samuels noting that I am a "model prisoner" and saying that I belong with my family, not in prison.

Thank you to Bishop Emeritus John McCarthy of the Catholic Diocese of Austin, Texas. Bishop McCarthy wrote directly to President Obama, saying that he was "disgusted" with my imprisonment and adding that, "John Kiriakou is an anti-torture whistleblower who bravely spoke out against torture. He never tortured anyone, yet he is the only individual to be prosecuted in relation to the torture program of the Bush administration. The interrogators who tortured prisoners, the officials who gave the orders, the attorneys who authored the torture memos, and the CIA officers who destroyed the interrogation tapes have not been held professionally accountable, much less charged with a crime. Please, Mr. President, how can you allow this terrible injustice to go on under your watch?"

Thank you to Lynn and Steve Newsom, the directors of the peace group Quaker House, who wrote to Director Samuels asking for nine months' halfway house and quoting Article 2 of the United Nations Convention Against Torture: "no exceptional circumstances whatsoever, whether a start of war or a threat of war, internal political instability, or any other public emergency, may be invoked as a justification for torture." They added that, "Mr. Kiriakou never tortured anyone, yet he is the only person to be prosecuted in relation to the torture program."

Thank you to Dr. Stephen Bowers, Dr. Chuck Murphy, and Jenna Collins, my colleagues at Liberty University, who have worked tirelessly to lobby Republican members of Congress on my behalf. Thank you to Alex Patico, Alex Georgiades, and Jim Gregorakis, who have worked the Greek Orthodox community for me. Thank you to John and Amy DeSanti, who spoke to their old friend Rep. Charlie Dent (R-PA) for me. Thank you to Jim Tjepkema and Susan Schibler, who reached out to their elected officials on my behalf. Thank you to Rob Shetterly for lobbying Maine's members of Congress. Thank you to the Santa Fe, New Mexico chapter of Amnesty International for appealing directly to Attorney General Holder for my release.

Thank you to Jesselyn Radack and the Government Accountability Project, who worked with Ralph Nader on a letter to Director Samuels asking for nine months' halfway house. Thank you to Jane Hamsher and the gang at firedoglake.com, who have had my back from the beginning of this nightmare. Thank you to my attorneys Mark MacDougall and Karen Williams at Akin Gump, whom I trust more than I trust myself. Thank you to the Peace and Justice Center of Sonoma County, California, for their confidence and support in giving me one of their Peacemaker of the Year awards, and for a personal hero, Daniel Ellsberg, for accepting it on my behalf. Thank you to my friend and former colleague, "Dave," whose steady advice has kept me sane for the past nine-plus months. And most of all, thank you to my wife and best friend Heather for, well, everything.

I thought that when I was denied the nine months that the easiest thing to do was to roll over and accept it. Maybe I would be released on November 1, 2014. Maybe February 1, 2015. But as more time passed, I realized that the situation is political in nature. And I realized further that if I just gave up, I'd never forgive myself.

So I am asking you to help me. The final decision on my halfway house will be made by the end of January by Erlinda Hernandez at the Bureau of Prisons. She can be reached at:

Erlinda Hernandez
Bureau of Prisons

Residential Reentry Office
P.O. Box 7000
Butner, NC 27509

Will you write to her to help me make my case for nine months? If
you are able please copy:

Mr. Charles Samuels
Director of Bureau of Prisons
320 First St. NW
Washington, DC 20534

Thank you for all your help, support, and the more than two
thousand letters I've received since I got to Loretto. I couldn't make it
through this experience without your kindness. More letters to follow.

Best regards,
John Kiriakou

I didn't expect what happened next. Erlinda Hernandez and BOP
Director Charles Samuels were inundated with letters and phone
calls—more than six hundred between the two of them—supporting
my request for nine months of halfway house. All it did was make
them angry.

So instead of nine months, instead of 151–180 days, I got nothing.
No halfway house at all. The warden pulled me aside one day after
lunch. "You know why they fucked you," he said. "It's because you
write those damn letters."

"It seems to me, Warden," I responded, "that they either retaliated
against me for my expression of freedom of speech, which is a crime,
or they showed you that they have absolutely no respect for you or for
your recommendations." We left it at that.

Nothing is "Corrected"

SOMETIMES IN PRISON YOU wake up in the morning and feel like you're beginning to go crazy. What am I doing in here? Why is everybody nuts? Why can't I have a normal conversation with people? I was fortunate, as I wrote previously, to make a few good friends in prison. But people are constantly being transferred to other prisons, sent to solitary, or released. So you can't even count on being able to maintain a long-term friendship. I did my best, and Letters from Loretto allowed me to vent.

February 2, 2014
"Letter from Loretto"

Hi again from the Federal Correctional Institution at Loretto, Pennsylvania. The term "Federal Correctional Institution" implies that the government is in some way "correcting" the behavior of prisoners here. In truth, that's just a bad joke. Nothing is "corrected" at Loretto. There is no therapy to help anybody with problems (except if you're a drug addict nearing the end of your sentence. More on that in a minute.) Pedophiles get no psychological therapy whatsoever. And the only classes offered by staff are GED prep courses and English as a Second Language (ESL) classes for the four hundred or so illegal aliens serving drug sentences. (After completion of their sentences, then deportation, knowing English will make it easier for them to reenter the US to restart their criminal enterprises.) If you already have a high school diploma, tough luck.

Here's how things work. We all get good conduct time, a maximum of forty-seven days off our sentences for every year of incarceration. (Congress mandated fifty-two days a year, but the Bureau of Prisons told Congress to go screw itself.) The only incentive to behave properly is a negative one: so you don't lose your good time. You get no tangible benefit from taking any classes taught by prisoners: Creative Writing, Introduction to Spanish, and History of Western Film, to name a few. The only way to actually collect your good time is to either get your GED, or be working on it, and to not get into trouble.

Everybody with a drug case wants to get into the drug program. If you're accepted, and you had no violence or firearms in your case, you're sent to the nearest prison that hosts the program, and you must complete five hundred hours of classroom work. If you complete the coursework, you can get up to one year off your sentence. The pre-course drug class is supposed to be forty hours. It's actually about ten hours and is comprised only of watching episodes of the A&E show Intervention. *If you're a drug addict and you come to prison, you have to get off drugs cold turkey, then wait until you near the end of your sentence to finally get into the drug program. That means you could wait five, ten, even as long as thirty years before you get any drug counseling at all.*

Loretto's "Education" Department scheduled a prisoner-led class last fall called Quantum Physics. Nobody bothered to check whether the prisoner-teacher was qualified to teach a course on quantum physics, nor did anyone request a lesson plan. As it turned out, the gay prisoner-teacher's only degree was from the Ringling Brothers Barnum & Bailey Clown College. The course had nothing to do with quantum physics. It was a self-help pity party for pedophiles, and it sought to help them expand their rationale of denial, with the theme from Rocky *playing in the background all the while. The teacher began the course by chanting, "We're homos and we're chomos! We're homos and we're chomos!" ("Chomo" is short for "child molester.") One African-American prisoner, who expected to learn something about quantum physics, got up, shouted, "This is fucked up!" and walked out. Otherwise, it was a very popular class among a certain demographic. I'm not kidding.*

Even more worrisome is the situation with pedophiles in general. Despite a recent Congressional Research Service report to the contrary, there is no treatment whatsoever for pedophiles and child molesters. Nothing. Indeed, these perverts find a welcoming community of like-minded offenders in prison, like we saw in the quantum physics class. They also trade pictures of children that they cut out of the Toys "R" Us catalogue or Parenting *magazine, photos of young-looking eighteen-year-olds in G-strings that they buy from mail-order houses that cater to sex offenders in prison, and even pictures of other inmates' children— stolen, of course.*

Pedophiles move in packs in prison. They sit together in the cafeteria, they take prisoner-led classes together, they watch movies together, and they congregate in large groups in the library and the chapel, all protesting their innocence and complaining that they're misunderstood.

My friend, cellmate, and former colleague, "Dave," and I took a prisoner-led Introductory Spanish course a few months ago. We quit after three sessions because the class was nothing more than a coffee klatch for pedophiles. After one asked, "How do you say in Spanish 'do you want some candy?'" we walked out and never went back.

The Bureau of Prisons doesn't do anything to dissuade pedophiles. Indeed, in an event right out of The Twilight Zone, *the warden sent a memo to all inmates, "Please join FCI Loretto and the Bureau of Prisons as we celebrate the United Nations' Universal Children's Day." The memo, announcing, "Happy Children's Day!" said, "Our Children's Day celebration will be held on the weekend of November 30 to December 1, 2013. Materials will be available for each family with visiting children ages three to ten."*

So we have a facility where pedophiles and pederasts are warehoused, where they get no therapy or medication for their perversion, where they spend all their time together exchanging tricks of the trade, and where the warden gives them advance warning of a children's event so they can schedule their own visits and be in the presence of young children from 8:30 a.m. to 2:15 p.m. over two days. You may recall from my third Letter from Loretto that a prison guard had to move my entire family during a visit because that pederast (Schaeffer) from Philadelphia was leering at my nine-year-old son. I'll say it again: if pedophiles must stay more than one thousand feet from a school on the outside, why are they allowed within five feet of my children in the visitor's room?

Even though I haven't been able to take (or at least complete) any classes since I got to prison, I have learned a lot. Among the things one can learn are how to cook methamphetamine; how to smuggle drugs across international borders without getting caught; how to steal food from the cafeteria and then cook an entire meal using only a live electrical wire and a garbage can full of water; how to make contraband cigarettes using chewing tobacco spat out by prison guards, dried, and rolled with toilet paper; how to self-medicate using home remedies and over-the-counter concoctions in lieu of real medical care; how to set up a Ponzi scheme; and how to defraud mortgage companies and the Department of Housing and Urban Development (another prisoner-led class).

So at the end of the day, I guess I have been educated in prison. Maybe I have been corrected. I'm confident now that I'm ready to re-enter civilized society.

Seriously, though, this lack of counseling, rehabilitation, and educational and training opportunities for prisoners is a long-term problem for society. The country is already home to an increasingly large population of uneducated, untrained, unreformed, pissed-off ex-felons who are not going to just sit around hoping to win the lottery. Lacking prospects for employment, they'll do what they do best—commit crimes. For the pedophiles, they will leave prison emboldened by the fact that they spent their entire sentence among like-minded sickos without once being challenged about their perversions. The BOP needs to get on the ball.

Yours,
John

February 10, 2014
"Letter from Loretto"

Hello again from the Federal Correctional Institution at Loretto, Pennsylvania. On February 7, I gave my first press interview since the prison administration reneged on our halfway house deal: they would put me in for nine months' halfway house and I would stop writing "Letters from Loretto," decline all media interviews, and withdraw two formal complaints against staff.

As you know from my previous letters, that agreement is no longer in effect, so on the seventh I spoke at length with Dean Sirigos and Demetrios Tsakas of The National Herald, the oldest, largest, and most highly-respected Greek-American newspaper in the country. We spent more than two hours together, and we discussed issues ranging from halfway house time to terrorism, drones, and Afghanistan. (The journalists had gone through the formal approval process weeks in advance, were approved, and arrived during normal business hours as instructed.)

Three hours after the interview ended, I was sitting in the TV room with my friend, former colleague, and cellmate, "Dave," when another prisoner approached us and said, "Guys, the cops are tearing up your room." We walked back to our room and, sure enough, two corrections officers were going through all of our possessions. I thought it was an odd coincidence, but I just shrugged. I didn't have any contraband so I lost nothing.

The very next night, Dave and I went for a walk around the outdoor basketball court. When we walked back into the housing unit, another prisoner approached us and said, "Hey, the cops are tearing you guys up again." We couldn't get to our cubicle because the gate at the head of the hall was locked. A half-hour later, the COs opened it and allowed us back in. This shakedown was different than the previous day's. (And I should note that in the previous year I had been shaken down a total of three times until the interview.) My locker door was left wide open (my cellmates' lockers were closed and locked.) Photos of my children were thrown on the floor. My mail was strewn all over the bed. And my books were tossed on a nearby chair.

I approached a CO and complained. Retaliation is one thing, I said, but this was just plain disrespectful. "Sorry" was the response. "We were just following orders." My cellmates were also disrespected. This shakedown was very thorough, and they had all lost property. One of my cellmates, a forty-ish African-American whom I like, respect, and consider a friend, made an important point. "Don't you see what they're doing? They're trying to make us mad with these shakedowns so that we'll turn on you." He imagined a conversation: "Let's piss off the big black guy so he pressures Kiriakou to stop writing and doing interviews." My cellmate urged me to "keep up the fight. Keep telling people what it's like in here." I promise to do that.

The issue here is not the bother and inconvenience of shakedowns. The COs are within their rights to shake us down whenever they want. The issue is retaliation and censorship, which are illegal. A senior prison official told me months ago that there have been active discussions about putting me in "diesel therapy" for the rest of my sentence. Diesel therapy is when a prisoner is transferred from one prison to another all across the country via prison van, bus, or "Con Air" plane, never staying in any one prison long enough to receive telephone, email, mailing, or visitation privileges. I could move to a different prison every week for the rest of my sentence and still not hit them all.

In the meantime, my family and attorneys wouldn't even know what time zone I was in. This would obviously be retaliation for "Letters from Loretto" and my press interviews, but the BOP could easily make up a lie that it was related to a "bed space" issue or for my own safety. Still, it would stink of retaliation for the exercise of my constitutional right to freedom of speech. I'm fortunate that my attorneys, among Washington's best, are willing to sue individual BOP employees, as well as the BOP as an organization, to ensure that such an assault on my rights doesn't take place. BOP officials should keep in mind what the Supreme Court said about diesel therapy in Frazier v. Dubois:

1210. Transfers:

Although prisoners enjoy no constitutional right to remain in a particular institution, prison officials do not have discretion to punish an inmate for exercising his First Amendment rights by transferring him to a different institution. Frazier v Dubois (1990, CA10 Kan) 922 F.2d 560.

Similarly, I have a constitutional right against retaliation, as the Supreme Court set forth in Bloch v. Ribar and in Skoog v. County of Clackamas:

460. Retaliation:

Plaintiffs had First Amendment right to criticize a public official's performance of his duties, and in action alleging retaliation by official against plaintiffs due to their exercise of their First Amendment rights, it was sufficient for them to allege injury in form of embarrassment, humiliation, and emotional distress. Bloch v Ribar (1998, CA6 Ohio) 156 F.3d 673, 1998 FED App 294P.

Right exists to be free of police action for which retaliation is but-for cause even if probable cause exists for that action. Skoog v County of Clackamas (2006, CA9 Or) 469 F.3d 1221 (criticized in Baldauf v Davidson (2007, SD Ind) 2007 US Dist LEXIS 53924).

These cases are freely available in the prison law library. Perhaps prison officials should acquaint themselves with them. Maybe they could also look at Largent v. Texas, which prohibits censorship:

306. Censorship:

Any regulation which makes dissemination of ideas depend upon approval of distributor by official constitutes administrative censorship in extreme form, and, subject to certain exceptions, any regulation which subjects communications to license infringes right of free speech. Largent v Texas (1943) 318 US 418, 87 L Ed 873, 63 S Ct 667.

Where do we go from here? First, understand that any monolithic bureaucracy will tend toward corruption without proper oversight. There is an internal "administrative remedy" process that's a joke. You write a complaint and they tell you to go screw yourself. Calling for an inspector general investigation is also a joke. An inspector general could make an entire career investigating where the money from the inmate trust fund goes. (Where did that new flat-screen TV in the CO medical lounge, especially during federal budget sequestration, come from?) The only alternative is to go to the top: BOP Director Charles Samuels.

Director Samuels worked his way up after starting as a line CO, moving up through the ranks to warden and then on to Washington to lead the BOP. Certainly, he knows the difference between right and wrong. Certainly, he wouldn't want his employees to violate the law (as I've documented in these letters). Certainly, he wouldn't want his people's actions highlighted in a press investigation.

Join me in writing Director Samuels and in demanding an end to these illegal and unconstitutional actions by his staff. We have to put our foot down and say, "Enough!"

I'll let you know how things develop.

Best regards,
John

PS: I wanted to thank Rep. Jim Moran (D-VA), who sent a second letter to Director Samuels last week saying:

"As you will recall, I sent a letter last September requesting that the Department of Justice grant my constituent, John Kiriakou, at least nine months of halfway house time. Despite the fact that twelve months of halfway house is well within BOP guidelines, I am disappointed to learn that John's return to society may be unnecessarily delayed. Thus, I am writing to reiterate the importance of John's release to a halfway house as soon as possible so that he can be a father to his five children and resume productive contributions to society."

Rep. Moran is a twelve-term congressman and a member of the House Appropriations Committee, which controls the BOP budget.

Addendum:

About twelve hours after I wrote this Letter from Loretto, I was called to the Special Investigative Service office. The CO there handed me an envelope containing the first twenty thousand words of this book. I hadn't even realized it was missing since the shakedown. The SIS CO said that the CO who had shaken me down had determined that the manuscript had "made threats against staff." He said he, too, had read it and believed that it did *not* contain any threats to staff. (The allegation was patently absurd, in any event.) He returned it to me in its entirety, although he most likely made a copy.

In one last swipe at my civil rights and my constitutional right to freedom of speech, the shakedown CO tried to remove my desk from the wall and confiscate it. After all, if I have no desk, I can't write "Letters from Loretto," right? After a while, he gave up. The bolts were stripped and wouldn't budge. (I had stripped them on purpose as a preemptive measure.) It was a temporary respite, though. The CO issued a work order to chip it off the wall. I had to go to the unit manager, who promised that the desk would not be removed.

These crude, amateurish attempts to deprive me of my rights don't originate with a low-level CO. They come from higher up, from officials who should know better. But I have the Constitution in my corner and I won't stop fighting.

After my letter was published, I taped a page from a legal pad on the desk, and I wrote on it, "This Desk Kills Fascism." This was a play on "This Machine Kills Fascism," which folksinger Woody Guthrie had famously written on his guitar in the 1930s. The sign hung on the desk only for a couple of hours before a CO tore it down, crumpled it into a ball, and threw it on the floor. I picked it up and mailed it home to myself. I keep it as a reminder that I was not alone as I went through this experience. I had thousands of friends whom I didn't even know. And they got me through it.

Los Angeles Times:
I Got 30 Months in Prison.
Why Does Leon Panetta Get a Pass?

By John Kiriakou

THE CONFIRMATION IN DECEMBER that former CIA director Leon Panetta let classified information slip to *Zero Dark Thirty* screenwriter Mark Boal during a speech at the agency's headquarters should result in a criminal espionage charge if there is any truth to Obama administration claims that it isn't enforcing the Espionage Act only against political opponents.

I'm one of the people the Obama administration charged with criminal espionage, one of those whose lives were torn apart by being accused, essentially, of betraying his country. The president and the attorney general have used the Espionage Act against more people than all other administrations combined, but not against real traitors and spies. The law has been applied selectively, often against whistleblowers and others who expose illegal, corrupt government actions.

After I blew the whistle on the CIA's waterboarding torture program in 2007, I was the subject of a years-long FBI investigation. In 2012, the Justice Department charged me with "disclosing classified information to journalists, including the name of a covert CIA officer and information revealing the role of another CIA employee in classified activities." I had revealed no more than others who were never charged, about activities—that the CIA had a program to kill or capture al-Qaeda members—that were hardly secret.

Eventually the espionage charges were dropped and I pleaded guilty to a lesser charge: confirming the name of a former CIA colleague, a name that was never made public. I am serving a thirty-month sentence.

The Espionage Act, the source of the most serious charges against me, was written and passed during World War I and was meant to target German saboteurs living in America. It was updated once, in 1950, when Americans got to thinking the country was awash in communist spies. The law is so outdated that it refers only to "national defense information" rather than "classified information," because the classification system had not yet been invented.

The act states: "Whoever, lawfully having possession of, access to, control over, or being entrusted with any...information relating to the national defense which information the possessor has reason to believe could be used to the injury of the United States or to the advantage of any foreign nation, willfully communicates...the same to any person not entitled to receive it...shall be fined under this title or imprisoned not more than ten years, or both."

A transcript obtained by the organization Judicial Watch shows that, at a CIA awards ceremony attended by Boal, Panetta did exactly that. The CIA seems to acknowledge that Panetta accidentally revealed the name of the special forces ground commander who led the operation to kill Osama bin Laden, not knowing that the Hollywood screenwriter was part of an audience cleared to hear him speak. But intent is not relevant to Espionage Act enforcement.

US District Court Judge Leonie Brinkema ruled in my case that evidence of the accidental release of national defense information was inadmissible, and she added that the government did not have to prove that a leak of classified information actually caused any harm to the United States. In other words, the act of disclosing the kind of broad information covered by the Espionage Act is prosecutable regardless of outcome or motive.

The sensitivity of what Panetta revealed is not in question. The spokesman for the former CIA director said Panetta assumed that everyone present at the time of the speech had proper clearance for such a discussion. When the transcript of the speech was released, more than ninety lines had been redacted, implying that Panetta had disclosed a great deal more classified information than the name of an operative.

Even the CIA's Office of Security concluded that "the agency's security policy and administrative procedures were not followed in allowing Mr. Boal, a member of the media, access to the classified bin Ladin [*sic*] Operation Award Ceremony."

If an intent to undermine US national security or if identifiable harm to US interests are indeed not relevant to Espionage Act enforcement, then the White House and the Justice Department should be in full froth. Panetta should be having his private life dug in to, sifted, and seized as evidence, as happened to me and six others under the Obama administration.

When the transcript of Panetta's speech and his inadvertent leak came to light in January, a CIA spokesman told the Associated Press that the agency had subsequently "overhauled its procedures for interaction with the entertainment industry." Such internal reviews are fine and good, but equality before the law is the rule in America. Your job title, your Rolodex, and your political friendships are not supposed to trump accountability. Except when they do.

General James "Hoss" Cartwright, once known as the president's "favorite general," was reportedly targeted as the source of information about the Stuxnet virus leaked to a *New York Times* writer. That investigation has dropped from sight, and Cartwright has so far faced no charges.

Yet when senior National Security Agency official Thomas Drake blew the whistle on waste, fraud, and abuse at the NSA—in the form of a bungled project that cost more than $1 billion—he wound up buried under espionage charges, all of which were eventually dropped, but only after his life was in shreds.

When former state department intelligence advisor Stephen Jin-Woo Kim talked to a Fox News reporter about North Korea, he was charged with espionage, and his prosecutors were absolved by the presiding judge from having to prove "that the information he allegedly leaked could damage US national security or benefit a foreign power, even potentially."

If Panetta and Cartwright aren't accountable while Drake, Kim, and I have been crucified for harming US national security—all of us accused of or investigated for the same thing: disclosing classified information to parties not authorized to know it—then what does that say about justice in America or White House hypocrisy?

The Espionage Act should be rewritten to deal with the issues of intent, such as accidental disclosures and real harm done. Until then, it is right and just to charge Panetta at least with espionage. Accidental though his revelation may have been, it's still a crime.

Prison Chapel

I CAN'T SAY THAT I liked anything at all about prison. But the chapel is probably the thing that I hated the least. It was usually quiet, people were generally friendlier to each other in the chapel, and the two chaplains were decent guys. I was able to use my time in the chapel to answer letters, watch movies, and help other prisoners organize their religious services.

March 31, 2014
"Letter from Loretto"

Hello again from the Federal Correctional Institution at Loretto, Pennsylvania. Many of you have written to ask me if I'm still working in the chapel. The answer is yes, and it occurred to me that I've not really said much about the chapel. So in the interest of broadening your understanding of this horrible place, here's some background.

FCI Loretto used to be a Catholic monastery in a town that is also home to St. Francis and Mt. Aloysius Colleges. The Bureau of Prisons bought the monastery and turned it into a low-security prison. A minimum-security camp came later. The monks' bedrooms were converted into prisoners' rooms. So instead of two monks per room, we have six or eight prisoners. Gross overcrowding is probably the one thing that the BOP is good at.

In the 1990s, the BOP added another housing unit, Central Unit, to cram another thirty-five to four hundred people into a ridiculously, and probably unconstitutionally, small space. That's where I live.

The chapel is the monastery's original chapel and is located in what is now North Unit. The BOP added two chaplains' offices and a small library by blocking off some space. They added a concrete block "worship room" across the hall, and the old choir loft became a TV room for North 2 Unit. Otherwise, it's a real chapel with stained glass windows and everything. There are crucifixes hanging and Stations of the Cross on the wall, but it's an ecumenical place. The altar and several large pieces of furniture are on wheels, so they can be moved out of the way depending on what group has the chapel reserved at any given time.

I'm an orderly in the chapel. On Tuesday mornings all nineteen chapel employees vacuum, dust, and polish the chapel, the auxiliary worship room, and the offices. Otherwise, my job is to provide prisoners with books and religious videos from the library. I work eight hours a week. I do this job because I enjoy the solace and the ability to sit at one of the prison's very few desks and write in peace.

FCI Loretto has two chaplains, both of whom are good men. In fact, they are the only two staff members to shake my hand since I arrived here. They are, of course, cops first and chaplains second, but the unfortunate fact of their BOP employment doesn't get in the way of their ministry to prisoners.

There is a myriad of faiths represented here. There are, of course, Catholics, mainstream and evangelical Protestants, Buddhists, Jews, and Muslims. We have a few Mormons and Orthodox, of which I am one. But there are a good number of faiths that I either knew little about or had never heard of. They include, in no particular order:

—Nation of Islam: originally founded by Wallace D. Fard in 1930 in the Midwest and popularized by Elijah Muhammad after Fard's disappearance in 1934. NOI followers believe that all humans were black until an evil genius named Yakub created a white race of devils. Believers maintain that upon the start of the end times, NOI followers will be taken to heaven in a spaceship currently buried in a field in Japan.

—Moorish Science Temple: founded in Newark, New Jersey, in 1913 by Timothy Drew, who took the name Noble Drew Ali, MST adherents believe all African-Americans are originally from Morocco. They use a version of the Quran written by Noble Drew Ali and completely unrelated to the Muslim Quran.

—Santería: combining elements of traditional Catholicism and voodoo, most Santería followers at Loretto are from the Caribbean.

—Messianics: also known as "Jews for Jesus," Messianics believe in combining Jewish and fundamentalist Christian teachings, refer to Jesus only as "Yeshua," and refuse to work on Saturdays, which they believe is the true Christian Sabbath. The group was founded in Northern California in 1970.

—Rastafarians: the Rastas are a messianic movement among poor Jamaicans founded in 1930 before spreading to the US and UK. Rastas believe that former Ethiopian emperor Haile Selassie is the messiah who came to liberate all black people, who are the true biblical Jews. Followers smoke marijuana as a sacrament, although not at Loretto.

—Native Americans: the various Native American tribes have a sweat lodge behind the chapel, which they use on Saturdays. One Native American friend of mine, who is a local tribal chief, told me that the "real Indians" stay away from the sweat lodge because it has been taken over by "fake Indians" who like to sit in the lodge for hours and "pretend they're Native Americans."

—Wiccans: I honestly don't know anything about the Wiccans, other than there are a lot of them and they represent a wide variety of beliefs. Some call themselves Druids, some Pagans, and others Satanists. (The Satanists can buy pentagram necklaces from a religious supply catalogue in the chapel office.) Know that your tax money is being well spent: the woodshop recently crafted an altar and magic wands for the Wiccans to use in their services.

One prisoner, a tax cheat, has taken it upon himself to create his own cult and to write his own bible by taking out the parts of the real bible that he doesn't like, then adding his own philosophy. I'm told that there's a lot of fire and brimstone. This prisoner has actually started "baptizing" people in the bathroom and now has several followers. He went so far as to write a letter to a visiting pastor saying that the pastor *would go to hell if he didn't join the cult. The chaplains do not recognize the cult as a legitimate faith group.*

We had a Seventh Day Adventist who worked in the chapel for one day. When he came in to start his shift, he looked at me and said, "What religion are you?"

"Greek Orthodox," I said.

He looked at the guy next to me. "What religion are you?"

"Mormon," he responded.

The Adventist looked at the third employee in the room. "What religion are you?"

"Catholic."

The Adventist shouted, "All of y'all's religions is false! You all going to hell!"

I said, "I don't think you're going to fit in very well here." The next day he was sent to solitary and fired for stealing milk from the cafeteria.

The chapel is supposed to be a place of contemplation, meditation, and prayer. It is sometimes that. More often it is a lounge for pedophiles, who congregate there because they can sit and relax undisturbed. (Honestly, they can sit and relax undisturbed anywhere because they have the run of the place. But they prefer the chapel and the library.) I've already beaten this dead horse so I won't get into it again.

I'm not trying to convey the notion that the chapel is all peace, love, and flowers. It's not. Many otherwise religious people refuse to go to services because there are so many pedophiles there. The chaplains' hands are tied. They can't, after all, have parallel pedophile and non-pedophile religious services. A separate dispute erupted a month ago in the Jewish group between Reformed, Conservative, and Orthodox Jews and instigated by a notorious pederast about whom I've written previously and who wanted to take over the group. The kerfuffle resulted in both a chair and a punch being thrown.

The chapel has other problems, too. In my year of incarceration there have been several sexual incidents in the chapel. Some prisoners have sex whenever they can, usually in the showers or under the stairwell near the mailroom, which have no security camera coverage. Unfortunately, the chapel also has no security cameras, and we have to occasionally tell other prisoners to stop making out or to stop fondling each other. When there are no religious services taking place, prisoners can watch movies or listen to religious CDs in the chapel. The low lights sometimes lead to make-out sessions, which we have to break up. I once had to ask a chapel employee to stop necking with his boyfriend. On another occasion, a pedophile was watching a movie that included a scene with a little boy in a bathtub. The pedophile watched the scene over and over and over again, becoming more excited with each viewing. We asked him to leave. Most recently, two guys were in the chapel with their hands up each other's shirts fondling each other's nipples. I'm told that security cameras will be installed in the next fiscal year.

I'm also told that funds have been appropriated in the past three years, but security cameras have never been installed. Of course, new TVs in the staff lounges have been installed during that same period. More soon...

Best regards,
John

PS: I'm proud to say that Oscar-nominated documentarian Jim Spione's film Silenced about the US government's war on whistleblowing will premiere at New York's Tribeca Film Festival on April 19. It documents my case in detail, as well as Tom Drake's and others. Don't miss it.

Retaliation

April 21, 2014

"Letter from Loretto"

Hello from the Federal Correctional Institution at Loretto, Pennsylvania. Yesterday, I had the pleasure of a visit from my friends Jane Hamsher and Kevin Gosztola of Firedoglake. It was two hours of terrific conversation, including, obviously, about my most recent Letter from Loretto, in which I came down hard on an officer here.

Today, my wife, my cousin Kip, and my three younger children came to visit. Visitation is scheduled from 8:30 a.m. to 2:15 p.m. They arrived at 8:30 a.m. and I was called to the visitation room at 8:45 a.m. The room was crowded, but not as crowded as it's been on other days they've visited. Indeed, the row behind us had twelve empty seats.

At 11:15 a.m., the prison facility manager, a short, portly, mustachioed middle-manager whom I have never seen before in the visitation room and who usually spends his time checking IDs in the cafeteria, made an announcement that he was worried about overcrowding and he wanted volunteers to leave to make room for other people who may or may not be waiting to come in. Nobody volunteered.

Fifteen minutes later, he called me into the strip search room. My family had to leave, he said. "You get lots of visits so I'm exercising my authority to end your visit."

I said, "You're throwing my family out."

"I'm not throwing them out," he responded. "I'm telling them to leave."

Semantics: I told him that the regulation said that a decision to ask a family to leave was based on the frequency of their visits and the distance of their travel. They visit once a month and drive 210 miles, leaving home at 5:00 a.m. He said the regulation related to the frequency of all visits and they had to go.

The facility manager said I could complain through the Administrative Remedy process, a joke of an appeal system that I'll address in a future letter. I told him I would instead write a Letter from Loretto.

I went back to my family to tell them they were being thrown out. When they got up and went to the door, a CO whom I respect came over and told me to bring them back to their seats. She said she thought the Facility Manager had misinterpreted the regulation and she would speak to him. A few minutes later, she returned and said she had been "overruled."

My cousin and the kids left. My seven-year-old daughter and two-year-old son cried all the way out the door. My wife was able to stay. Of the four seats my family vacated, two were filled with new visitors. Within an hour, another two dozen visitors left, calling it a day.

I normally don't complain about the petty daily inconveniences that are a normal part of life here. But I have to call this out for what it is: retaliation for Letters from Loretto. There was no space problem in the visitation room. There were plenty of seats. There were even more an hour later. Only a "troublemaker" from Detroit and I were told that our families had to leave. We were the only ones. Coincidence? I think not.

This is yet another example of the power of the written word. A temporary inconvenience in the visitation room won't stop Letters from Loretto. Nothing will. There's a lot more truth to tell in the coming months.

In the meantime, to learn more about my case, please visit defendjohnk.com.

Update: the day this letter was published, the "friendly" prison administrator about whom I've written called me into his office. He had the letter up on his computer screen. "Is this true?" he asked. "It sure is,"

I said. "It took everything I had to hold my temper." He looked at me sympathetically. "I'm going to give you some advice," he started. "But I'll deny that we ever had this conversation if anybody asks me. You have to file a complaint against the facility manager. What he did to your family was wrong. He shouldn't get away with it." I thanked him, but I said that I was in no way sanguine that a complaint would do anything. "The complaint system is set up to take a year for the process to work. And I'll get nothing out of it in the end. I'd rather go public, like I did. I get it. I'm under their control. I'm a prisoner here. They can throw my family out and get away with it. But I'm going to speak out, and it's that that the facility manager doesn't want."

John

The Daily Beast:
Time to Reopen the Case on CIA Torture

by John Kiriakou

June 3, 2014

He blew the whistle on CIA waterboarding, but the government keeps trying to sweep the issue, and him, out of sight. From prison, John Kiriakou says it's time for a special prosecutor.

It has been a year and a half since the United States Senate Select Committee on Intelligence finished its six-thousand-page report on torture by the Central Intelligence Agency. It's been two months since it voted to declassify portions of it. But what we've seen leaked so far is next to nothing.

I was at the CIA when the torture program was conceived. I refused to be trained in the techniques, and when I left government I confirmed that torture was official US policy. Partly as a result, I have been locked away almost as long as the Senate report. But the issues remain, not only as a matter for history, and a question of justice; they remain because we still can't be sure whether ours is a nation governed by people who condone torture or not.

It is vital that we know this at a time when so many headlines raise questions about intelligence gathering that intercepts phone calls and emails, or analyzes metadata from millions of different sources. Even if we accept that much of that work is necessary, we should have— we must have—confidence that the government will deal honestly, fairly, and with restraint to keep our country and its people safe, and without violating the Constitution.

How can we have such confidence if the government leaves the door open to torture by pretending it can close that door behind us, that we can just walk away, holding no one accountable for the actions that were taken?

The most revealing defense of what the CIA did was published in *The Washington Post* in April when the Senate voted to declassify a few pages of its vast report.

Former CIA official Jose Rodriguez, the agency's most vocal torture defender, wrote to defend his indefensible position that torture worked, torture was good, and that the Senate Select Committee on Intelligence (SSCI) report highly critical of the program is wrong. Rodriguez's strategy is not new: repeat the lie often enough that the public comes to believe it as truth.

Rodriguez, remember, was the head of the CIA's Counterterrorism Center (CTC) when the agency created the torture program. He implemented the program, oversaw it, and defended it, to say nothing of the secret prisons, which he also directed.

When the press began reporting that torture was taking place and was official US Government policy, Rodriguez, who was by then the CIA's deputy director for operations, did not work toward the "transparency" that he recently lauded in the *Post*. Instead, he took it upon himself to destroy videotaped evidence of the torture, an act many would call "obstruction of justice."

Rodriguez protested in the *Post* that the torture program was "effective" and "authorized," and that the Senate report is flawed. He even condemned the SSCI vote to declassify only the report's conclusions. His position is that he knows the truth because he was there and that the SSCI wrote the report with 20/20 hindsight.

I can tell you that he is wrong. I was there, too, at the same time.

What of the report's conclusions is so objectionable? Among other things, the SSCI found that torture did not work: agency officials, including Rodriguez, repeatedly and routinely misled the Justice Department, the White House, and Congressional leaders, and underreported the program's brutality. The report concludes that the agency deliberately misled the media by leaking classified information, which "inaccurately portrayed [the program's] effectiveness;"

that Rodriguez's management of the program was "deeply flawed throughout its duration"; and that the program "damaged the United States' global reputation and came with heavy costs, both monetary and non-monetary."

Surely, Rodriguez is not solely to blame for the government's immoral decision to torture prisoners. Others in and out of the CIA were up to their necks in the program. There are the torturers themselves, the CIA officials who conceived of and implemented the program, the attorneys at the CIA, the Justice Department, the Bush White House officials who wrote specious legal opinions justifying the torture, and the CIA officials who blocked internal and external investigations.

In the eyes of history, President Barack Obama's legacy will be tainted by his 2009 decision that the Justice Department would "look forward, not backward" on torture. This denied justice and attempted to cover up a dark chapter in American history, putting us at risk for repeating this immorality in the future. It also allowed people like Rodriguez and his former minions to go to the press and repeat their lies over and over again.

This is not to say that the Justice Department has done nothing. After I blew the whistle on the CIA's torture program in 2007, I became the subject of a selective and vindictive FBI investigation that lasted more than four years. In 2012, the Justice Department charged me with "disclosing classified information to journalists, including the name of a covert CIA officer and revealing the role of another CIA employee in classified activities." What I had revealed was that the CIA had a program to kill or capture al-Qaeda members—hardly a secret—and that the CIA was torturing many of those prisoners. I'm serving thirty months in a federal prison.

The Senate report apparently does not offer any suggestions for next steps. Clearly, the White House will not reverse itself and pursue criminal charges against anyone involved in the torture program. Rodriguez will continue to brag, as he did last year on the CBS program *60 Minutes*, that he put on his "big-boy pants" to lead the torture program. He'll continue to deny that anybody was tortured, and then out of the other side of his mouth argue that the torture worked and American lives were saved.

What the Senate can do, however, is to demand that President Obama appoint an independent prosecutor, and to hold public hearings on the torture program. Further, the SSCI can declassify the report in its entirety, subpoena witnesses, demand the truth, and vow never again to allow the abomination of torture to become US Government policy. This is the only way that the United States can reclaim the moral high ground on torture and enable the international community to trust our leadership on human rights. We must learn from our past mistakes, embrace the report's conclusions, and not allow the likes of Jose Rodriguez to set the terms of the debate.

Prison Sentencing Reform

June 23, 2014
"Letter from Loretto"

Hello again from the Federal Correctional Institution at Loretto, Pennsylvania. We're grossly overcrowded at Loretto, like just about every other prison in America. Rooms for two now house four. Rooms for four now house six or eight. And rooms formerly used for recreation now house fourteen to twenty, all on steel-slab bunk beds. A staff member told me recently that when he began working at Loretto in the 1990s, there were 645 prisoners. We now have over 1,400. Besides making disease control nearly impossible, overcrowding leads to short tempers and increases in violence—never a good thing.

(Prison Legal News magazine reported this month that federal prisons as a whole in 2011 were 40 percent overcrowded. They will be 45 percent overcrowded by 2018. Meanwhile, the Supreme Court last year ordered the State of California, the prisons of which are 41 percent overcrowded, to begin releasing prisoners. There was no such order for federal prisons.)

The United States has 5 percent of the world's population and 25 percent of the world's prison population. The US, on a per capita basis, has more prison inmates than Russia, China, and Iran. This inexcusable fact is a result of our government's ill-conceived and ill-advised "War on Drugs" and of Congress' propensity in election years to prove that it is "tough on crime." Indeed, according to the Congressional Research

Service, Congress has created fifty new CRIMES per year over the past ten years.

Harvard Law School professor Harvey Silverglate argues in his book Three Felonies a Day that the US is so overlegislated and daily life is so over-criminalized that the average American going about his normal business on the average day commits three felonies. Every day! It's no wonder that the Bureau of Prisons accounts for a quarter of the Justice Department's budget. It's no wonder that, according to the American Civil Liberties Union, there are 3,278 prisoners in the US serving sentences of life without parole for nonviolent drug and property crimes.

In prison, from the time you wake up in the morning until the time you go to sleep at night, most people want to talk to you about their cases. At first it's fascinating. After a while, it's tedious. Later it becomes a real pain. But the truth is that many of them have been wronged, whether by a racist system, by incompetent attorneys, by overzealous prosecutors, or by judges whose hands are tied because Congress has mandated long minimum sentences, especially for drug crimes.

This year, though, some members of Congress and some Justice Department officials have initiated at least the beginning of change. On March 6, the Senate Judiciary Committee passed the Recidivism Reduction and Public Safety Act (S. 1675), sponsored by Senators Sheldon Whitehouse (D-RI) and John Cornyn (R-TX). The bill will next go to the Senate floor. Majority Leader Harry Reid (D-NV) said recently that the Senate would also take up the Smarter Sentencing Act this spring. That bill has the support of dozens of advocacy and civil rights groups ranging from the Heritage Foundation to the ACLU, former prosecutors, police and prison guard organizations, victim advocates, prominent conservatives, and faith groups. The bills would allow for widely expanded good time credits, diversionary programs, and educational opportunities. For many progressives and libertarians, punitive overpunishment calls out for redress. For many conservatives, it simply costs too much to incarcerate so many people.

More importantly, on April 10, the US Sentencing Commission voted unanimously to lower the drug sentencing guidelines by two levels for all drug offenses. (Career offenders and those who used firearms or violence in their crimes get no relief.) Critically, the Commission will decide on retroactivity for the reduction by the end of November.

Here's what this means. Let's say that "Scott" is involved in a methamphetamine case along with a bunch of other people. The charge is conspiracy to manufacture and distribute one kilo of meth. Let's also say that Scott is a first-time nonviolent offender. He has no gun in his case. Because he has no criminal history, Scott falls under Criminal History Category I on the chart. Prosecutors prefer not to go to trial. Indeed 98.2 percent of all federal inmates take a plea, rather than go to a trial, according to Pro Publica. If Scott takes a plea, his federal guideline would put him at a level twenty-five to fifty-seven to seventy-one months. But Scott says he's innocent. He never made meth, sold meth, or used meth, although some of his friends did. He pleads not guilty, reasoning that a jury will see the truth. He goes to trial.

Unfortunately, when the government claims a "conspiracy," it pretty much has to prove only that the people involved knew each other, not that they personally committed the crimes charged in the conspiracy. Scott is found guilty. When he goes for sentencing, he gets a level twenty-five. But he also now faces "enhancements." Enhancements are additions to a sentence that are given for a variety of reasons. Scott gets an extra two "points," or levels, for "failure to accept responsibility." (He argued his innocence, after all.) He gets another two points for "obstruction of justice" because he wouldn't testify against his codefendants. Although he's never been prosecuted for a serious crime before, he did have a DUI in college. That's an extra four points for "criminal history," even though it doesn't raise his Criminal History category. No federal taxes were paid on the proceeds of the meth so that's another two points. At sentencing, instead of the 57 to 71 months that he might have gotten (or the 36 to 48 months he was probably offered as part of a plea deal) Scott goes from a level 25 to a level 35, which means 168-210 months. He'll do around fifteen years. This happens every day in America, where judges have no concept of time and prosecutors simply don't care.

If the Sentencing Commission's two-level reduction is made retroactive, thousands of current prisoners will get relief for the first time since Congress outlawed parole for all federal prisoners convicted of a crime before November 1, 1987. In addition, the Justice Department has begun a new clemency program that would allow drug offenders to apply for a pardon or commutation of their sentences. Prisoners would have to meet six criteria, which would serve to weed out the bad apples and keep the public safe.

Inmates:

1. *Would likely have received a substantially lower sentence if convicted of the same offense today;*
2. *Must be nonviolent, low-level offenders without any significant ties to large-scale criminal organizations, gangs, or cartels;*
3. *Must have served at least ten years of their sentence;*
4. *Must not have any significant criminal history;*
5. *Must have demonstrated good conduct in prison; and*
6. *Must have no history of violence before or during imprisonment.*

Realistically, pardons and commutations probably won't happen. As President Obama has issued only eleven pardons and forty commutations, the fewest of any president in American history, the two-level reduction is probably the only relief most prisoners will have to look forward to unless Congress passes a sentencing reform bill. [Note: Obama finished his presidency with a flurry of commutations, finally issuing more than the previous twelve presidents combined.]

These are not nameless, faceless people we're talking about. There is a human side to this. We're talking about people who made a mistake, usually in their youth, and are paying for it with their lives. Their families are also victims. Rather than being in prison, where each prisoner costs the American taxpayers $29,291.25 per year, they could be out working, paying taxes, paying child support, and contributing to society. Remember, career criminals are exempt from this plan. Only those who deserve it would get relief.

President Obama can do the right thing to correct these wrongs. He can announce his support for retroactivity of the Sentencing Commission's two-level reduction. He can grant commutations and pardons. And he can sign the bipartisan legislation for reform that Congress sends him. Fairness in sentencing—"mercy," I would call it—can be his legacy. With barely more than two years left in his presidency, he can be a part of the problem or a part of the solution.

Best regards,
John

Both the Recidivism Reduction and Public Safety Act and the Smarter Sentencing Act died in the Senate without a vote. Then-Majority Leader Harry Reid never brought them up for a vote. They have not been reintroduced in the new Congress. Indeed, the new Senate Majority Leader, Sen. Mitch McConnell (R-KY), said the bills would no longer be considered.

The Sentencing Commission's two-point reduction was implemented, however, and prisoners began to be released in November 2015.

The Big Challenge, Part III

I TOOK THE "RULES" very seriously when I was in prison, and I tried hard to live by them. They had served me well and, I believed, had kept me safe overseas. But near the end of my sentence, I nearly went off the rails because I let emotion get in the way of the rules.

After dinner one evening in August 2014, just six months before the end of my sentence, Frank walked into the room after going to the insulin line for his evening shot. "Hey, John. There was a guy in the insulin line talking trash about you tonight."

I was surprised, to say the least. "Who? What did he say?"

"I never saw him before," Frank said. "He must be new. He was telling people that you were a rat."

I could feel my blood pressure rising. I genuinely don't care what people think of me. But calling somebody a rat in prison usually results in blood being spilled. I had to defend my honor or die trying. "Point this guy out to me, Frank. I want to see who this asshole is."

The next morning, I met up with Clint for our daily walk around the track. As soon as we saw each other, he said, "There was a guy in Medical this morning telling everybody that you were a rat. You might want to take care of this before it goes any further."

I was incredulous. "Point this guy out to me, Clint. Who does this guy think he is? Those are fighting words."

I frankly wasn't sure what to do. By saying that I was a rat, in public, he was asking for a hearty ass-kicking. I knew that if I were to deliver it, I would likely spend the rest of my sentence in solitary. I didn't care. I was furious. And God knows I had lived in worse places over the previous twenty-five years than the solitary confinement unit in Loretto, Pennsylvania.

At dinner that evening, both Frank and Clint pointed out the transgressor. I had never seen him before. He was definitely new. He was about my age, thinner, six feet tall, and with a bushy beard covering a severely pockmarked face. He got a tray of food and sat with the Aryans. I was at the next table sitting with the Italians.

I fixed a stare on him. "Hey!" I shouted. "You have a problem with me?" About fifty heads turned, including several COs. The cafeteria is the only place where the COs worry about their safety. It's the only place where they're generally outnumbered fifty to one at any given time. Consequently, they are always attuned to any hint of trouble.

"You know what I said. You know where I live," he responded.

"Fuck that!" I shouted it too loudly. Again heads turned. "If you have something to say to me, say it now and we'll settle this! Right here!"

A young Aryan ran over to me. "Please don't fight here. If you do, the cops will send all of us to solitary." I didn't care. I was ready to do it. In the meantime, the bearded guy and I were in a staring contest.

As I weighed in my mind what to do next, Pete, the Bonanno family captain, gently tugged my sleeve. "What in the world are you doing?" he asked quietly. "Are you crazy doing this in the cafeteria?"

"As God is my witness, Pete, I'm going to kill this guy," I said, still staring.

"No, you're not. You're going to go to Mark's room and you're going to read the USA Today while we take care of this." I was still furious, but I knew that I wasn't thinking straight. I took Pete's advice, sat down, quickly ate dinner, and went to Mark's room.

Mark and Paulie showed up a few minutes later. They were bemused by how angry I was. I was spewing epithets. I wanted to kill the guy, or at least I wanted everybody around me to believe that I wanted to kill the guy. I was so furious that I had completely forgotten the rules. I should have been thinking about "eliminating potential problems using dirty tricks" and about "knowing my enemy." But as things stood, I just wanted to see the guy lying in a pool of his own blood.

Mark smiled at me. "I've never seen you this worked up before. Why did this guy get to you? Nobody else has." I couldn't explain myself. Maybe it was because I had worked so hard to cement relationships with such diverse groups all over the prison. Maybe it was because nobody had ever called me a rat before. Maybe I just didn't want to take any shit from this piece of white trash. Mark handed me a soda and said that he and Paulie would be back in a few minutes.

I perused the *USA Today* sports section, unable to focus. Mark and Paulie returned about fifteen minutes later. "Everything's taken care of," Mark said.

"What's that supposed to mean?" I was still incredulous.

"It means it's all taken care of. The guy's not going to be a problem." Mark and Paulie were smiling at me. Mark continued, "The guy apparently didn't realize that you were a highly-respected member of the prison community—and especially of the Italian community. We made him understand that."

"OK," I said. "I'll take your word for it." A moment later came the call for a ten-minute move. I went back to my room.

Five minutes later, I was sitting on the edge of my bed reading *The Wall Street Journal*. It was the middle of the ten-minute move. "Excuse me." The voice was to my left. I turned, looked up, and saw "the guy." It looked as though his face had recently undergone a serious rearrangement. His left cheek was swollen, blood was drying in his left nostril, and his hair was askew.

Now was not the time to feel sorry for him. "What the fuck do you want?"

He hung his head down. "I'm very sorry for what I said about you," he said, near tears. "I should never have said it. I want you to know that I'll never say it again." I looked at him for a moment. I had to appear tough.

"Get the fuck out of here before I decide to break your legs, too."
He turned and walked quickly, all the way out of the housing unit.

I went back down to Mark and Paulie's room at the next move.
"I really appreciate you guys stepping up for me," I said.

They laughed. "You're always talking about those damn rules,"
Mark said. "I figured someone should take them seriously."

Marked as Dangerous

O NE OF THE FIRST lessons I learned, on my first day in prison, was that prison officials can do virtually anything they want to you, and there is no recourse. Officially, of course, there is an Administrative Remedy Process that is supposed to allow prisoners the chance to challenge wrongs against them and to have them corrected. Well, the process is as corrupt as the Bureau of Prisons is. The BOP ignores its own rules relative to the Administrative Remedy Process, it refuses to abide by the time restrictions placed on it for responses, and I've never heard of anybody ever winning an appeal. Really, the whole purpose of the thing is to allow the BOP to throw the complaints out based on the technicality that the prisoner did not file in time, hope that the prisoner loses interest and gives up, or hope that the prisoner is transferred or released before the BOP has to make a decision. It's all just a paperwork exercise to pretend to show the courts that the BOP is doing something to address grievances. For prisoners, it's just a sick joke.

August 7, 2014
"Letter from Loretto"

Hello again from the Federal Correctional Institution at Loretto, Pennsylvania. I have begun counting down the days until my release on February 3. I have just over six months to go. You may remember that when I first arrived here on February 28, 2013, I expected to be placed in the minimum-security camp. Instead, I was taken to the prison, where I remain. I wanted to tell you about the appeal process.

First though, I wanted to say thank you from the bottom of my heart to Medea Benjamin, Jane Hamsher, and the members and supporters of Code Pink and Firedoglake. Your selflessness and generosity have literally saved our home. Heather, the children, and I are eternally grateful for your kindness. I won't forget this. And I can't wait to get home and begin to pay it forward.

Many of you know from some of my earlier letters that the Bureau of Prisons has given me what is called a Public Safety Factor (PSF) designation. What that means, for all intents and purposes, is that I am so dangerous and such a threat to the safety of the public that I will never be allowed to serve any of my sentence in a minimum-security camp. I have to be behind a double fence for my entire sentence. Some nameless, faceless, junior bureaucrat half-wit in the BOP's Grand Prairie, Texas, Designation and Sentence Computation Center (DSCC) is responsible for this designation. Others with a PSF include murderers, terrorists, arsonists, members of organized crime, and child molesters.

With six months to go before release, I don't care about the PSF anymore, except as a matter of principle. You see, on the day I was arrested, the judge released me on a signature bond, meaning that I didn't have to put any money down, just an assurance from my wife and my brother that I would show up for trial. I was thus free to go about my business—among the public—for thirteen months. When I took a plea to violating the Intelligence Identities Protection Act (IIPA) in October 2012, I remained free pending formal sentencing in January 2013. At the formal sentencing, the judge, a Clinton appointee with twenty years experience on the bench, recommended that I serve my time in a minimum-security camp. The US attorney, who represented the government in my case, also recommended camp. Neither believed I was a threat to the public. And on top of that, I was not cuffed at sentencing and I was not taken to prison. I remained free for another five weeks before driving up to the prison and turning myself in. Again, nobody in any position of authority thought I was a threat to anybody.

I arrived at Loretto on February 28, 2013, and was immediately put in the prison, rather than the camp. I called my attorneys and they wrote to the BOP to point out the "mistake." They made several points, the most important of which was that the BOP had placed the Public Safety Factor designation on me erroneously because my offense was categorized as "espionage." I had not committed, nor was I convicted of, espionage.

My attorneys also argued that the judge and the prosecutors had both recommended camp, and they went into great legal detail on how the Intelligence Identities Protection Act had nothing to do with espionage.

The Designation and Sentence Computation Center, which placed the PSF on me, ignored my attorney's letter and instead sent it to the warden for a response. This was a cynical and disingenuous attempt to pass the buck because the warden has no authority whatsoever to initiate or to remove a PSF. A month after receiving my attorney's letter, the warden responded that, "Prior to an inmate's placement in the correctional facility, the DSCC conducts a thorough review of their record. The 'Greatest Severity' Public Safety Factor was placed on inmate Kiriakou by the DSCC. According to Program Statement 5100.08, Security Designation and Custody Classification Manual, crimes involving espionage, treason, sabotage, or other related offenses fall within the Greatest Severity scale. If inmate Kiriakou feels this Public Safety Factor was placed on him erroneously, he may file an administrative remedy by following the procedures outline in Program Statement 1330.17, Administrative Remedy Program."

I know the warden. I respect him. I have found him to be a man of his word, and these were clearly not his words. Besides the fact that espionage, treason, and sabotage often carry the death penalty, while I was sentenced to thirty months with a camp recommendation, the warden in his letter just parroted back the same language my attorneys used in their letter to the DSCC, but with a different conclusion. I would have to avail myself of the BOP's corrupt and inefficient Administrative Remedy Process.

A reminder: around this time, July/August 2013, I filed a Freedom of Information Act (FOIA) request on myself. The BOP's 157-page response included 8 pages marked "FOIA Exempt: Do Not Release to Inmate," which were apparently included inadvertently. One of the pages, dealing with security, said, "CAUTION—Inmate has extensive access to the press." Another said, "CAUTION: Publicity." This Public Safety Factor was clearly put on me to curtail or inhibit my freedom of speech and not for any other reason. Nonetheless, I had to go through the BOP's motions.

Here's some background on the Administrative Remedy Process. If a prisoner has a problem with staff, food, medical, or pretty much anything else, he must file a form BP-8 1/2. (The courts will not hear a prisoner's complaint until the Administrative Remedy Process is exhausted.) This form, with the prisoner's complaint, goes to the unit manager for resolution. If the prisoner is not happy with the decision, he has one week to file a BP-9, which goes to the warden. If the prisoner finds the warden's decision unacceptable, he can file a BP-10, which goes to the BOP's regional office. If the prisoner is unhappy with the regional decision, he can file a BP-11, which goes to the BOP's headquarters in Washington. The BOP rarely meets its deadlines. But the prisoner must meet his deadlines or the entire complaint is dismissed.

I filed a BP 8 1/2 on November 6, 2013. I wrote, "I hereby request that the Public Safety Factor placed on me be lifted. I believe the PSF has been placed on me inappropriately. Please see the attached letter from my attorneys. My crime should not fall under 'greatest severity' because it is not in any way associated with espionage, treason, sabotage, or 'other related offenses.' It is not even in the same part of the US Code." I also attached a copy of my plea agreement, which contained the judge's and the prosecutor's camp recommendation. On November 18, 2013, the unit manager responded, "According to PS 5100.08, Security Designation and Custody Classification Manual, crimes involving espionage, treason, sabotage, or other related offenses fall within the Greatest Severity scale. Your offense is considered an 'other related offense.'" Sound familiar?

On November 21, 2013, I filed a BP-9 with the warden, to whom I wrote, "I hereby request that the Public Safety Factor placed on me be lifted. I believe the PSF has been placed on me inappropriately. My crime should not fall under 'greatest severity' because it is not in any way associated with 'espionage, treason, sabotage, or other related offenses,' as per PS 5100.08 of the Security Designation and Custody Classification Manual nor is it even in the same part of the US Code. Please see the attached information from my attorneys."

The warden responded on December 20, 2013, saying, "A review of this matter reveals you were found guilty of Intentionally Disclosing Information Identifying a Covert Agent [capitals as original]. Prior to your placement in a correctional facility, the DSCC conducted a thorough review of your record. Due to your conviction, the DSCC felt it was appropriate to apply a Greatest Severity Public Safety Factor. According to Program Statement 5100.08, Security Designation and Custody Classification Manual, crimes involving espionage, treason, sabotage, or other related offenses fall within the Greatest Severity scale. Accordingly, your Request for Administrative Remedy is denied." Again, sound familiar? It's my attorney's language, along with a denial that utterly ignores the facts. But note that the warden claims that my crime is an "other related offense."

Although the warden's response was dated December 20, 2013, I didn't receive it until December 31, 2013—and we're in the same building. So on January 2, 2014, I wrote a BP-10 to the BOP's regional director. I said, "I request that the Public Safety Factor placed on me be lifted. I believe the PSF has been placed on me inappropriately. Please see the attached letter from my attorneys. My crime should not fall under 'Greatest Severity' because it is not in any way related to 'espionage, treason, sabotage, or other related offenses.' Although I was charged with espionage, all of those charges were dropped for the simple reason that I had not committed espionage. Thank you."

In a letter dated February 11, 2014, the BOP's regional director wrote, "Your total offensive behavior is to be considered utilizing the most serious offense or act committed when determining offense security level." Aha! So the cat's out of the bag. The security designation has nothing to do with your crime. It has to do with whatever the government accuses you of doing, whether the charges were dropped or not. What happened to due process? If I had actually committed the crimes I was charged with, why didn't the government insist on going to trial? Why did they make five different plea offers? Why did they drop four of the five charges? And, if I'm so dangerous, why didn't the BOP put me in a maximum-security penitentiary?

Until I received this letter I believed that many BOP officials were either lazy or stupid. I was wrong. They're malicious. (Well, some are also lazy and stupid.) The regional director added, "Appendix A of the Inmate Security Designation and Custody Classification Manual Offense Severity Scale classifies espionage, treason, sabotage, or related offenses as a Greatest Severity offense. Accordingly, your appeal is denied."

Concluding that I would like to waste as much of the BOP's time and money as I possibly could, I sent an identical appeal, a BP-11, to the BOP's headquarters in Washington on March 4, 2014. Although the BOP's response was dated May 21, 2014, a full month past the April 22, 2014 deadline, I did not receive it until June 22. The response was a slightly less nasty and confused version of the regional director's response, although no less nonsensical. As if writing with a case of brain damage, the Administrator of National Appeals wrote, "When considering the severity level of the current offense, staff are to refer to the Offense Security Scale, Attachment A, of Program Statement 5100.08. The Offense Security Scale provides that any offense that involved espionage (defined as treason, sabotage, or related offenses) is classified as a greatest severity offense. Your current offense is correctly classified as a greatest severity offense."

On the one hand, I can't believe that so many people in such positions of authority don't even know the definition of espionage or that the Intelligence Identities Protection Act has nothing to do with espionage. I can't believe they are so incompetent as to not check their own records to see that the only other person ever convicted of violating the IIPA (five counts!) served two years of a five-year sentence in Camp Cupcake.

On the other hand, this isn't about competence. It's about punishing me for exercising my constitutional right to freedom of speech. But I'm a patient person. I can wait six months. I'm going to have a lot to say.

(FYI, according to a July 2014 article in Prison Legal News *entitled "BOP Grievance System Contributes to 'Compliance of Defiance' by Prisoners," a study conducted jointly by David M. Bierie, the US Marshal's Service, and the Department of Criminology and Criminal Justice at the University of Maryland, found that "the failure of BOP officials to adequately respond to grievances contributes to higher levels of violence in federal prisons. The research study determined that (a) benefit of the BOP's grievance system is deflecting or reducing potential litigation. Indeed, many federal court decisions have been decided in the BOP's favor based upon prisoners' failure to exhaust administrative remedies."*

The article went on to say that, "The BOP's grievance system is perceived by some prisoners as overly formal and more concerned with procedural practices and deadlines than the substance of a complaint. Accordingly, data suggest that a higher volume of late or rejected grievance responses will increase violence…Two features of the grievance process consistently predicted violence: the proportion of responses which were late, and the proportion of responses which were substantively rejected."

Thanks again for everything. Six months to go.

Until next time,
John

One more note on this letter: I thank a lot of people in my Letters from Loretto. That's because a lot of people opened their hearts—and their wallets—to help my family and me. But what Medea Benjamin, Jane Hamsher, Code Pink, and Firedoglake did was over and above. They paid off the second mortgage on my house and literally saved it from foreclosure. When I say that I'm eternally grateful, I really mean it.

Wrong Medication

IN FEBRUARY 2015 AS many as 2,800 prisoners at the Willacy County Correctional Center in Texas seized control of the facility to protest the low quality of medical care there. The Associated Press said, "inmates reported that their medical concerns were often ignored by staff and that corners were often cut when it came to health care." An attorney with the Texas Civil Rights Project said that he was "not surprised inadequate medical care could ignite a riot. It's pretty abysmal with regard to modern standards of how people should be treated."

And this wasn't just an isolated incident. What any normal person would consider to be malpractice on the "street," was a common occurrence in prison. My bunkmate, Frank, was a sixty-five-year-old man with diabetes and a history of heart trouble. He was insulin dependent and took more medications than I could shake a stick at. We were sitting in our room one evening when he said he felt a tightness in his chest. I told him that he should speak with a CO immediately, and I walked with him to see the CO on duty in our housing unit.

Frank told the CO that he felt tightness in his chest and he added that he had also been short of breath during the day. The CO said there was nothing he could do. Sick call was from 6:00 to 6:15 a.m. on Monday, Tuesday, Thursday, and Friday, and he would have to go to Medical Services the next morning. He did so, only to be given Tylenol. The physician's assistant on duty said that he would apply to the regional medical officer to approve a request for an EKG. *Great*, Frank thought.

Months passed. Frank continued to feel tightness in his chest, and he occasionally told me that he felt like somebody was sitting on his chest. I urged him to go back again to Medical Services, which he did. But the physician's assistant told him there was nothing they could do for him until they had heard back from the regional office.

Another two months passed. One morning Frank awakened early to go to the insulin line. I slept in until about 8:00 a.m. I got out of bed and began walking to the shower when a prisoner who lived near the front of the unit called my name. "Yo, John! Frank had a heart attack in insulin line! He just dropped to the ground, unconscious."

I felt dizzy with anger. Frank had been telling Medical for months that he was sick. He showed all the classic signs of a man either having a heart attack or on the verge of having one. And they had ignored him.

Frank spent eleven days in a local hospital, where he underwent surgery for two angioplasties and to install two stents. Why not bypass surgery? It was too expensive, the BOP said. He was later transferred to a "prison hospital" in Massachusetts, fifteen hours from his family.

Similarly, there was a prisoner who lived near the chapel, where I worked as an orderly. We had some mutual friends and I used to greet him when I went to work in the morning. One day he appeared to be a little hunched over. "Larry, are you ok?" I asked. "My back is really killing me," he said. He had gone to Medical earlier that morning at sick call and was given the usual Tylenol. He said that he had been having back pain for nearly a year, but that every time he went to the Medical Unit, they gave him Tylenol and sent him on his way. The pain persisted. Actually, it got worse. But the physician's assistants refused to request any testing at an outside hospital.

A couple of weeks later I saw Larry walking with a cane. "Larry, what's up with the cane?" I asked. "Is your back that bad?" He told me that he had never experienced back pain like this before. The Tylenol did nothing, and he otherwise couldn't get any relief. I recommended that he have his family call their congressman. Somebody had to do something for the poor guy. He was clearly in agony.

A few weeks later I was sitting in the weekly chapel staff meeting when the chaplain mentioned that he was going to stop by Larry's cell to see how he was doing. I asked if there had been any change in Larry's health, and the chaplain responded that Larry had moved from the cane to a walker, and now to a wheelchair. I told the chaplain about Larry's history of back pain, about how Medical had ignored him, and I asked the chaplain to intervene.

The chaplain did intervene. He went to Medical and demanded that Larry be taken to a hospital for testing. Another two weeks passed, and the regional medical office finally agreed to pay for the test. Larry was taken to a hospital where he underwent an MRI. He was diagnosed with Stage 4 cancer of the spine and sent back to the prison, where he died in his bed two weeks later. He never underwent any treatment of any kind. He was never considered for compassionate release. He was simply left to die.

There were a lot of bad people at Loretto. But none of them had been sentenced to death. They deserved at least basic medical care, as well as some human compassion.

Meanwhile, my own problems with the Medical Unit weren't over yet.

September 12, 2014
"Letter from Loretto"

Hello again from the Federal Correctional Institution at Loretto, Pennyslvania. I had a scare a few weeks ago that I wanted to tell you about because it's so typical of the BOP experience. By way of background, I have Type 2 diabetes, although I'm not insulin dependent. A month ago, I had a routine quarterly blood test. I have no idea what, if anything, that blood test revealed, as my physician's assistant (PA) never put me on call-out to inform me. (A "call-out" is a scheduled appointment.)

A few days later, I was put on call-out, but to the pharmacy, not to the PA. I went to the appointment and the pharmacist handed me a bottle of pills. "What is this?" I asked.

"Glyburide," he said, as though that should mean something to me.

"What's it for?"

"Diabetes," he said.

Growing worried, I asked, "Do I have a problem?"

"I don't know," he said. "Your PA called it in. He'll put you on call-out." Only insulin-dependent diabetics are allowed to have testing meters so I had no idea what my blood sugar numbers were. I took the pills back to my room.

The instructions on the bottle were to take a pill a day with food. That's what I did. At 2:00 a.m. on the second day, I woke up covered in sweat. I got down off my bunk, got my bearings, and then went to my locker for a cookie. I figured my blood sugar had dropped, and I felt better almost immediately. I drank some water and went back to bed.

I felt fine the next morning. That evening with dinner I took the third glyburide. I went to bed at 11:00 p.m. and slept through the night.

I woke up at 7:00 a.m., again soaked in sweat, and lowered myself onto a chair. For a minute, I thought I was going to throw up. It passed, so I got up to wash my face. The bathroom is about one hundred feet from my cubicle, and I started to make my way up there. After a few steps, I started to get dizzy. I heard somebody say, "John! Are you okay?" I mumbled, "I'm not sure what's happening." A friend and fellow prisoner, Wahid, who was a pharmacist on the street, said, "Your blood sugar is crashing. Sit down." I sat down on the concrete floor while Wahid ran and got a Coke. I took two sips, then everything went gray and I passed out on the floor.

I woke up fifteen minutes later in a wheelchair in the medical unit. A nurse helped me onto an examination table and took my blood pressure. Eighty-eight over sixty. He took it a second time. Eighty-eight over sixty. He asked what medications I was taking. I told him about the glyburide. He suggested, rather directly, that "perhaps you're not taking it the way you're supposed to." I assured him that I was and that

I had only taken three pills in three days. The nurse then suggested that I passed out because I was dehydrated.

"Okay," I said. "Are you going to give me an IV?"

"No," he said. "We don't do that here. Let's do an EKG to make sure you didn't have a heart attack." The EKG was normal.

I told the nurse that I was certain this was a case of low blood sugar because of the glyburide. He tested my blood, which was 135. (Normal fasting levels should be between seventy and one hundred.) I told him that I had had two sips of Coke, which would account for the higher level, but he went back to the dehydration diagnosis. He took my blood pressure twice more: ninety over sixty then ninety over seventy.

The nurse told me to sit in a chair in the hall, and when the regularly scheduled move was called at 8:25 a.m., I should go back to my unit and "take it easy for the day." I never saw a doctor. I never saw a PA. That was three weeks ago, and I still have not seen a medical professional.

I've mentioned before that my father-in-law is a highly respected physician (and former pharmacist) in Cincinnati. I called him immediately. STOP THE GLYBURIDE! he said. Glyburide is a medication meant as a last resort before diabetics go on insulin. I'm not at that stage, he said. And, besides, glyburide can ruin the pancreas. That's why so many physicians refuse to prescribe it. He added that if I continue the glyburide I could expect to eventually go into heart failure. I tossed it all. Interestingly, on the day I wrote this Letter from Loretto, I received an electronic message that my refill of glyburide was ready.

I feel fine now. I use a friend's blood sugar meter to test my blood each morning, and it's been between "normal" and slightly elevated. What happened to me is minor compared to what happens to other prisoners, systematically, across the BOP.

Ask any federal prisoner anywhere in America about medical care and he'll tell you the same thing: The BOP generally ignores prisoners' medical problems, hoping they'll either go away or that the prisoner will be released and will become someone else's problem. This isn't just John Kiriakou talking. This is a documented policy in every BOP facility in America.

I have a friend who was sentenced to two years in prison for having an illegal poker machine in his bar. He suffers from Hepatitis C, and, as soon as he got to Loretto, he told the medical unit about his condition. He said he needed treatment. "We'll think about it" was the response. He asked repeatedly over the next eighteen months for treatment. He was ignored. Finally, two weeks before his release, he was called to Medical. They would give him the treatment, they said, if he would agree to forego his halfway house and home confinement time. In other words, "We'll treat you, but you have to stay in prison." He declined. The BOP now can cover itself by saying that they wanted to treat him, but he refused. They knew he would decline. That was the plan from the beginning. That night he called his wife to tell her what had happened. He was upset and angry, and his language reflected that. The next morning he was thrown into solitary for insolence, where he remained until his release.

Judy White is a contributor to OpEdNews, a fantastic website that frequently covers BOP malfeasance. Her husband, Gary White, is a former Jefferson County, Alabama, commissioner who was caught up in the Karl Rove–instigated political case involving former Alabama governor Don Siegelman. Gary White is serving ten years in a federal prison in Forrest City, Arkansas. Judy White recently told OpEdNews about the experience of one of her husband's friends at FCI Forrest City. Here's what she said:

"Today we are very concerned about Dave, one of Gary's fellow prisoners in Forrest City. Dave is seventy-one years old and should have already been released to a halfway house. For the past two years, Dave has sought medical treatment because of blood in his urine. As his condition has become dramatically worse and Dave has become much sicker, his medical needs and efforts to obtain treatment have been consistently ignored or denied by prison employees. The BOP routinely and purposely withholds treatment, then releases sick prisoners to get whatever help they can get on their own. Dave's medical needs became even more urgent when he began passing blood clots, along with lots of blood.

"Dave understood that he was in serious trouble and that prison employees live by their unofficial motto: we don't care! So he begged to be taken to the hospital. Denied, and told to go back to his housing unit, Dave had no choice but to take a stand. He told the prison employees he was not leaving Medical and that he had to be taken to the hospital. Eventually, Dave was taken to the hospital, where it was quickly and easily determined that he had multiple tumors and needed emergency medical intervention and surgery. The emergency room physician told Dave that if he had not gotten to the hospital he would have been in the newspaper. In the obituaries.

"Want to guess what happened next? Nothing. Dave was taken from the hospital back to the prison, where he remains today, without surgery and without a plan to save his life."

The US media has largely ignored this abominable denial of medical care. It has not, however, been ignored by everybody. According to Prison Legal News, *the European Court of Human Rights (ECHR) refused to extradite suspected terrorist Haroon Rashid Aswat from the United Kingdom to the United States "on the ground that his mental and physical health would face significant deterioration in the more hostile US prison system." (Aswat v. United Kingdom, ECHR Case No. 17299/12.) The ECHR ruled that, "In light of the medical evidence before it, there was a real risk that Mr. Aswat's extradition to the USA, a country to which he has no ties, and to a different and potentially hostile prison environment, would result in a significant deterioration in his mental and physical health." Most notably, the ECHR found that "such deterioration would be capable of amounting to treatment in breach of Article 3 of the European Convention on Human Rights, which prohibits inhuman or degrading treatment."* I wish we had a court like that.

I have less than 150 days to go until my release on February 3, 2015. The first thing I'm going to do is to go see my doctor. I'm one of the lucky ones.

An update: A new guy moved in across the hall from me last week. [WITHHELD] is a heroin dealer who sold tainted junk to a friend, resulting in the friend's death. [WITHHELD] got twenty years in *prison and was given a "Greatest Severity" security classification, the same as mine. [WITHHELD] appealed the classification, just like I did, arguing that he is not a threat to society and should be in a minimum-security camp. This week he won his appeal. His security classification was downgraded to "high" and he will be transferred to camp soon. Meanwhile, I am far more dangerous than a drug-dealing murderer, and I'll remain behind the barbed wire fence. That's how our "Justice" Department works.*

Best regards,
John

Roommates, or The Road to Hell is Paved with Good Intentions

ONE OF THE GOOD-AND-BAD things about prison is that roommates (or cellmates, depending on your situation) constantly come and go. This is good in the respect that if you have an idiot for a roommate, or somebody who is loud or dirty or a child molester, the chances are good that he'll eventually move to another room, be released, or be sent to solitary for some infraction. If you have a good room, you do everything you can to maintain the status quo. If you have a bad room, you either move to a good one or do what you can to convince the trouble roommate to move on.

When Dave was taken to the SHU after the incident with Schaeffer, Frank and I scrambled to clean out his locker. I learned when I arrived in prison that this was something friends did for each other: when one was sent to solitary, his friends got to his locker before the cops did, bagged everything, and held it until he came back. Otherwise, the cops would just set aside the uniforms and throw everything else away—food, books, paperwork, you name it. Frank and I got two empty laundry bags and filled them with Dave's belongings, which we stowed under our bunk.

SIS told me soon after they took Dave that he wouldn't be coming back onto the compound. He hadn't received a charge, or even a disciplinary report related to Schaeffer, but he was very unpopular among the Aryans and other whites at the front table for his constant accusations that everybody he disliked was a "rat," a "chomo," or a "fag," and they had had enough. The three white shot-callers had gone to SIS to say that they wouldn't guarantee Dave's safety on the yard. That was none-too-subtle code for "if you let him out we're giving him a beatdown."

I went back to the room to tell Frank. I gathered Dave's legal paperwork and mailed it to his attorneys. I sent his books to his grandmother. And I gave his clothes to indigent prisoners. Several of the books I had loaned to Dave, so I just put those back in my locker. Leafing through one of them, though, I got a shock. In it was a piece of paper in Dave's handwriting. It was, for lack of a better term, a "rat list," that is, a list of people along with an accounting of their "misdeeds" that Dave had taken to the cops. I was dumbstruck. My name was at the top of the list.

Every time I wrote one of my Letters from Loretto blog posts, I would make several copies—one for the publisher of firedoglake.com, one for my attorney, one for myself, and one for Dave. I made one for Dave because he said he would keep a copy of each letter for me at an undisclosed location so that, in the event I was shaken down and my letters confiscated, I would still have the hidden copy. I shouldn't know the location of the letters so that if I were called into SIS, I couldn't incriminate myself. In fact, Dave was giving the copy to SIS. That was how they always seemed to know what I was doing. I had assumed that the letters were hidden in Art's room. In reality Dave was passing them to the unit manager, a former SIS officer, who then passed them to SIS. I'd been duped, and I felt like a fool, especially because I had violated one of my own rules: trust nobody.

The list had many others on it. "Mark Lanzilotti—bookie— hiding place" was one entry. The cops shook down Mark's room and confiscated 1,200 books of stamps. They put him out of business. Another entry said "Luke—porn—kill party." A former neighbor of ours, Luke Davis, a bank robber, had some hard core adult porn hidden in his locker. He was also writing a "novel," as were about a thousand other prisoners. But in his novel, he had what he called a "kill party," where he invited his judge, prosecutors, his own attorneys, his codefendant, and others to a Christmas party, then killed them all in a hail of machine gun fire. Not only was Luke taken to the SHU, he was then upgraded to a medium-security prison.

Of course, there were dozens of entries for Schaeffer and for Al the arsonist, with whom Dave feuded constantly, as well as for just about everybody else who had ever offended him in any way. He had even ratted on a staff member with whom I had once had a conversation about pedophiles. Dave had exaggerated the story when he reported it, so when the SIS called me down to make a sworn statement, it was easy for me to tell her truthfully that her rat, whoever he was, was lying. The story was simply untrue. Even more bizarrely, as soon as Dave got to his next prison, he wrote a letter to my wife, followed by a phone call, asking for $1,000. She told him no, kept the conversation very short, and hung up, but only after Dave told her that he had "stood up" for me while he was in the SHU. He said that SIS had visited him several times to ask him for any information they could use against me, even if he had to make it up. This was ridiculous on its face. SIS could have put me in the SHU for up to six months "pending investigation" for no reason at all if they had wanted to. They didn't need Dave's help.

Four months after Dave was taken to the SHU, I was still dealing with fallout from his time at Loretto. When I first got to prison, one of my best friends got me a subscription to Vanity Fair, my favorite magazine. The subscription had stopped around the time Dave went to the SHU. Finally, four months later, my friend emailed me and said, "Do you still want the Vanity Fair subscription? I got a letter from Vanity Fair saying that it's undeliverable and that the name on the subscription was changed from yours to David Phillips. Who's David Phillips?" Dave had sunk so low as to actually write to Vanity Fair in my name and ask that the subscription be turned over to him. All I could do was shake my head in disgust.

This string of events reminded me of a conversation I had had with an attorney friend of mine a year earlier. Dave was appealing his sentence and was looking for an attorney. He wanted to know if my friend would take his case. I said I'd ask. I told my friend about Dave, said he was a former colleague of mine, and said he needed legal representation as he appealed his sentence. Would my friend think about taking the case? My friend said he'd look up the case and give it some thought. A few months later he came to visit me. "I decided not to take Dave's case," he said.

I was surprised. "Why?" I asked.

"Well," he said, "I went through the whole case and came to the conclusion that he's just a common criminal. A con man." It stung when he said it, but it made perfect sense a year later.

I googled Dave when I got home. What I found, in about five seconds, infuriated me. He was indeed a con man. His sentencing judge actually called him a "brazen con man." He had never worked at the CIA. He had briefly been a contractor, and that's how I had met him. As far as his crimes were concerned, he ripped off family members, getting credit cards in the names of his elderly grandparents and his daughter. He scammed a former girlfriend and a pal from high school. He was a financial predator.

Dave and I would often walk around the track at Loretto and talk about our careers. He would go into detail about some of the operations he said he was involved in and the awards he had received for heroism. There were a couple of things that bothered me about these conversations, though. First, Dave could generally "talk the talk." But he frequently made mistakes with the lingo—something no former CIA officer would ever do. He would also mention training courses that he supposedly had gone through, but he got the locations wrong. I knew this because I had taken several of those same courses, and I knew for a fact where they were held.

Another thing was that Dave claimed a twenty-five-year career at the CIA, but he didn't know any of the players. I'm not talking about people undercover. I'm talking about the CIA's leadership.

Even average Americans who follow the news by reading the papers every day would know these people. Dave always said he had been under deep cover. That was fine with me. But that shouldn't have meant that he lived so deep under a rock that he didn't know his own organization's leaders.

I should have reminded myself to stick with the lessons the CIA had taught me. I should have gone with my gut. I shouldn't have allowed myself to get close to anyone. This was prison, after all. But when I first arrived I was alone, in shock, and depressed. Dave and I had a certain life in common. I exhibited a weakness, a vulnerability. Lesson learned. The whole experience made me tougher, stronger, and more self-reliant. And it helped to pass the time.

Dave went to the SHU on May 1, 2014. My roommates and I let the bed remain open for two weeks, thinking initially that he would be released and would come back. Frank, Beard, and I heard, finally, that he was being shipped to another prison, so we began the search for a roommate. Doc Grivas, a Medicare fraud doctor from Staten Island, couldn't get a lower bunk pass; Chin, a crooked and incontinent concrete mogul, didn't want to move farther away from the bathroom; Joey the Kid, who was my first choice, was out of favor with the counselor, who was in charge of bed assignments. So the bed sat empty for five weeks.

In the meantime, Mark received an email from one of his attorneys telling him to be on the lookout for another of his clients. Sher Mawlani was a naturalized citizen of Afghan origin. He had emigrated to the United States in 1980 after the Soviet Union invaded his country, arriving in Washington's Virginia suburbs. He drove a cab until the September 11 attacks, when he was recruited by a defense contractor to be a translator for US forces in Afghanistan.

During an operation in eastern Afghanistan, Sher's armored Humvee hit an improvised explosive device and flipped over. The vehicle then came under enemy fire. Everybody in the Humvee was killed upon the initial impact except Sher and one soldier. They crawled through a broken window, and when Sher stood up, he was shot in the shoulder and stomach by a Taliban fighter with an AK-47. The American soldier pulled him down, called in reinforcements, and tried to stanch the flow of blood. They were eventually rescued, but Sher was near death. After emergency surgery at a field hospital, he was sent to a US military hospital in Germany, where his mangled arm was amputated just below the shoulder. He remained in a coma for six weeks.

When he awoke, surrounded by his family, his body was an utter mess. His right arm was gone and he had one of the most ghastly scars anybody had ever seen, courtesy of the bullet to the stomach. It stretched from his breastbone to his pubic bone and was nearly a foot across at the center, in the shape of a diamond. His belly-button had been moved to his side, literally.

The psychological scars were much worse, though. Sher came out of the attack with severe cases of post-traumatic stress disorder (PTSD) and depression. His body was wrecked, he would have to learn basic tasks all over again, and he was angry—very angry—at everything and everyone. A multimillion-dollar settlement and drugs for PTSD and depression didn't seem to help. He was arrested after a family dispute when he beat his wife and threw a vase through the screen of his new seventy-two-inch television. He was sentenced to six months of anger management classes. His psychiatrist suggested that perhaps he should volunteer to go back to Afghanistan to confront his demons. He went back to work as a translator and made several trips per year, spending most of his time at the US Air Force base at Bagram.

Mark told me about Sher and asked if I could track him down and make him feel comfortable when he arrived. He thought we could talk about shared experiences in Afghanistan and that I could take him to the chapel to introduce him to the Muslims. Sure enough, five weeks after Dave's departure, a CO accompanied a five-foot-four-inch, bearded, one-armed Afghan man to my room and said, "Here's your new cellie." Surprised, I asked if he was Sher Mawlani; he said he was. We shook hands and I said we had been expecting him. I gave him a pair of shower shoes, a toothbrush, toothpaste, soap, and shampoo, took him to the chapel to get him a Quran, and introduced him to Wahid, another Afghan inmate and a former pharmacist.

I told Sher, when we got back to our cubicle, that we had a good room—quiet and respectful. We all got along and respected each other's privacy. We were also honest with each other. "I don't know anything about your crime," I told him, "but everybody is going to ask you. Everybody. You have to be honest if you hope to get along here. What did you do?"

He smiled, threw up his hand, and said, "Silly craziness!"

I very seriously told him, "That's a really bad answer for prison. What did you do?" A look of tension and embarrassment swept over him.

"Computer," he said.

"Pictures on the computer?" I asked. "Pictures of children?"

"Yes," he answered meekly.

"Well," I said, "you're going to have to be honest about it. But you should know that there are a lot of people here who won't talk to you."

Just then, Beard walked in. Beard was the perfect roommate. Unbelievably easy to get along with, he was an all-around good guy. Six feet three inches of rock-hard muscle, he was, in his own words, a career criminal and drug dealer from Lansing, Michigan. Beard liked prison. All he did all day, every day, was eat, sleep, work out, and watch TV. Life was good. Beard trusted Frank and me to choose roommates, and he frequently offered us sage advice on a variety of issues learned through his many years in prison. He was almost never in the room, preferring his reserved seat in the TV room.

"Are you the new roommate?" Beard asked bluntly.

Sher nodded and offered his hand.

Beard shook it and said, "What's your crime?"

"Well," Sher started uncomfortably, "I just made a stupid mistake."

"What kind of mistake?" Beard gave him a hard look and said, "We have a rule in our room. Child molesters can't have visitors. Got it?"

"Yes," Sher answered quietly.

Beard looked at me, his eyes saying, "Not another fucking child molester!"

One of the first things Sher did when he arrived was to ask me to take him to the chapel to show him the library and to introduce him to the chaplain. We walked down to the chapel after dinner and I showed him where all the books on Islam were kept. We then went to the chaplain's office. I introduced Sher to the chaplain and noted that he was one of a very small number of Shia Muslims in the prison. Sher asked if he could buy any religious items he may need. Sure, the chaplain said. We have a catalogue and any inmate can order what he needs. "What I need," Sher explained, "is a ritual bowl to wash my penis and testicles before I pray." The chaplain looked at me; he knew I had earned a degree in Middle Eastern Studies with a concentration in Islamic theology. I gave him a perplexed look and shrugged my shoulders. "Sorry," the chaplain said. "I can't help you there." We thanked him and walked out. On the way back to the room, Sher said, "I think he hates Muslims."

From the very beginning, Sher was overly comfortable with prison, acting as though he was instead at a men's club. He slept most of the day, played soccer in the evenings, and prayed all night. He swore a lot—at people he didn't know—and I warned him that this would eventually result in a hearty ass kicking. And Sher was not a guy who could easily defend himself. At fifty-four years old, he was short and weighed about 140 pounds. And he had one arm.

We had problems with Sher from the day he arrived. He told me privately that his crime was more serious than he had let on. He had been having an "affair" with his fourteen-year-old niece. She sent him a nude photo of herself, which he kept on his computer. His teenage daughter saw the photo and called the police, who in turn called the FBI. He was arrested, took a plea, and was sentenced to six years. "But I forgive them," he told me.

"Who?" I asked, perplexed.

"My niece and my daughter. I forgive them."

236 J O H N K I R I A K O U

I was indignant. Why do pedophiles always do this? "Sher," I said. "That's really not a healthy attitude for a whole bunch of reasons. My advice is that you shouldn't talk about your crime at all."

He lit up. "If people don't like it, I will FUCK THEM UP THE ASS!" This was to become an ongoing theme.

Sher was a filthy slob. He would return from soccer drenched in sweat, take off his clothes, and then hang the soaked, smelly clothes on *our* lockers. This included his underwear, socks, shirt, shorts, and towel. We were all shocked. "Are you kidding me?" I asked him. "Get your shit off my locker!" On top of that, he had a large, festering herpes sore on his upper lip, and he put his washcloth on Erik's bed. I thought Erik would lose his mind. Beard's only reaction was to shout, "This shit stops NOW!"

Sher then hung a string for his clothes from one end of his bunk to the other. This was against regulations, and would never pass weekly inspection. The problem was that Sher was on the bottom bunk and Erik was on the top, so the string was actually on Erik's bed, rather than Sher's. Of course, Sher put the herpes washcloth inches from Erik's face, next to his pillow. This resulted in the first blowout.

When Erik opened his eyes after a nap to see the herpes washcloth next to his face, he flipped out. He jumped out of bed, pulled the string, snapped it in half, and shouted at Sher, "Don't EVER fucking do that again!"

Sher went nuts. "I will fuck you in the ass! I will fuck your mother in the ass!"

The craziness had begun. Erik walked out, and for the next forty minutes Sher ranted about Bill Clinton and Monica Lewinski, Nancy Reagan being pregnant before she married Ronald, and the fact that he shouldn't be in prison because his niece's parents had forgiven him and, "according to Islamic law, I haven't done anything wrong." Frank and I tried to calm him, which took more than an hour, during which he admitted that he suffered from severe PTSD, took strong medication for mental illness, and had previously been arrested for beating his wife and smashing his television. We finally calmed him down, but we were both worried about this ominous development. Sher's presence in the room wasn't going to work out.

That night Sher picked a fight with Erik after lights out. I was still up reading and Frank was sitting on the edge of his bed. Beard was in the TV room and Steve was asleep. Erik could feel some movement beneath him and he looked over the side of the bed. Sher had restrung the string and had hung the herpes washcloth right by Erik's head again. Sher looked up at Erik defiantly, saying nothing. Erik, also saying nothing, broke the string again. The washcloth fell on the floor. After a quick exchange of "fuck you!" Sher ran out of the room. Frank looked at me and said, "Oh, no."

A moment later, eight Muslims rushed into the room. "Out of bed, kid!" one of them shouted.

I jumped up. "Whoa, whoa. This can't get out of hand."

One of the Muslims said, "The kid stabbed the brother with a pencil." Frank and Erik both said that was ridiculous. Meanwhile, one of the senior Muslims motioned for me to step into the hall.

"What happened?" he asked. I told him about the herpes washcloth. He asked if Erik had stabbed Sher.

"Absolutely not," I said. "He was in bed, half asleep." We walked back into the room, where the Muslim addressed Sher.

"Sher. Where did he stab you?"

"Well," Sher said. "He tried to stab me."

"Where's the pencil?" Sher knew there had never been a pencil in the first place.

"But he WANTED to stab me!" The Muslims, clearly embarrassed, apologized to Erik and walked out.

I looked at Sher. "So now you're a rat in addition to being a pedophile? Don't ever fucking do that again."

The next day we had a room meeting and decided that Sher had to go. I wrote a Request to Staff, which Sher signed, asking that he be moved to another room. He gave it to the counselor, who rejected it with a terse "tough luck." We were stuck with him.

From the moment he arrived, Sher flouted the rules of the prison and of the room. He prayed constantly, upward of twenty times a day. This would have been fine if he had prayed in the designated prayer area down the hall, but he insisted on praying in the room. Six of us were crammed into 160 square feet, so having Sher on his prayer rug in the middle of the room simply didn't work. For a while he prayed on his bed, then he moved to the prayer area with the rest of the Muslims. This was only a temporary respite for us, however.

Sher never cleaned the room, never took out the garbage, and walked around without a shirt, exposing his stump and his absolutely grisly stomach wound. Nudity, even partial nudity, is anathema in prison, and we told Sher repeatedly to cover up. His reaction was to shout, "Fuck you! Everybody should see what the US Army made happen to me!"

I told him, "Nobody gives a shit what happened to you. Cover up before somebody gives you a beatdown."

Sher also had a bad habit of not being in uniform. The rules in prison are clear: all inmates must be in full uniform from 6:00 a.m. until after lunch. If you are asleep during the day, you must be in uniform and sleeping on top of the covers. If you are under blankets, your pillow will be confiscated, and you will be given an administrative sanction, such as three months' suspension of commissary, telephone, email, or visiting privileges. Sher didn't care. Because he was up praying all night, he slept all day—in shorts and a T-shirt, and under the covers.

One day the warden walked by on one of his periodic "walkabouts." He saw Sher in bed, woke him up, and said, "Get up! Get your uniform on! You can't sleep under the covers."

Sher popped out of bed, looked at the warden, and said, "And who the hell are you?"

The warden raised his eyebrows. "I'm the warden."

"What does this mean—'warden'?"

"It means he's the boss of the whole prison," I interjected. I looked at the warden, and with my index finger, circled the side of my head to indicate that Sher was insane.

"Get up and get dressed," the warden said, and he walked out.

"What was all that about?" Sher asked.

I said, "Sher, I said it before and I'll say it again. You are not in a men's club. You're in prison. You have to follow the rules or things are going to get hard for you." Still, though, he scoffed. Things got steadily worse.

Sher was the only Shia Muslim in a large group of Sunnis. Most of the Muslims were prison converts, knew little about the Sunni/Shia split, cared even less, and didn't want a lesson from a one-armed Afghan child molester on why they should instead be praying to some obscure eighteenth-century Iranian ayatollah. Sher soon began lecturing the Muslims about how their prayers were "wrong," how they repeated Arabic sayings without knowing the meaning, and how none of them were "real" Muslims. For good measure, he added that he didn't like praying with African-Americans because "they're stupid, they smell bad, and they don't know the prayers." This caused an irreconcilable rift. Sher was thrown out of the group and told he couldn't pray with the Sunnis anymore. His only reaction, later, was to say he would shove his prayer rug "up their mothers' cunts." Very pious.

Sher had further angered just about everybody in the unit by standing in front of the large floor fan outside the bathroom after playing soccer for two hours, pulling down his pants, and airing out his balls, a violation of just about every kind of prison protocol imaginable.

A few days later, somebody entered our room and gave Sher's locker a vigorous shake. When he opened it, nearly all of its contents fell on the floor. This is a relatively common event in prison. If you piss someone off, rather than fight you, and have you both go to solitary and lose good time, they will instead shake your locker. Frank, Erik, and I thought it was pretty funny, and it was obvious that one of Sher's many enemies was messing with him. His reaction, though, was irrational—again. He blamed Wahid, the Afghan Sunni who had befriended him upon his arrival, introduced him to the other Muslims, and had given him clothes and a watch to get him started. Sher challenged Wahid: "You shook my locker! If you do it again, I'll kill you!"

"I didn't do shit to you!" Wahid responded. "You're out. You can't pray with us. Don't talk to us. You're on your own."

By then word had gotten around that Sher was a pedophile, not just a "clicker," someone who looked at pornographic pictures of children, but a "toucher," the lowest of the low. One of the leaders of the Hispanic Pisces gang, with whom Sher had played soccer, asked him directly if he had committed a sex crime. Sher answered that his case was "very complicated." The gangbanger wanted none of it. "You can't play soccer with us anymore. You're cut off."

Sher's response was typical. He said, "Fine," then waited until the guy was out of earshot. "I don't care about their soccer! I fuck them all! I fuck their mothers! I will shove my fist up their asses!" I called him a Sodomite and walked out.

It was clear to all of us that Sher had serious mental problems. I went to Mark's room to ask some advice on prison etiquette. "If I tell the chief psychologist that he's nuts, he's depressed, and he's potentially violent, does that make me a rat?"

His answer was clear. "Yes. Stay away from it." So what do I do? "You're always talking about your CIA rules," Mark said. "Do what you need to do to protect yourself." A light went off in my head. Remember, "if stability is not to your benefit, chaos is your friend, and eliminate potential problems using dirty tricks." I would get Sher to check himself into the SHU, where he would be out of our hair, and where he would get much closer psychological observation. It wouldn't win me any "nice guy" contests, but we just couldn't live with this monster any longer.

The first thing I did was to crush up a sleeve of Saltine crackers and spread them all over Sher's bed while he was outside walking the track. When he came into the room and saw the crumbs, he shouted, "Fucking pieces of shit!"

I said, "Sher. Obviously you have enemies. This harassment is going to continue. Maybe you should check into the SHU. It's quiet down there and nobody will bother you."

Frank agreed. "Listen to him, Sher. This will just get worse. Go to the SHU."

With a tense smirk on his lips, Sher exploded, naturally. "I fuck their SHU! I am not afraid of the blasphemers [the Sunni Muslims]! I am Sher Mawlani, follower of Ali, follower of Husayn! I will give my life to kill the enemies of Islam!" He beat his breast with his fist. Well, that didn't work.

The next day I mentioned to Joey the Kid, one of the Italians who lived across the hall, that we were facing a challenge in our room. I told him that we wanted this guy in the SHU, but that it was too risky for us to do things to him ourselves. It would be much better if things "happened" while everybody in the room was outside exercising. We knew from a friendly CO that the nearby security camera didn't work, so Joey said he would take care of it. We all went outside.

Frank, Erik, and I talked about what we thought would happen. I said there were several "rules" involved here: "eliminate potential problems using dirty tricks;" "if stability is not to your benefit, chaos is your friend;" and "be the power behind the throne." Joey could and would do the dirty work.

We got back to the room and immediately saw Joey's handiwork. He had broken into Sher's locker and stolen ten bags of mackerel, he had taken a pair of scissors and cut the pockets out of Sher's pants, and Sher's prayer beads were missing. Joey later told us that he had flushed them down the toilet. A minute after we entered the room, Sher arrived with a CO. "Look what they did to me!" he shouted. "I demand that you check the security tape."

"Buddy," the CO responded. "The cameras are not for you. They're for us. If you have a problem with somebody, you deal with it."

Sher protested. "I want you to investigate this and arrest who did it."

The CO was getting bored. "I'm not here to protect you. I am here to protect people *from* you."

He walked out. I could see Sher's explosion coming, and I knew his rant would continue for hours. "Sher, you should check into the SHU. Otherwise, this'll get out of hand."

Frank concurred. "Just go to the SHU."

Sher could barely contain his rage. "I will feed them their own balls!"

Sher responded the next day by getting "protection." He hired another Muslim pedophile, a Roma, or Gypsy, from Cleveland, to keep an eye on our room. He paid the Roma by having his wife transfer money into the kid's account to buy a radio and an MP3 player—strictly against the rules and punishable by confinement in the SHU, ironically. I had to take the bull by the horns. I went up to the Roma and said, "Why are you hanging around my room?"

"I'm just looking for Sher."

"Pedophiles don't have visitors in our room. Get lost before I do something I'll regret later." He left.

Joey wanted to act quickly, but I called him off. "We've heated up the area," I told him, using a phrase from my CIA surveillance training. "Let's let a week pass before we move on him again. Besides, I can try to convince him again to go to the SHU." The SHU conversation was a nonstarter. Sher would have none of it. Finally, the week passed. Joey asked me what I wanted him to do. "I don't care," I said. "But have some fun with it."

Two hours later, we got back to the room after walking the track. Sher was standing in front of the bed with the same CO as during the previous incident. They were looking at Sher's bed, in the middle of which Joey had used a Sharpie permanent marker to draw a huge erect cock and balls.

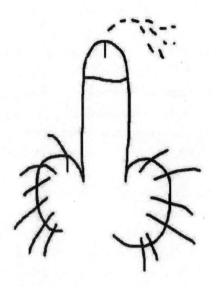

When I saw it, I said, "Sher, this is out of hand. Whoever your enemy is, make peace."

Beard, who was not in on the plan, exploded. "Do you know what this means?" he spat at Sher. "It means somebody is coming into our room when we're not here! Our room is being disrespected because YOU have enemies! End this shit or go to the SHU!" The CO offered no encouragement. He walked out, smiling again.

Word spread around the unit like wildfire that somebody had humiliated Sher. He blamed everybody—the Hispanics who had thrown him off the soccer team, the blacks he had insulted, the Muslims. He confided in Frank that the only thing worse would have been if the perpetrator had called him an asshole. "There is nothing worse than the asshole," he said. "It is the most disgusting thing imaginable." Frank got a chuckle out of this and mentioned it to Doc Grivas.

A few uneventful days passed. Sher was a nervous wreck, but he wasn't even sure who his enemies were. He had threatened to remain in the room twenty-four hours a day to "catch and kill" his tormentor. That only lasted a day. Finally, several days after the most recent incident, we all went to dinner, and then went outside to walk the track. An hour later, at about 6:30 p.m., Frank, Joey, and I ran into Doc Grivas. "There's a present waiting for you in your room," he said excitedly. *Oh, no*, I thought. Either he decided to take a swipe at Sher or Sher had finally gone off the deep end. We rushed back to the room just as Sher was arriving. There was Sher's prayer rug, laid out upside down on the bed. It was festooned with another huge erect cock, and above it was written, "Asshole, you are." It was signed "Yoda."

Sher was physically shaking with anger. He tore off the underside of the carpet and threw it away. "Don't go to the cops," I told him. "It'll just make you more of a rat."

"Fuck you!" Sher shouted.

I shouted back. "You're a rat, you're a child molester, you're always talking about who you want to fuck up the ass! Fuck you! Get out of here! We don't want you here! Go to the SHU!" Of course, Sher ran straight to the CO again, who told him there was nothing he could do. Sher was incensed, but he went about his business, muttering to himself and praying the rest of the night. He didn't sleep. In the morning he didn't speak to any of us. He went to breakfast and then up to the library for his pre-GED class.

By 8:00 a.m. Frank and I were alone in the room together. "Frank, I think I can push him over the edge today," I said.

Frank's response was quick. "How can I help?" I asked him to be my lookout. When the coast was clear, I quickly opened a package of sliced pork pepperoni that I had gotten from the commissary and spread it under Sher's pillow. (Terrible. I know. I don't care. You try living with this monster.) Sher spent most of the day outside, not returning to the room until 2:30 p.m., giving the pepperoni the entire day to get nice and ripe.

Again, of course, Sher ran to the cops. They didn't want to have anything to do with him. The only response was "take care of your own problems, buddy." This was the time to provoke Sher. His rantings had attracted a sizeable crowd. I stood up and shouted, "I think YOU'RE doing this to yourself for attention! We're tired of your bullshit! We're tired of you! Just get out!"

"Sure," Sher said rhetorically. "I'm doing it to myself!"

"So the truth comes out!" I retorted.

Sher walked into the hall surrounded by a dozen people. "I will fuck you all! I will kill you all! I am not afraid of your prison! I am not afraid of death! I am not afraid of your government! You created al-Qaeda! I fuck al-Qaeda! I fuck the Taliban!" He was utterly irrational. It was a breakdown.

I quickly ran down to the unit manager's office. It was his last day on the job before transferring to Washington, and he was just about ready to leave the office. "Sher's gone nuts," I said. "I think he needs psych attention." I walked back to my room just as the announcement came over the PA system. "Sher Mawlani report to the unit manager's office."

"I won't go!" he shouted. The announcement came a second time. Still he wouldn't budge.

I went back to the unit manager's office. "He refuses to come," I said. The unit manager picked up his walkie-talkie and called SIS.

"Can I get two COs with cuffs?" he asked. "I have one for the SHU, and he won't go peaceably."

We could all hear the jingling of keys for what seemed like a whole minute before the SIS COs arrived. When Sher saw what he was up against, he gave up. Because he had only one arm, the CO fastened a dog chain around his waist, cuffed his hand to it, and took him away. The only thing we heard him say was, "Can I take my prayer rug?" He could. It was all over.

Frank and I stood there and watched as the cops led Sher away. "Thank God that worked," Frank said. "If it hadn't, I was seriously going to poop in his boots."

A couple hours later, two Muslims stopped at the entrance to the room. They looked at Sher's empty bed. Finally, one turned to the other and said, "Wow. They done him in with the swine." Another two weeks passed. Finally, a guy in the next cube got out of the SHU,

I asked him if he had encountered Sher. "The one-armed guy? He's having a tough time down there." I asked what was going on. "He kicks the cell door all the time and shouts things like 'I fuck you!' and 'I fuck your mother.' So the cops wait until he's asleep, then they kick the door, wake him up, and say, 'I thought you liked to kick the door, you piece of shit!'" That's Sher.

Prison Health Care, Mental Health, and Suicide

CORRECTIONS OFFICERS SUFFER FROM post-traumatic stress disorder (PTSD) at more than double the rate of military veterans, according to a study by Desert Waters Correctional Outreach, a Colorado nonprofit organization.[6] I can tell you from firsthand experience that this has a direct effect on prisoners. I've had PTSD myself, after serving overseas. Sometimes it wears off; sometimes it doesn't. I can spot it, and at Loretto I spotted it frequently among the COs, many of whom were veterans of the Afghanistan and Iraq wars.

The Desert Waters Correctional Outreach report found further that 34 percent of COs suffer from PTSD. This compares to 14 percent of veterans. "The suicide rate among corrections officers is twice as high as that of both police officers and the general public, according to a New Jersey police task force. An earlier national study found that corrections officers' suicide risk was 39 percent higher than all other professions combined." The stress causes COs to become "cynical, withdrawn, and aggressive, the study found."

An article in *The Guardian* (UK) newspaper said that COs experience stress unlike any other profession. "The biggest stress factor is not knowing when crisis situations may arise. This leads to permanent hyper-vigilance." One CO related that this is "because we go into a place where we have control because the inmates let us run the prison. If they wanted to, they could take it. They're compliant until they choose not to be."

This constant stress takes a toll. Sometimes it manifests itself in violence against prisoners. Sometimes a CO will take his own life. That's what happened at Loretto.

January 22, 2015
"Letters from Loretto"

Hello from the Federal Correctional Institution at Loretto, Pennsylvania. A CO at Loretto committed suicide yesterday. I didn't know him nor did I ever have any contact with him. But from all accounts he was a nice guy—friendly, reasonable, and honest. The response by staff to his death has been fascinating to me.

First some background. Over the course of my fourteen-plus years at the CIA, several of my colleagues were killed in action. A star for them was then placed on the Wall of Honor at CIA headquarters, eulogies were made, and we got on with our mission. There was work to do.

Things are quite different here. Although the COs death occurred at home, the prison was "locked down." All prisoners had to return to their housing units, all work and classes were canceled, and the recreation yard was closed. Today there is still no work, and all activities were canceled. "Grief counselors" are in the building for staff members who need them. All 1,200-plus prisoners are just sitting around.

Again, I've heard that this CO was a nice guy, and I'm sorry for his wife and children. But this whole experience smacks of utter hypocrisy. Last night I was walking through a nearby housing unit when a CO walked into the TV room and announced, "Nobody better fuck with me tonight because tonight I can beat the shit out of anybody I want and get away with it!" Is that grieving?

An inmate also died this week. Shaba had told the medical unit for months that he wasn't feeling well. It took a formal written complaint to force the prison to take him to a nearby hospital, where he was diagnosed with Stage 4 cancer. He suffered for weeks before dying, chained to a hospital bed surrounded not by his family but by two COs more interested in watching television than in comforting a dying man. He was to be released to a halfway house next month. There were no grief counselors or work cancellations for Shaba. He was a prisoner, a non-person.

Three close family members of mine have died since I got to Loretto: my aunt, who played a major role in raising me and was like a second mother; my mother-in-law, who died suddenly and unexpectedly in November; and my cousin, who at thirty-eight had a heart attack while pumping gas. In the cases of my mother-in-law and my cousin, nobody here even bothered to inform me of their deaths. And because I have a multi-day delay on my emails, I had no idea that they had died. (And when the chaplain told me that my aunt had died, he followed it up with an uncomfortable, "Well, now you can say you've had the complete prison experience.")

Why are our lives and the lives of our loved ones worth less? BOP regulations allow for prisoner travel to the funerals of immediate family members. But this travel is never permitted at Loretto. Never. I've lost count of the number of prisoners I've encountered in tears because they'd lost their wives, their parents, or their children. The prison administration's response is typical: Tough luck. Get over it. There are no grief counselors for us.

On another issue, I have eleven days to go in my sentence so I'm just biding my time. I was taken aback last week when the prison (again) served an overtly racist meal for Martin Luther King Jr. Day: BBQ chicken, collard greens, macaroni and cheese, corn bread, and bean pie. Last year it was worse: fried chicken, collard greens, black-eyed peas, and corn bread. I would venture to guess that the only reason we didn't have watermelon was that it's out of season.

How are these decisions made? I wonder. The president of the United States, the attorney general of the United States, and the director of the Bureau of Prisons are all African-Americans and still something as simple as a holiday meal reeks of racism. Is there a committee of white people sitting around a table asking, "What do they eat? I heard they like chicken." My African-American friends here were appalled, and this was a topic of much discussion. But, sadly, they're used to this kind of backhanded racism.

The Italians with whom I'm friendly, however, were angered. There's a precedent here, so where's the Italian food on Columbus Day? (We had tacos.) Last year in March I was asked to give a speech in the chapel to commemorate "Greek Heritage Month." Where's my Greek food? I'm tired of chicken and tacos. But I've been patient for two years. I can be patient for another eleven days.

All the best,
John Kiriakou

A Day in the Life: Vignettes

Scene: Central 1 TV Room.

Setting: Middle of the day. A small group of prisoners are watching CNN coverage of the Steubenville, Ohio, rape case, where several high school football standouts are accused of raping an unconscious sixteen-year-old girl.

CNN ANNOUNCER: "Police say the girl was also digitally violated."

PRISONER #1: "What's that mean? 'Digitally violated'?"

PRISONER #2: "It means they stuck a camera up in there. Took pictures. Put that shit on the Internet."

PRISONER #1: "Yeah. (*Long pause.*) I'd have just killed the bitch."

PRISONER #2: (*Long pause.*) "Yeah. Me, too."

Scene: Outside on the walking track.

Setting: Two prisoners who hadn't seen each other in a long time. One had just returned to prison after having been to court to respond to a paternity suit.

PRISONER #1: "Where you been all this time?"

PRISONER #2: "Had a paternity suit. Had to take a DNA test."

PRISONER #1: "Me too. Last month."

PRISONER #2: "Mine came back positive."

PRISONER #1: "Me, too."

PRISONER #2: "Mine was ninety-nine-point-ninety-nine percent."

PRISONER #1: "Mine too!"

PRISONER #2: "Damn! We got some strong DNA!"

PRISONER #1: "We're ninety-nine-point-ninety-nine and those stupid bitches are only point-zero-one!"

PRISONER #2: "True that!"

Scene: Prison law library.

Setting: One prisoner explaining to another how he's going to make sure his appeal gets a full hearing in court.

PRISONER #1: "What they want you to do is to file a two-two-five-five Notice of Appeal."

PRISONER #2: "OK."

PRISONER #1: "But that way they can find out what arguments you're going to use."

PRISONER #2: "OK."

PRISONER #1: "Well, I ain't filing shit! That way they HAVE to hear my appeal and they won't know what's coming!"

PRISONER #2: "You're a genius."

Scene: Prison law library.

Setting: One prisoner explaining to another the benefit of the law allowing a 2255 Notice of Appeal.

PRISONER #1: "The great thing about the two-two-five-five is that you get to lay out all your arguments to explain why the cops was wrong and that you're innocent."

PRISONER #2: "Right."

PRISONER #1: "It's called the Statute of Liberty. That's why they got the statue of it in New York."

PRISONER #2: "Riiiight."

Scene: The prison cafeteria.

Setting: A prisoner who is a long-time member of a New York–based "La Cosa Nostra" family stops me to ask if I would write a letter for him to a prominent law school, asking for help in reducing his forty-year sentence for his role in a gangland murder in 1983.

MOB guy: "John, would you do me a favor? I want to write a letter to this university law school dean to ask if she can get her students to help me get out of here."

ME: "Sure. I'll help you write a letter. What's your crime?"

MOB guy: "Well, I'm a member of a certain New York 'family.'"

ME: "OK."

MOB guy: "There was this guy who was a real problem for me."

ME: "OK."

MOB guy: "Unfortunately, some violence ensued."

ME: "I think I understand."

MOB guy: "Don't get me wrong. If I could, I'd dig the guy up and kill him again. But forty years! It's unreasonable!"

I wrote the letter, but the dean never responded.

Scene: Outside the prison in the parking lot.

Setting: A first-time prisoner has arrived to self-surrender for a ten-year prison sentence. His stripper girlfriend has driven him, and they're making out in the parking lot as they say goodbye. A lieutenant comes out of the building to confront them. He happens to be the only African-American officer on staff. It is 10:00 a.m.

LIEUTENANT: "Hey! Take that shit out of my parking lot!"

SOON-TO-BE PRISONER: "Fuck you! I don't have to surrender until eleven."

LIEUTENANT: "I said take that shit out of here!"

SOON-TO-BE PRISONER: "Shut up before I slap the black right off of you!"

The lieutenant goes back inside the building. Soon-to-be-prisoner and stripper girlfriend drive to a nearby Wal-Mart for an hour, then return to prison.

LIEUTENANT: "Ah. Welcome back."

SOON-TO-BE prisoner: "I told you I was surrendering at eleven."

LIEUTENANT: "Well, all our beds are full. But we've made arrangements to house you in solitary."

Where the loud-mouthed prisoner spent the next two months.

Scene: A prison cell in North 1 Unit.

Setting: An uncle and nephew, both members of an organized crime family, are reunited. Both have been sentenced to five-year terms for drug trafficking. The drug was methamphetamine, but there were allegations that the nephew was selling cocaine on the side.

UNCLE: "Good to see you, kid."

NEPHEW: "Good to see you, too. We're lucky they put us together."

UNCLE: "What's this shit I hear about coke? You were dealing coke?"

NEPHEW: "I thought I could make a little extra money."

UNCLE: "And you kept this from me? Your flesh and blood? What, I shouldn't eat, too?"

NEPHEW: "I didn't mean any disrespect. I should have cut you in. What's that square thing under your shirt?"

UNCLE: (*Touching the square thing.*) "This? Uhh, it's an insulin pump. I got diabetes."

NEPHEW: "I thought those hooked to your belt or something."

UNCLE: "No. This one sticks to my chest. Anyway, tell me everything. Start from the beginning."

The nephew confesses his entire drug conspiracy. The insulin pump is, of course, a digital recorder. The uncle turns the recording over to the DEA and is quickly released. The nephew gets an additional fifteen years.

Scene: Central 1 Unit.

Setting: Every prisoner is writing either a book about his case, or a movie script. Because I was one of a minority of prisoners who was literate, one would-be screenwriter asked me to review his script and to give him comments.

PRISONER: "The plot is that the CIA discovered the cure for cancer, but they don't want to tell anybody, so they keep it a secret. But these two CIA agents [*sic*] figure out what's going on and they try to get the CIA director to give the cure for cancer to the newspapers."

ME: "Well, you know, the CIA doesn't really do stuff like that. They collect and analyze foreign intelligence."

PRISONER: "Yeah, but people in foreign countries get cancer, too. That's why the CIA is involved."

ME: "OK. Read me a passage."

PRISONER: "The two CIA agents run up to the director's limo and shout 'Yo! You gotta release the cure for cancer.' The director shouts 'Yo! You don't know what you're talking about!' The female CIA agent shouts 'Yes we do!' But the director's limo takes off. The male CIA agent turns to the female CIA agent and says 'Look what you done gone and did now, girl!'"

ME: "Wow. That's great. But this really isn't for me. I've never written a script before. Good luck, though!"

Scene: The Education Department

Setting: A prisoner explaining to friends why he's opted out of the GED program, despite the fact that doing so will prevent him from accumulating time off for good behavior.

PRISONER: "A mothafucka can't go to school and hustle the streets at the same time. And a mothafucka needs his money. That's why I ain't going to no bitch-ass school. Cause I need my mothafuckin' money."

Scene: The Central 1 TV Room

Setting: Dave walks in to watch TV. It's 4:00 p.m.

DAVE: "Hey guys. Do you mind if I put one of the [six] TVs on CNBC? I want to see what the markets did today."

PRISONER: "We don't give a shit about no bitch-ass stocks!" Translation: You may not change the channel.

(*An ad comes on for the 2015 Jaguar, followed by an ad for the 2015 Buick.*)

PRISONER: "Those bitch-ass Jaguar engineers made the Jaguar look like a Buick!"

DAVE: "I think the Buick engineers made the Buick look like a Jaguar, actually." (*Angry looks and silence follow.*)

Scene: The commissary.

Setting: The first thing a prisoner does when he walks into the commissary is to look at the white board, where the "Out of" list is written. This is, obviously, a list of items that are currently out of stock. Sometimes tensions run high when a prisoner has been looking forward to buying something, only to find that it is out of stock, or when a needed item has been out of stock for multiple weeks. At 6:00 a.m. one day, a member of the Latin Kings street gang came in for the sole purpose of buying a tube of A+D ointment.

LATIN KING: (*Sees the "Out of" list.*) "They're out of A+D ointment again? Again?" (*Murmurs follow.*)

LATIN KING: "How the fuck can that happen? How the fuck do you run out of A+D ointment?" (*Several other prisoners nod in agreement.*)

LATIN KING: "What…the…FUCK is this place coming to? Where's the fucking A+D ointment? I want my fucking A+D ointment!" (*Prisoners begin to move away from the Latin King.*)

LATIN KING: "WHERE'S THE FUCKING A+D OINTMENT? I WANT YOU MOTHERFUCKERS TO GIVE ME MY MOTHERFUCKING A+D OINTMENT!!"

CO CASHIER: (*On the loudspeaker.*) "Hey! Shut the fuck up!"

LATIN KING: (*Leaping over the railing toward the CO.*) "I'LL FUCKING KILL YOU!! I'LL FUCKING KILL YOU!! GIVE ME THE FUCKING A+D OINTMENT!!"

The Latin King was tackled by three COs, cuffed, and taken to solitary. I never saw him again. He did not get his A+D Ointment.

Scene: Central 1 Officer's Conference Room.

Setting: I was asked to teach a class on how to build a small business for inmates preparing to go home soon.

ME: "Why don't we go around the room and talk about what we want to do when we get home?"

PRISONER #1: "I'm a certified welder, so I'll go back into welding when I get out."

PRISONER #2: "I had a heating and air-conditioning company before I came in. I'll probably do the same thing when I go home."

PRISONER #3: "I'm a mechanic. When I get out I want to open an auto body and detailing shop."

PRISONER #4: "I want to be a rap mogul."

ME: "A mogul? Not a rapper."

PRISONER #4: "I don't know how to rap. I want to be a mogul, like P. Diddy. Plus I wrote a movie script about how the CIA has a cure for cancer, but they won't share it."

ME: "How does one become a rap mogul like P. Diddy?"

PRISONER #4: "First you write a hit rap song, then you play it in the strip clubs in Atlanta. Then it gets onto the radio because the strippers use it as their official song, then you make millions of dollars from it."

ME: "Great!"(*Looking at Prisoner #5.*) "How about you?"

PRISONER #5: "I'm an outdoorsman." (*He clearly was NOT an outdoorsman.*) "I want to create a business called the Adventure Club. I'll take boys between the ages of nine and thirteen out into the woods for weekends of hiking and camping. They can link their Facebook pages to mine and we can stay in touch that way."

ME: "Do you mind if I ask what your crime was?"

PRISONER #5: "Well…child molestation."

ME: "I don't think you're allowed to have any contact with children."

(*Later in the day, I went to see the counselor, who had asked me to teach the class.*)

ME: "There's a pedophile in the class who wants to open a business where he takes young boys into the woods for the weekend. I think we should report him."

COUNSELOR: "Nobody's going to take boys into the woods! They're all going to end up selling drugs or going into food service! Now get the fuck out of my office!"

The class was not renewed for a second session.

Scene: Walking path on the way to the recreation yard.

Setting: Two inmates are walking past the prison's bright blue, one-hundred-foot-tall water tower as a CO comes out of it.

PRISONER #1: "CO! What is that thing, anyway?"

CO: (*Motioning toward the water tower.*) "That? That's the water tower. You've never seen a water tower before?"

PRISONER #1: "No. There's water in there? For the prison?"

CO: "Yeah. It supplies all the prison's water."

PRISONER #1: (*Completely seriously.*) "How come when you came out of it water didn't come gushing out? Your clothes are dry."

CO: "You're an idiot."

Scene: The Aryan table in the prison cafeteria.

Setting: A new prisoner has arrived and is introducing himself to the Aryans and assorted hillbillies at the table.

PRISONER #1: "So what are you in for?"

NEW PRISONER: "Meth. Like everybody else."

PRISONER #1: "How much time did you get?"

NEW PRISONER: "Twenty years."

PRISONER #1: "Why so much time? Did you go to trial?"

NEW PRISONER: "No. I got an extra five years because my wife ratted me out."

ME: "What do you mean?"

NEW PRISONER: "My wife ratted me out to the cops for making meth. So when I got out on bail I had to beat that pussy. It gave me an extra five years."

ME: "I'm not understanding you. What do you mean you 'had to beat that pussy?' Are you saying you raped her?"

NEW PRISONER: "Yeah. But I forgive her. She's waiting for me to come home."

Scene: Outside, in the recreation yard.

Setting: During softball season there are dozens of softballs laying on the field at any given time. The prisoner with the stripper girlfriend picked one up, walked to the rec building, and, once inside, began bouncing the softball on the concrete floor. A CO came out to see what the loud noise was.

CO: "Hey! What the hell are you doing?"

PRISONER: "Bouncing a ball."

CO: "Well, cut it out! Put that ball in the storage locker where you found it!"

PRISONER: "I didn't find it in the storage locker."

CO: "You gonna get smart with me? Put it back in the storage locker!"

PRISONER: "I didn't find it in the storage locker."

CO: "If you don't put it back where you found it, you're going to solitary!"

(*The prisoner walks to the door and heaves the ball back onto the softball field.*)

CO: "Alright. You're going to solitary. See you in six months."

Scene: *The prison cafeteria.*

Setting: *I'm sitting at the Aryan table when Tommy sits next to me. I hadn't seen him in a month.*

ME: "Tommy! Long time no see. Where've you been?"

TOMMY: "I was in solitary for a month."

ME: "You were? What for?"

TOMMY: "You know Fred the tow-truck driver?"

ME: "Yeah."

TOMMY: "He put the moves on my boyfriend, so I had to fuck him up."

ME: "Your boyfriend? What are you talking about?"

TOMMY: "You know Richie with the long blond hair?"

ME: "Yeah."

TOMMY: "He's my boyfriend and Fred tried to steal him from me."

ME: "I didn't know you and Fred were gay."

TOMMY: "We're not. I'm married and I have four kids. I just like to party."

ME: (*Long pause.*) "But if you put your dick in a man's ass and you let a man put his dick in your ass, then you're gay."

TOMMY: "That's just what *society* says. But if you tell my wife I'll kill you."

Scene: Outside, in the rec yard.

Setting: A group of guys are sitting in the bleachers watching a softball game, talking about their glory days as high school football stars.

PRISONER #1: "I was a star running back at Steel City High. I had this awesome coach. He was the coach there for, like, thirty-five years. He was always smoking cigars. When the cigar got down to a little stub, he would put it out, then chew it."

PRISONER #2: "He must have really loved cigars."

PRISONER #1: "The poor guy got tongue cancer. They had to cut his tongue out."

PRISONER #2: "All that tobacco catches up with you."

PRISONER #1: "Nah. He got cancer from eating pussy."

PRISONER #2: "But tobacco causes tongue cancer."

PRISONER #1: "This guy ate all kinds of pussy—dirty pussy, clean pussy, hooker pussy. It was definitely the pussy."

The Council of Europe Takes an Interest

J UST A COUPLE OF weeks before my departure I received a letter from the Parliamentary Assembly of the Council of Europe asking me to testify the following week before a committee investigating whistleblowing. I couldn't testify in person, of course, but the committee agreed that one of my attorneys, Jesselyn Radack, could read my testimony into the record. This is what I had to say.

Statement by ex-CIA officer and whistleblower John Kiriakou, currently in prison in the US, to the hearing of the Committee on Legal Affairs and Human Rights of the Parliamentary Assembly of the Council of Europe (PACE) on "Improving the protection of whistleblowing", held in Strasbourg on 29 January 2015:

Ladies and Gentlemen,

Thank you allowing me to address the esteemed Legal Affairs and Human Rights Committee of the Parliamentary Assembly of the Council of Europe. I am honored by this opportunity and humbled by the notion that I may help you to help American leaders end the abomination that is torture. I address you from my prison cell at the Federal Correctional Institution at Loretto, Pennsylvania.

I served in the Central Intelligence Agency for more than fourteen years, first as an analyst and later as a counterterrorism operations officer. Like all of you, I was appalled and sickened by the events of September 11, 2001, and like most CIA officers that day, I volunteered to go to the Middle East or South Asia to bring the perpetrators of that terrible crime to justice. The CIA had several very important successes in the immediate aftermath of the attacks, capturing several senior al-Qaeda leaders and their associates. Most of us thought these terrorists would be returned to the United States and brought to justice. We were wrong.

My first inkling that a decision had been made to violate both US and international law was in mid-2002, when a senior CIA officer asked if I wanted to be "certified" in the use of torture techniques. I declined, saying that I had a moral problem with torture, that it was wrong, and that it was a slippery slope that would lead to disaster. Dianne Feinstein, the chairwoman of the Senate Select Committee on Intelligence, later said that the torture program was a "brutality that stands in stark contrast to our values as a nation. It is a stain on our history that must never be allowed to happen again." She was right.

There is precedent for how the US government dealt with torture in the past. The Washington Post on January 21, 1968, published a photo of a US soldier waterboarding a North Vietnamese prisoner. The Defense Department investigated, court-martialed the soldier, and convicted him of committing torture. It was wrong to torture in 1968 and it was wrong in 2002.

Many CIA leaders, past and present, will argue that torture led to unique intelligence that saved American lives. This is simply not true. But even if it were true it would be irrelevant. The question isn't whether torture works. The question is whether it is right, whether it is moral.

On my first day at the CIA in January 1990, all newly hired officers were welcomed and briefed by a senior officer. All these years later, I still remember one thing he told us. He said that as CIA officers we must always act ethically. We should never do anything that we would be ashamed to see on the front page of The New York Times. Torture is something we should be ashamed of. It is something we must ensure never happens again, whether as a part of official government policy or not. *If any American President fails to hold CIA officers accountable when their actions merit it, that failure doesn't strengthen the CIA. It weakens it. The fact is, by holding CIA officers accountable, the government would honor all officers who act lawfully.*

In December 2007, in a nationally televised interview, I said that the CIA was torturing prisoners and that torture was an official US government policy approved by the president. I was called a liar and a malcontent. Indeed, one US senator said I should be tried for treason, a death penalty charge. I was fired from my job, and the Internal Revenue Service began to audit my finances, an annual harassment that continues to this day. The FBI began investigating me, and after four years I was charged with five felonies, including three counts of espionage, all for talking about torture. Facing forty-five years in prison, I took a plea to a lesser charge so that I would be out of prison to see my five children grow up. Even still, my wife, a CIA officer, was forced from her job simply for being married to me; the government confiscated my pension, at a cost to me of nearly $1 million; and I accrued another $1 million in legal fees. I lost everything, including my freedom, for thirty months.

But it was worth it. Somebody had to stand up and say, "Enough. This is wrong. And the world has the right to know it." I'm proud that I could play that role.

There is also a broader bureaucratic problem here. That is, where does a national security whistleblower go when the chain of command— including the CIA director, senior CIA officers, the CIA inspector general, the CIA general counsel, the Justice Department, the White House, and even the Congressional oversight committees—are a part of the conspiracy of silence? The short answer is that there is nowhere to go but to the media. Indeed, in the United States, the Whistleblower Protection Act does not apply to national security and intelligence whistleblowers—the ones who have revealed torture, secret surveillance, and war crimes. The Intelligence Community Whistleblower Protection Act is little more than a tool of entrapment.

There is now an untested Presidential Policy Directive, but it was not in existence when I blew the whistle and does not cover contractors *like Edward Snowden, from whom you heard testimony last April. The Whistleblower Protection Enhancement Act of 2012 provides millions of federal workers with the rights they need to report government corruption and wrongdoing safely, but federal employees still lack most of the basic rights available to whistleblowers in the private sector such as a trial by jury. Additionally, it excludes national security whistleblowers. A modest improvement was passed two years later, but it still excludes contractors and the enforcement mechanism is far inferior to that for other federal employees.*

Meaningful, effective, and enforceable "best practices" whistleblower protection is needed in the United States and Europe, especially in national security fields and cultures of deeply-rooted secrecy, in order to hold governments to account. Otherwise, the whistleblower must be prepared to be ruined personally, professionally, and financially, and to face decades in prison. An employee should not have to choose his conscience over his career, and especially his very freedom.

Thank you for shedding light on this important issue. Perhaps Congress can learn from your leadership.

John Kiriakou

Farewell from Loretto

YES, THIS LETTER IS probably mean-spirited, but I felt that I had the right to take a parting shot. One passive-aggressive comfort that I always had was the knowledge that the COs would have to spend a lot more time in prison than I ever would. I was headed home and I could vent without reprisals. So here it is:

February 3, 2015
"Letter from Loretto"

Farewell from the Federal Correctional Institution at Loretto, Pennsylvania! I'm leaving this morning to check into a halfway house and then to go home for eighty-six days of house arrest.

First, I want to say thank you. Thank you to Jane Hamsher, Kevin Gosztola, Brian Sonenstein, and the readers and supporters of Firedoglake; thank you Medea Benjamin and the angels of Code Pink; thank you to the more than eight hundred people who wrote me more than seven thousand letters (from forty-six states and eighteen foreign countries) since I arrived here and who kept me flush with books, magazines, and news articles. I literally could not have survived this nightmare without your support, friendship, and generosity. It means the world to me. And thank you to Heather. What I put that poor woman through over the past seven years...

I've made several good friends here at Loretto. Two of them have been transferred to other prisons and, even with legislative relief, they probably have many years in prison ahead of them. I'll miss them, I'm pulling for them, and I wish them the best. The justice system is broken in our country. We have a lot to learn about crime and punishment from more enlightened countries, especially in Europe. The current state of the Justice Department and its Bureau of Prisons is something that all Americans should be ashamed of. But that's not the subject of this letter. That's the subject of a future book.

I will miss absolutely nothing about prison. Indeed, I'm elated by what I won't have to deal with anymore. Here's what I won't miss:

1. Staff lies: before I even got to prison, a former CIA colleague who had done a couple of years in a camp warned me about prison staff. He explained that I would encounter a warden, several deputy wardens, a unit manager, a case manager, and a counselor. His most important advice: "They're all liars, and their job is to fuck you, not to help you." Truer words were never spoken. "We'll put you in for nine months halfway house." A lie. "You'll get six months halfway house if the nine months doesn't work out." A lie. "If you need stamps for all those letters you write, just ask us every week and we'll authorize it." A lie. The funny thing about all these lies is that I would have respected a staff member who just said, "Look. You're a high-profile inmate, you're a pain in the ass, we can't send you on diesel therapy because the press would kill us, but we're going to screw you while you're here." No staff member ever had the balls to state the obvious.

2. Pretending to respect staff: I'm just going to say it straight out. Ninety percent of the staff members here are semiliterate half-wits who couldn't cut it anywhere else in government. Let's face it. Most of them are here only because their parents are here and helped them get jobs. If I was a loser with nowhere else to go, and my dad was a BOP official in the regional office, maybe I would have ended up here, too. Wait. No I wouldn't have. And so many of them try to come off as tough guys, wearing jackets and T-shirts with slogans like "FCI Loretto Incident Response Team," or, my favorite, "Either You're SWAT or You're Not." Well, guess what! You're not! Many of the COs are rejects from the military or from local police departments. And there aren't any

"incidents" at Loretto. It's low-security, not a penitentiary. And another thing: my title is "Mr." Maybe in a year or two, "Dr." It's not "Inmate."

3. Bullies and punks with something to prove: so many of the dim-witted COs I've encountered are young, power-hungry bullies in their first positions of authority, serving alongside their parents or siblings and constantly bragging about how tough they are. Walking down the hall just last week I heard one obviously disturbed CO bragging to another, saying, "You should hear how I fucked up this inmate the other day." All I can say now is, "So long, tough guy." He'll have many more years in this prison than I ever did.

4. Nosy cops listening to my phone calls: my wife Heather is awesome. She's so crazy smart and intuitive that we've developed a certain "code" that we use over the phone. She knows when I'm serious, when I'm conveying important information but don't want to come right out and say it and when I'm making something up for the nimrod COs and lieutenants who get their jollies by listening to other people's private conversations. The joke's on them. Losers.

5. COs harassing my visitors: the COs in the visiting room are almost universally decent folks. The guards at the front gate, however, can sometimes be bullies and complete idiots. Even Jane Hamsher was harassed once. The CO said she was too sexily dressed or something like that. She had to go to a nearby Wal-Mart, probably where the prison administrators buy their one-hundred-dollar suits, and buy something to cover herself. My friend and former CIA colleague Ray McGovern had a CO bark at him for sitting on the edge of a low wall while waiting to be processed in for a visit. Ray told him, I'm sure in a much nicer tone than I would have used, to go fly a kite. Another friend, a woman, was sent to Wal-Mart to buy pants because the CO on duty arbitrarily decided that her skirt was too short. I won't even get into the incident where my children were thrown out of a visit because of "overcrowding."

6. Staff members acting like they're doing me a favor for doing their jobs: at any given time, a prisoner may have only ten "active" visitors on his list, so depending on who's planning to visit, I'm constantly taking people off and putting others on the "active" list. (I have sixty-two

approved visitors.) The problem is when there's a holiday. The counselor is the only person who can switch out names on the visitors list. But when there's a holiday, every counselor goes on vacation at the same time. Need to switch out a name? Tough luck, unless you can convince a unit manager to do it. I approached a unit manager after waiting for four days for a counselor to show up for work. It was the day before a visit, and he huffed and puffed before telling me to go to his office an hour later. I did, along with my visitors list. This unit manager never liked me. I don't know why nor do I care. I vowed when I arrived never to seek the approval of anyone I don't respect. Anyway, I handed this unit manager my visitors list, he made the changes, yelled at me for "waiting until the last minute," and handed me my list back. As I turned to leave, he stopped me. "Give me that list back." I handed him the five-page printout. "I don't trust you," he said. "Let me see that list. I want to make sure you didn't steal any papers off my desk." I laughed out loud. Who did this mini-Napoleon think he was? It struck me as so incongruous that I just laughed, watched him leaf through the list, and walked out still laughing. I guess he really showed me who was boss! Haha.

7. Waiting for four days to send or receive an email from my family or attorneys: unlike other prisoners, I have a four-day delay on my incoming and outgoing email. Officially, this is because I'm somehow viewed as being "dangerous." In reality, and I know this from BOP documents accidentally released to me through a FOIA request, that the BOP is afraid of the broad access that I have to the press. Anytime my attorneys, wife, brother, or sister send me an email or I send them one, it sits in queue in the computers of the Special Investigative Service, where it is eventually reviewed and passed onto me. Needless to say, I rely on email for nothing, but I still send and receive it, if only to waste SIS's time and money. You see, the time they spend reading my email could be used to investigate actual criminals. But my personal goal has become to waste as much of the BOP's resources as I possibly can. Multiply that by 1,125 prisoners and nothing gets done.

8. Waiting days for my mail, only to have it tampered with, destroyed or rejected: all of my incoming mail goes to the mail room, where it is

opened by a "slicing" machine, read, probably copied, and sent to the FBI, stapled shut, and finally sent to me. The slicing machine damages easily half of my incoming letters. When people send handmade cards, they are literally taken apart in a search for contraband. SIS often reads my mail and even cuts open my outgoing mail to see what I'm saying. They're not even good at it, and they frequently make a mess of the envelopes. Did I mention that most of these guys are rejects from local police departments and the military?

9. Ten-minute moves: prisoners are only allowed to move from point A to point B during ten-minute moves (which are frequently seven or eight minutes). These moves are at 7:00 a.m., 7:45 a.m., 8:25 a.m., 9:25 a.m., 10:25 a.m., 12:25 p.m., 1:25 p.m., 2:25 p.m., 3:25 p.m., 6:00 p.m., 7:00 p.m., 8:00 p.m., and 9:00 p.m.. If you go from A to B and finish your business but can't get back to A within the ten minutes, tough. You're stuck there for an hour. My view is that they can shove their ten-minute moves.

10. Locked doors during ten-minute moves: during the moves, there are as many as 1,100 people in the prison's single hallway, all trying to get from A to B. What many of these sadistic bully COs do is to keep one of the double doors locked at the entrance to each unit so there are 1,100 people going in both directions squeezing through one door all within ten minutes. Why do this? To encourage violence. If a fight breaks out because one prisoner cuts in front of the other to get through the door, or because two prisoners brush shoulders, COs can call out the vaunted "Incident Response Team." Put down a fight and there might be a performance bonus or even a promotion in it for you. Remember, either you're SWAT or you're not!

11. Commissary: this is the single worst experience in prison. The commissary is run by an incompetent boob who wouldn't last fifteen minutes in a 7-Eleven on the outside. Until he was unceremoniously transferred to the warehouse, the commissary guy would write and circulate lists of everything the store was out of. Some weeks it was faster and easier to write a shorter list of things that were actually in stock. Once the new commissary manager got things running smoothly, the

boob was transferred back and put in charge again. They're welcome to him.

12. *Begging the staff for permission to buy stamps:* I go through an insane number of stamps (and thanks to Billy Halgat I can afford it). Some weeks I get more than one hundred letters, and never fewer than forty. The problem is that prisoners are only allowed to buy twenty stamps a week. I wrote a request to the warden asking permission to buy sixty stamps a week. He gave a provisional approval, saying that I had to ask my unit manager every week for authorization to buy sixty. This was a pain in the ass, but it worked until the unit manager transferred. I then had to get permission every week from the unit manager who wanted to know if I had stolen papers from his desk when I asked for a visitor change. He always said yes but would "forget" to inform the commissary so I was turned down every week. I went up to the warden at lunch one day and asked for blanket permission to buy sixty stamps a week. He said no. As I walked away, the assistant warden asked him, "What was that all about?" I turned to look, only to see the warden roll his eyes; they both laughed. From that day on, every stamp I bought was from a bookie or contraband dealer. That's what happens when you try to follow the rules. I was a fool for even asking in the first place.

13. *Medical:* people under the care of the medical unit at Loretto die with terrifying frequency. I intend to report on and to write about the unit's malfeasance soon. You already know about my own experience with glyburide. Since passing out last August, I have never been called down to see a medical professional. My friend Frank complained for three months about chest pains and shortness of breath. He was told to wait: Medical would ask permission from the BOP's regional office for him to see a cardiologist. Frank heard nothing for those three months and then one day, while waiting for an insulin shot, he had a massive heart attack. Paramedics rushed him to a local hospital, where he had a successful surgery. He was in the hospital for two weeks, barely having lived through the experience. Two weeks ago, I happened to be in the medical unit when I saw a prisoner wheel in another prisoner who was clutching his chest and crying. The seventy-year-old told the technician

on duty that he was having a heart attack. Her response? "Well, you're just going to have to wait because nobody else has gotten to work yet."

14. The cafeteria: yes, it's as bad as you imagine. What it comes down to is a low-quality "all carb, all the time" diet. A typical dinner from last week was lasagna, rice, beans, and bread. Disgusting. I also won't miss seeing cases of food marked "Not for Human Consumption— Feed Use Only," or "For Sale Only in China," or "Broccoli-Floret-free." Even our Christmas baskets (which we prisoners paid for with profits from the commissary) were full of off-brand cookies, chips, and candies nobody had ever heard of. The Christmas cookies were marked "Made in Mexico Exclusively for Pedro's Discount Mart, Tijuana." I sold my basket for a book of stamps.

15. Standing in line: like citizens of the Soviet Union, we stand in line for everything here. This is due primarily to unconstitutional overcrowding. From the time you wake up in the morning until the time you go to sleep at night, you wait in line to eat, take a shower, brush your teeth, go to the bathroom, buy food from the commissary, use the phone, photocopy legal documents, or even go to sick call. I've had enough.

16. Involuntary servitude: seriously, that's what it comes down to. You must work. If you don't, you go to solitary. The problem is that we're so grossly overcrowded that there aren't enough jobs for everybody and there isn't enough money to pay people. As a result, hundreds of prisoners are "stand-by orderlies," earning sixty cents a month. I made $1.08 a month in the chapel. And in UNICOR, where an army of illegal aliens makes cable for the US military, the prisoner-employees still make less than they'd make in a Bangladeshi sweatshop. How is this legal?

17. Not being able to change the TV channel because I'm white: whether we like it or not, every new prisoner is hit in the face with every racial stereotype he's ever heard. Absolutely everything in prison is racial. Where the TVs are concerned, the Hispanics control half of them and the African-Americans control half. White people are forbidden from touching the TVs. If you do, you get a sharp, "Hey! White people can't touch the TVs!" This is followed by a meeting between the white shot-caller, the black shot-caller, and the "Spanish" shot-callers. You

must then apologize to the blacks and/or Hispanics for touching their TV. You get a beating if you do it again. For the record, I don't watch TV here.

18. Count time: all prisoners must stand at attention and be counted at 4:15 p.m. and at 9:30 p.m., seven days a week, as well as at 10:00 a.m. on weekends and holidays. There are also non-standing counts at midnight, 3:00 a.m., and 5:00 a.m. You would be shocked by the number of recounts necessary because some COs have trouble counting. I'm sick of it.

19. Pedophiles: I've said a lot about these guys in previous letters. The only good thing, at least for society, is that many of them will die in prison. The world will be a better place without them in it.

By the time you read this, I'll be home. Now the real work can begin—the struggle for human rights, civil liberties, and prison reform. I can guarantee you that I am unbowed, unbroken, uninstitutionalized, and ready to fight. Thanks for being there for me these past two years.

Your friend,
John Kiriakou

Letter to Loretto

May 1, 2015
"Letter to Loretto"

Hello from Arlington, Virginia! I thought I would write a letter to Loretto to tell you about my experience since going home. I learned a lot about the halfway house process, while the Bureau of Prisons' bumbling ineptitude was made even more crystal clear after I left than it had been when I was still inside.

Imagine that! I even recently saw a YouTube video of the BOP Director Charles Samuels testifying on Capitol Hill. One Congressman asked him the average size of a cell in solitary confinement. He hemmed, hawed, and generally made a fool of himself. The bottom line: he had no idea how big (or small) a cell is in solitary confinement, despite the fact that he's spent his entire career in the BOP and is a former warden! That says a lot.

I completed my house arrest on May 1 and began three years of probation, or what Ronald Reagan called "supervised release." (Technically, there is no such thing as probation anymore, although the person to whom I report is called a "United States Probation Officer.") Anyway, I wanted to tell you how things have gone since I left FCI Loretto on February 3, 2015.

My last hour at Loretto was a little stressful, not because I was anxious to get out (although I was), but because of a little troll who tried to set me up just as I was leaving. The details aren't important, other than to say that this prison employee was furious when I wouldn't take *her bait. She taunted me and threatened to put me in solitary because I asked to go to the release office at a time other than a formal "move." And when I just repeated, "I'm not going to let you set me up. I'm going home and you can't stop me," she blew me a cynical kiss. (This secretary, the sister and daughter of Corrections Officers, has a reputation for sending prisoners to solitary for "leering" at her. Take my word for it: she's nothing to leer at.)*

I was met in the parking lot by my wife Heather, my three youngest children, and my friend Joe Burns, who took the day off to drive me to the halfway house, where I was to check in before being sent home. We stopped at the nearest McDonald's for an Egg McMuffin. (I know, I know. But it just goes to show you how sickening the food is in prison when you can't get to a McDonald's fast enough upon release.)

Heather, Joe, and I briefly toyed with the idea of stopping for lunch somewhere, but I only had five hours to get to the halfway house, so we decided to drive straight through. I'm glad we did. The trip to Washington is normally three hours, but there was a lot of traffic entering Washington, and I got to the halfway house with only forty-five minutes to spare.

The halfway house to which I was sent is called Hope Village. Residents call it Hopeless Village. I've seen it referred to in the press as "Abandon-All-Hope Village." It's a former housing project on the worst block in the worst neighborhood in the worst part of Washington. It's nowhere near a Metro station and transportation by bus is inconvenient, to say the least.

I had done a little research on Hope Village before my arrival. The Washington Post found the facility's "job training services lacking and access to mental health services anemic." There is no money for "residents" to use public transportation to job interviews, and phone calls and Internet access are forbidden.

In addition, according to Prison Legal News, a 2013 report by the District of Columbia's Corrections Information Council (CIC) found that Hope Village "lacked the ability to help residents find housing and employment, and hindered them from accessing mental health services.

Residents said they felt unsafe and the halfway house did not have an effective system to handle grievances." The report continued that "the CIC heard on multiple occasions that incarcerated DC residents would prefer to stay at secure BOP facilities than to reenter DC through Hope Village." The then-chairman of the CIC added, "I would say that there are some things that are obviously dysfunctional" at Hope Village.

So I was prepared for the worst. I arrived at Hope Village at around 11:45 a.m. and went to the office to check in. I was told that I had to speak to several different people before being sent home, and I was told to go to apartment 301 and wait until somebody came to get me. I told Heather and Joe to go home, and I said I'd call them when I was done.

Several things came immediately to my attention. First, everybody was friendly. And I mean everybody. The staff greeted me with, "Hello, Mr. Kiriakou. Welcome to Hope Village." The apartment was sparsely furnished, but had everything important: two bunk beds, a couch, two chairs, and a color TV with broadcast channels.

There was a schedule waiting for me. I was to see a case manager, an employment counselor, a drug counselor, and a social worker. That also meant that I couldn't just check in, check out, and go home. Instead, check-in took nine hours. With that said, the food in the cafeteria, which everybody complained about, was absolutely delicious to me: white bread with a slice of turkey and a slice of cheese. I had never tasted anything so wonderful.

The case manager finally gave me a list of fourteen mandatory classes that I had to complete in the coming weeks, and then sent me home. I was told that I had to go to the halfway house every day to check in, go to class, and get drug tested. That sounded fine, but became a colossal pain in the ass.

First, I wasn't allowed to drive, so I had to take public transportation. I had to leave my house, walk to the Metro station, take the Metro to the Eastern Market station on Capitol Hill, catch a bus for Washington's Anacostia neighborhood, get off on Alabama Avenue, then walk the rest of the way to Hope Village. This took at least two hours each way. I would spend an hour or two at Hope Village, and then make the two-hour trip home. This was killing six hours every day in the middle of the workday. The problem here is that I'm supposed to be working every day. If I don't work, I get violated, and I have to go back to Loretto. I saw these daily visits to the halfway house as an utter waste of time.

Perhaps out of laziness or perhaps out of rebellion, I didn't sign up for any of the classes the first two weeks that I was home. These classes included Life Skills, Kicking Your Drug Addiction, Suicide Prevention, Prison Rape Prevention, How to Write a Resume, and others. I frankly didn't need any of them. I've never done a drug in my life, my life skills are just fine, etc. I told the case manager that the prison rape prevention class should be given before the person goes to prison, not after release. It seemed like closing the barn door after the animals get out.

At the end of the second week, I got a call from my case manager. "Come to Hope Village right away. We need to have a team meeting." I had no idea what this meant, but I began the long trek to Anacostia. When I got there, I was ushered into a dilapidated conference room. Sitting around the table were the director and deputy director of Hope Village, the case manager, the employment counselor, the social worker, and a representative of the Bureau of Prisons. The case manager angrily said, "You haven't signed up for a single class since you got out. Unless you want to be violated you better start taking the Life Skills classes!"

I paused for a moment, looked at her, and said, "Have you ever seen the episode of The Simpsons where Homer has to take a life skills class? He walks into the classroom and the instructor is saying 'put a garbage can lid on the garbage can, people. I can't stress that enough.' Is that what you're going to teach me in your life skills class? To put a garbage can lid on the garbage can?" There was silence for a moment, then the director asked me to step outside.

I stood in the hall for about a half hour, and then I was called back in to the conference room. "OK," the director said. "We're waiving all the classes. You don't have to take any of them." I thanked him, and continued: "There's another thing. I want permission to drive. I kill four hours in travel time, plus however much time I spend being here every time I come up. I can drive here from my house in fifteen minutes. I can use the rest of that time to work. And isn't that what I'm supposed to be doing?" There was another period of silence. Then the director said, "OK. You can drive. Give the employment counselor a copy of your license, insurance, and title. I'll approve it."

I later made one more minor complaint to my case manager. I told her that our meetings, by then three times a week and scheduled in the middle of the day, further interfered with my ability to work. She moved them to Tuesdays and Thursdays at 7:00 p.m. Again, BOP take notice! This is how to treat people.

Hope Village's employees showed leadership, flexibility, pragmatism, and respect. It's a recognition that some newly-released prisoners need less help and oversight than others. It's a recognition that resources are better spent on some prisoners than on others. I have said cynically that I'm happy to waste as much of the Justice Department's time and money as I possibly can. But that's not really true. I simply don't need the oversight or the hassle.

So for eighty-seven days, from my release from Loretto on February 3 until the end of my house arrest on May 1, this was the deal: I couldn't leave my house except to go to Hope Village or the doctor. The halfway house's "officer in charge of quarters" called me every morning between 7:10 and 8:00 a.m. to make sure I was home. There was a second call every night between 9:15 and 10:15 p.m. Sometimes they called as late as 11:20 p.m. The "employment counselor" stopped by the house randomly, usually on a Tuesday or Wednesday, to make sure I was home. If I left the house for any reason whatsoever, even for an emergency, I had to call Hope Village and say, "John Kiriakou leaving the house," even if it was to go to Hope Village. I also had to call when I got home to say, "John Kiriakou. I arrived home."

The only exception to movement was on weekends. On Saturdays and Sundays I was allowed to leave the house for five hours, I had to return home for at least an hour, and then I could go back out for four hours, for the purpose of "family reintegration." I could go to a movie, a restaurant, the park, whatever, with my wife and kids.

Every Tuesday I had to meet with my case manager and give her a copy of my proposed movement for the week—a list of doctor's appointments, movement to Hope Village, or meetings with my attorneys, and plans for the weekend. I also had to give her receipts from the weekend to prove that I did what I said I would do, and a copy of my monthly phone bill.

I also had to pay "rent" to Hope Village for the bed I didn't use. That rent was 25 percent of my gross pay. You see, like all halfway houses, Hope Village is a for-profit enterprise. Lip service to job training, mental health, and reintegration are fine, but the truth is that the goal of Hope Village and every other halfway house is to get released prisoners in and out as quickly as possible.

Every resident has to pay rent, and the only way the halfway house can make any money is to rent out the bed to three, four, or more people at the same time. The goal, then, is to get people into home confinement quickly. That way, they don't cost the halfway house anything in the way of food or other resources, but they still pay rent.

You would think that would be an incentive for Hope Village to help people find a job, but it's not. Aside from a bulletin board in the office listing job openings at fast food restaurants, car washes, and motels, there is no program to get anybody a job. Just get a job—any job—on your own, and go home and pay your rent.

For me that was no big deal. I had a job lined up before I even left prison. This was, however, a temporary job. I set out immediately to find something permanent. I was finally offered a job as an associate fellow with Washington's preeminent progressive think tank, the Institute for Policy Studies. IPS is one of the oldest and most highly-respected independent policy institutions in the city. Its experts appear on network news programs all the time, they publish countless books, magazine articles, and syndicated columns, and they speak around the world on issues as varied as the Middle East peace process, climate change, gender equality, human rights, civil rights, and the environment. My job would be to write articles, papers, and op-eds on prison reform, intelligence reform, torture policy, terrorism, and the Middle East.

I've always admired IPS and the work they do, and I was excited at the prospect of working there. I filled out the relevant paperwork for the halfway house. The employment counselor visited the office to make sure there was such a place and that they knew I was a felon. (They had approached me, incidentally. No problems there.)

But two weeks later my case manager showed me a note from the Bureau of Prisons regional office in Baltimore. It said, "We feel it is inappropriate for Inmate Kiriakou to work in a job that would allow him to comment on foreign affairs and prison reform, given the nature of his crime."

The BOP's opinion is, of course, nonsensical. First, there's that pesky issue of the First Amendment to the Constitution of the United States, as in "freedom of speech." Second, it's not up to the Bureau of Prisons to decide where I can and can't work. I could have gone to court to file a motion overturning the BOP's decision. But that would take months, so I decided to wait them out. The BOP no longer controls me, and on May 4 I started my job with IPS.

My only other problem also has been with the BOP. When I got home on February 3, I tweeted a photo of myself sitting on the couch with my three youngest kids, and the caption, "Free at last. Free at last. Thank God Almighty, I'm free at last. MLK Jr. (And John Kiriakou.)" That tweet was picked up by the major alternative news websites, as well as the Russia Today television news network, Al Jazeera, and others. Consequently, I received dozens of interview requests over the next couple of weeks.

Before I accepted any of them, I looked at the BOP's regulations related to press interviews at bop.gov. The regulations were clear. I needed to get BOP approval for interviews while incarcerated. I then checked the halfway house's website. It said that residents of Hope Village had to get the director's permission before speaking to the press. I was neither incarcerated nor a resident of the halfway house. So I accepted a number of interview requests, including with Democracy Now, RT, and several print outlets. Within days, I received a call from a BOP official in Baltimore. He said that he was "very concerned" that I had had unauthorized contact with the press. I told him that, on the contrary, I had read the regulations and I knew that I did not need BOP approval. Furthermore, I had read the Hope Village regulations, and I didn't need their authorization either.

The BOP guy said that while that may be true, he was insisting that I get approvals. If I continued to grant interviews without his approval, he would violate me and send me back to prison. Again, a motion before the court would take months to get a hearing. And I likely would have had to argue it from prison. I know when to make a strategic retreat, and I did so. Fine. I would bury him in paper.

That's what I did. I sent him as many as a dozen forms per week. I put him in touch with every blogger, podcaster, reporter, and photojournalist I came into contact with. There were reporters from most major American news outlets and a dozen foreign countries. There were radio hosts from the far left, the far right, and everything in between. I even did an entire one-hour radio program on how folk singer Pete Seeger influenced the course of my life.

This turned out to be too much for the BOP guy. He just ignored many of the requests when he was too busy. I resubmitted them. And when he told one freelance journalist that he couldn't speak to me because he wasn't a "real" journalist, I countered that I then didn't need to ask permission to speak with him. After all, it would be a conversation between two private citizens. The BOP guy backed down. Again, if I needed to, I could just outwait him. He only controlled me until May 1.

So now I'm home and, generally, free. The future looks promising. I intend to make a living writing, speaking, and teaching. I will write op-eds for IPS's syndication service and other outlets, I'll write articles for The Nation magazine, I'll speak at colleges, universities, nonprofits, and other groups, and I'll teach a university course I've developed on ethics in intelligence operations.

My voice will be heard on prison reform no matter how much of a pest I have to make of myself. Our country's prison system is broken. It is racist. And it needs to be torn down and rebuilt. Overcrowding is unconstitutional and out of control. Sentences are draconian, especially *for minorities. And the quality of medical care is criminal. There's no other word for it. The Bureau of Prisons' neglect of sick prisoners is tantamount to abuse and, in some cases, manslaughter. I hope to help put an end to that.*

In the meantime, I want to say thanks again to the more than seven hundred people who wrote to me in prison. Thank you for remembering me. Thank you for your support. Please also remember those still inside.

Best regards,
John

I SOMETIMES TELL REPORTERS that the government has turned me into a dissident. I only say that half-jokingly. I don't feel like a dissident. I do feel, though, that our government demonizes people who disagree with the official line. This has become especially bad since the September 11 attacks. And that's where I now find myself. I don't feel like I've changed over the years. I feel like the government has changed.

When I was on a rotation to the State Department in the mid-1990s, I was the human rights officer at the American Embassy in Manama, Bahrain. The Bahraini government at the time was trying to put down a popular uprising, and was using force to do it. It was my job to document the Bahraini government's use of force against unarmed civilians, its extrajudicial killings of protestors, and its use of torture and solitary confinement against people never convicted of a crime. This was all documented in my human rights report, a document mandated by Congress, and was used to pressure the Bahraini government to respect human rights.

But much of what the Bahraini government did to its people in the 1990s was then done by the American government to its prisoners in the so-called "War on Terror" just a few years later. We tortured prisoners. We murdered people—including at least three American citizens—using drones and without the benefit of trial. We held people incommunicado in secret prisons around the world. And we worked hard to ensure that our prisoners either had no access to an attorney or, if they did, never saw the inside of a courtroom. That's not the American way. Again, I didn't change. The country changed.

This all started with the so-called "Patriot" Act. The Patriot Act has legalized government actions against American citizens that were unthinkable and intolerable only twenty years ago. When I first entered government, one rule was that if NSA intercepted the communications of an American citizen—even accidentally— heads would roll. Congress had to be informed, an investigation was launched, and the intercept was purged from the system.

Today, NSA has an enormous facility in Utah big enough to save copies of every email and every phone conversation made by every American for the next five hundred years. I don't know about you, but I don't want my government trampling my civil liberties. We Americans have a constitutional right to freedom of speech. The Supreme Court has interpreted the Constitution to also give us a right to privacy. The issue isn't what's being said in our private communications. The issue is that it's none of the government's business.

People frequently will ask me why they should care if the government is reading their emails or listening to their phone calls. "I have nothing to hide, so why should I worry about it?" This question sends chills up my spine.

First, anybody who has ever spent any time working in the intelligence community will tell you that even if you have "nothing" to hide, metadata—just the raw information about whom you are calling or what websites you're visiting—are incredibly revealing. Analysts don't need the actual content of the calls or emails to know what you're up to. Are you calling an abortion provider? A divorce lawyer? A secret girlfriend or boyfriend? A substance abuse counselor? What kind of porn do you like? What kind of chat rooms do you go to? What websites do you visit? What organizations do you belong to? Anybody can be made to look like a troublemaker, a suspect. Anybody. Anybody's life can be twisted to make them look like a threat or a potential criminal. Of course you're not. But the truth doesn't matter here. Everybody is a suspect. And that means that the government needs even more money to spy in more sophisticated ways on more people.

The problem doesn't end with data collection, of course. Daniel Ellsberg, who is probably the most important and highly-respected American whistleblower of the past half-century, once told me that every dirty trick that the Nixon White House pulled on him in order to convict him of espionage for leaking information about the Vietnam War is now legal under the Patriot Act. With a "national security letter," not even a warrant, the FBI can get your medical records, treatment notes from your psychiatrist, your phone records, what kind of books you buy, or what you borrow from the library. They can build a case against you whether you've done anything or not.

Harvey Silverglate, whom I've mentioned earlier in this book, posits in his book *Three Felonies a Day* that the United States is so over-legislated and over-regulated that the average American, on the average day, going about his or her normal business, commits three felonies. The moral of the story is that if the government wants to get you, they're going to get you. And that's what they do "legally" to silence dissent. It's all about that pesky Constitutional amendment guaranteeing freedom of speech. It doesn't quite fit into the government's program to protect us from enemies real or imagined.

The Founding Fathers saw this coming. James Madison, who wrote the Constitution's Bill of Rights, argued that the First Amendment must protect the minority from the majority, ensuring that even in the face of overwhelming pressure, the minority would still have a Constitutionally-guaranteed right to freedom of speech, press, religion, assembly, and to petition elected officials. The Bill of Rights is the only thing standing between us and fascism.

So am I a dissident? I don't know. I don't care. The important thing is that I've become passionate in my defense of our Constitutional rights. I have a Constitutionally-mandated freedom of speech and I'll continue to exercise it. It has already meant a stint in prison.

Again, I don't care. The more of us who are willing to tough it out in prison, the less powerful the government is in trying to take our rights away from us. The more of us who are willing to write, speak, or blog about government overreach, the better our chances of preserving our freedoms. It's worth it, no matter the costs.

It's an old adage that you don't go to prison to make friends. With that said, I really did make a few friends. You've read about Mark, who is trying to get through a thirty-year sentence as a first-time, nonviolent drug offender; Clint, who went to trial, convinced that once a jury heard his story they would realize how ridiculous his drug conspiracy charges were; Frank, the former auditor of Cuyahoga County, Ohio, who became like a big brother to me; Art, the cat burglar and jewel thief who was a steady source of good advice; and Dave, who professed to be a former CIA officer.

I wish I could stay in touch with them, but as convicted felons, we're not allowed to "consort," lest I be sent back to prison. I am, however, allowed to call their parents and spouses and inquire as to their well-being. That's how I keep up on all the news.

Mark applied to the Justice Department's Clemency Project, which allowed convicted felons with appallingly long sentences to petition for an ease in their sentences. A major Washington law firm, Latham and Watkins, agreed to take his case pro-bono, and prepared a commutation request for the president's consideration. Even better, Mark's prosecutor wrote a letter supporting his commutation request, saying that while what Mark did was wrong, he did not deserve the draconian punishment he received. Indeed, he even wrote that he had dreamt of the injustice of Mark's sentence over the years. Mark's coconspirators each got five-and-a-half years. Mark should have gotten ten years after going to trial. The prosecutor asked the president to send him home. I was prosecuted by the Obama Justice Department, so it's personally difficult for me to compliment this president. But he did the right thing. In August 2016, the White House announced that 111 prisoners would have their sentences commuted and would be released. Mark was one of them. He'll be home by the end of 2017.

Clint was transferred to a low-security prison in Fort Worth, Texas. He, too, applied for a commutation, but no attorney stepped forward to help him. In Texas, Clint was able to reconnect with his daughter, who is now married and whom Clint had not seen in ten years. Ever the optimist, he believes that his prison sentence is a test from God, and that he will be released from prison soon.

Frank is in poor health and is in the federal prison hospital in Devens, Massachusetts. His family is an eleven-hour drive from the facility, versus three hours from Loretto, but his family still makes the trip every single week. Frank cooperated with the authorities in his case and is awaiting a sentence reduction, hoping that his sentencing judge will reduce his sentence to ten years. That would make him eligible to go to a minimum-security prison camp hospital. But as things stand, Frank still has about twenty more years left on his sentence. He knows that he is unlikely to survive it.

After being caught up in the dispute with Schaeffer, the pedophile, Art was transferred to a low-security prison in Big Spring, Texas, and then to the same Fort Worth, Texas, prison where Clint is incarcerated. He was later transferred again to a low-security prison in California. Art's only brother died in 2015; Art has no children of his own, and he hopes to live with his only sister when he's finally released in 2022. He will be in his early eighties.

Robert was the first of us to get out of prison. He served a few weeks in a halfway house in Buffalo, New York, never bothered to make contact with his wife, who was living minutes away, and then absconded to the United Kingdom to avoid the nuisance of probation. I have heard that he's living somewhere in a small English town and selling used cars.

Dave hated pedophiles more than anything in the world. Ironically, the Bureau of Prisons relocated him to FCI Elkton, the Ohio-based home of the federal pedophile program. He will likely remain there until his projected release in 2019.

I don't think about people like Dave or Schaeffer or Sher anymore. Loretto is behind me, water under the bridge. I don't dwell on it because nothing good can come of that. I've even forgotten the names of nearly everybody I knew there, prisoners and staff alike.

The important thing is to remember how important our Constitutional right to freedom of speech is. I hadn't even thought about it until the Bureau of Prisons tried to take mine away from me. For the rest of my life, though, I'll go to the mat to protect that right.

Prison is a terrible place. But my time at Loretto made me a better person—more serious, more patient, and much more appreciative of the civil liberties that our Founding Fathers gave us. I take the Constitution very seriously, and I'll work to help those inside and outside prison to preserve their Constitutional rights, especially that of freedom of speech.

In the meantime, I'm getting on with my life. I've become something of a national voice on prison reform issues. I've appeared on CNN, Fox News, MSNBC, *Democracy Now*, and elsewhere to talk about the prison system, mandatory minimum sentencing, and my own experience. I have a weekly column at *Reader Supported News*. I'm thrilled that people actually listen.

On the day of my arrest, my brother Emanuel told me, "I know you can't see this right now, but this is going to turn out to be the best thing that ever happened to you." As crazy as that sounds, he was right. My wife was asked to leave the CIA on the day of my arrest, only because she was married to me. She went on to an incredible and hugely successful career with a major defense contractor. She's worth her weight in gold to them. I partnered with Oliver Stone to create and produce a television series about the CIA for the History Channel. We hope to go to production around the time this book is released. I've been a lot of things in my life. I never expected that "television producer" would be one of them.

My kids are doing well. They're all crazy smart, inquisitive, hardworking, and, most important of all, happy. They all understand fully what has happened to us over the past five and a half years, and they're proud of me.

And I have the "rules." I am not so cynical that I will use them in real life outside the prison walls. But they're there if I ever need them.

Acknowledgments

PUBLISHERS GENERALLY HATE IT when authors go on and on in their books thanking people. I ask their indulgence, however, because I really do have a lot of people to thank. My family and I could not have gotten through this nightmare without the support of friends and family. That support was both emotional and financial, and I am truly indebted to them.

Thank you to my brother Emanuel Kiriakou; my sister and brother-in-law Tina and Spiro Moulis; my father-in-law Dr. Mike Armentrout and his wife Ruth Anne Armentrout; my aunt and uncle, the late Chysanthie and Harold Davis; my cousins Maria Vournous, Stella Leftheris, and Kip Reese; my brother-in-law and sister-in-law Jason and Karen Armentrout; and my cousins Mark and Jody Kiriakou.

Thank you to Medea Benjamin, Jodi Evans, and the angels of Code Pink; to Jane Hamsher, Kevin Gosztola, and Brian Sonenstein of firedoglake.com, now called shadowproof.com. Thank you to Jesselyn Radack and Kathleen McClellan of the Whistleblower & Source Protection Program at exposefacts.org; Nick Mechanic, Tom Drake, Peter van Buren, Daniel Ellsberg, Dan Froomkin, Naomi Pitcairn, Tom and Julia Fitzpatrick, Don Roberts, Alan Cohen, Merrill Kinstler, Rick Santos, Jim Clarke, Rabbi Ed Harwitz, John Jordan, Bruce and Elizabeth Riedel, the late Gus Moshos, the American Hellenic Educational Progressive Association and the Brothers of AHEPA Chapter 438, Plato Cacheris, Bob Trout, John Hundley, Jesse Winograd, Mark MacDougall, Karen Williams, Nikos Mouyaris, Rob Shetterly,

Jim Spione, Daniel Chalfen, Michael-Patrick Hogue, Dr. Athan Georgiades, and Dr. Lydia Georgiades.

Thank you to John Cusack, Oliver Stone, Rosie O'Donnell, Roseanne Barr, Susan Sarandon, Yoko Ono, and the late Pete Seeger for their support and help in getting word of my case out into the open.

Thank you to my friends and family members who visited me in prison: my mother-in-law, the late Linda Armentrout, Dr. Stephen Bowers, Joe and Kristin Burns, Michael Carney, Jenna Collins, Damien Enderle, Tom Geanopulos, Alex Georgiades, Jim Gregorakis, Ed Guminski, Mihalis Ignatiou, Fr. Michael Kallaur, Jeremy Kareken, Sandy Kelson, Rich Klein, Jason Leopold, Dr. Spiro Macris, Pete Mazurkiewicz, Theo McCracken, Ray McGovern, Tara McKelvey, Frank Mollica, Dr. Charles Murphy, Nancy Murphy, Eric and Jennifer Pesanelli, Michael Ruby, Gary Senko, Tom Tolstoy, Ray Vazquez, Phil Yamalis, and His Eminence Metropolitan Savas Zembillas. *Matthew 25:36*

Thank you to those who provided much-needed political support, including Rep. Jim Moran (D-VA), Rep. Lloyd Doggett (D-TX), Governor Gary Johnson (R-NM), Bishop John McCarthy of the Catholic Diocese of Austin, Quaker House, Ralph Nader, Jill Claybrook, Bruce Fein, Ambassador Jonathan Weiner, Dennis Meheil, and Alexi Giannoulias.

Thank you to the 650 people from around the country and the world who wrote to me, especially my regular correspondents: Vone Bowly, Jeffrey Bradshaw, Russ Cletta, Peggy Corbin, Mike and Chiriyan Dominick, Chuck Fager, Lynn Faulkner, Michael and Angela Ferraro, Jane Fitzpatrick, Martin Gugino, Chuck and Marybeth James, Lynn and Steve Newsom, John Papathanassiou, Scott Seligman, John Spezzano, Jim Stoucker, Sarah Barrentine, Karina Aguilar, Deirdre Balaam, Peggy Bull, Catherine Bodin, Vivienne "Benson," Carol Ballou, Eloise Bates, Pat Connolly, Les Davis, Lynn Chong, Juan Fernandez, Desiree Fairooz, Jason Gulledge, Freda Giamenos, Jeanie Glass, Barbara Grothus, Andy Irwin, Julie Kempken, Alanna Lazarowich, Jackie Martin, Tresa Roth, Kirk

Snavely, Will Shapira, Annie Shaw, Brad Thacker, Sandy Winters, Beatrice Williams-Rude, Marion Ward, Anne Zielinski, Chris Bartels, Jim Becket, Larry Baschkin, Robert Cooper, Alex Cox, Alina Dollat, Pamela Drew, Catherine Frompovich, Amber Garlan, Dr. Iris Diamond, Pamela Gude, J.S. Hedegard, Billy Halgat, Brandon Jordan, Zeke Johnson, Michelle Lassaux-Harlan, Janice Lopez, Heidi Lucken, James McCullagh, Ryan Maxwell, Alex Patico, Joe Papp, Floyd Rudmin, Ann Rick, Susan Schibler, Stevon Scott, Pinky Stanseski, Jackie Schmid, Craig Shepard, Russell Tice, Sandy Winters, Elaine Woods, Fr. Chris Wallace, Gwen Zabicki, Dr. John Pittman Hey, Mary Hendrix, Dr. Lori Handrahan, Chesa Keane, Nevra Ledwon, Jackie Martin, Brian Montgomery, Larry McGovern, Alan Marwine, Faith Madzar, Natalia Megas, Ruth Ann Monti, Alex Panos, Sharon Powell, Dan Raphael, Paul Scott, John Stanton, and Linda Weltner.